Preach the Word

Including over 850 sermon outlines from the Bible

George Duncan

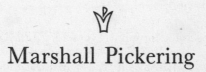

Marshall Pickering

Marshall Morgan and Scott
Marshall Pickering
34–42 Cleveland Street, London, W1P 5FB. U.K.
Copyright © 1989 George Duncan
First published in 1989 by Marshall Morgan and Scott
Publications Ltd, Part of the Marshall Pickering Holdings Group

British Library Cataloguing in Publication Data
Duncan, George B. (George Baillie), *1912–*
    Preach the Word
    1. Christian church. Sermons
    I. Title
    252

ISBN: 0–551–01939–5

Text Set in Baskerville by Input Typesetting Ltd, London

Printed in Great Britain by Cox & Wyman, Reading, Berks

Contents

Dedicated to My Father
The Rev J. M. B. Duncan M.A.,B.D
A Faithful Minister of the Word
and
A Faithful Pastor of the Flock

Mr. Duncan has three special qualifications. Firstly, he is a more than competent biblical scholar. Secondly, he is one of Britain's most famous preachers in the evangelical line. Thirdly, he has a very unique ability to express himself lucidly and to arrange his thoughts in an orderly and compelling manner.

WILLIAM BARCLAY

George Duncan has exercised in Britain and across the world a ministry of immense spiritual power. His preaching is at once biblical and contemporary, expository and evangelical. What gives his kind of preaching its unchallengeable force is the note of living conviction and exciting discovery running all through it. It is a true 'ambassador for Christ'.

JAMES STEWART

Introduction

The BBC recently broadcast a radio programme entitled *Where Are the Preachers?*. This implied that the subject of preaching needed looking at. Numerous books on preaching have been published but many of them have been written by preachers of such outstanding ability and learning that what they write is sometimes well above the standard that more ordinary mortals can ever hope to reach! Also, some of them seem to be able to spend much more time in their studies than most preachers, although perhaps some of us could and should spend more time there than we do. This book tries to bring the whole subject more within the reach of the majority of those who have the privilege and responsibility of preaching the word, whether as clergy, laypreachers, R.E. teachers in school, Sunday school teachers or Bible Class leaders.

The book falls into two parts. The first looks at what goes to make a good preacher. Our Lord said, 'The good shepherd knows his sheep,' and no man can know his sheep by looking at them only from a pulpit. Bishop Lightfoot of Durham used to say in his addresses to his ordination candidates, 'No man can be a good preacher unless he is a good pastor.' The flock may be a small one like a Sunday school class or it may be a large congregation, but the same principle applies. As Samuel Rutherford used to say, 'A minister must always be found upon his knees and among his people!'

Preaching has been defined as 'truth through personality'. What goes into the making of the preacher himself has a great deal to do with the success or failure of the preacher's work. Someone with great knowledge of the Bible is not necessarily going to be a good preacher. Teaching merely reaches the head, but preaching reaches the head and the heart. While a teacher may not preach, a good preacher will certainly teach as well.

The second part of the book is a selection of sermon outlines based on texts ranging from Genesis to Revelation. Most are from the New Testament. The outlines are designed not to do all the work of the preacher for him or her, but to provide structures around which the message can be built. A thorough study of the biblical passage on which the outline is based is indispensable. Each outline seeks to define the main truths contained in the text. The use of headings enables the listener to look at the passage in three different ways and so to maintain his interest. It also helps him to remember what the message was all about. Of course, this is not the only way of preaching but is one that helps the preacher to know what he wants to say and the hearer to know what the preacher has said.

I want to acknowledge the debt I owe to the writers of the countless books I have read; to those who have prayed for me, whether in the weekly prayer meetings in my churches or in their homes; to the very many prayer partners I have all over the world; to the members of the various churches in which I have sought to preach the word, half of which had seen better days by the time I was called to serve in them; to those who have helped in the typing of the manuscript of this book – Carol Witt in Denver, Milton Worthington and his secretary in Royal Oak, Michigan, Bette Owens in Cornwall and Hazel Cripps of Great Walstead School. Above all I have to thank God who in his grace and mercy has for more than half a century enabled me to preach all over the British Isles and in many other countries around the world.

Finally I end by quoting the words of Robert Murray McCheyne 'What a minister is on his knees in secret before God almighty, that he is and no more.' Words which cut each and all of us down to size!

George B. Duncan.

Part I

The Preacher and His Work

Chapter 1: Preachers of the Word

Study to show thyself approved unto God, a workman that needeth not to be ashamed, rightly dividing the word of truth (2 Tim. 2.15).

I charge thee therefore before God, and the Lord Jesus Christ, who shall judge the quick and the dead at his appearing and his kingdom; Preach the word; be instant in season, out of season; reprove, rebuke, exhort with all longsuffering and doctrine (2 Tim. 4. 1–2).

The Sources of his Material

First of all let us look at the sources of the material the preacher will use. We begin, of course, with something that is fundamental: namely, *The words of Holy Scripture*. Throughout fifty years of ministry I have recognised that it is my task to preach the word. When I was ordained in Chichester Cathedral in 1937 I was ordained to the ministry of the word and the sacraments, in that order. The word has priority over the sacraments.

When we come to study the word we will no doubt find there is a battle here which must be won. The last thing that the enemy wants us to do is to get alone with the word of God and yet God told Joshua that if he meditated upon the word day and night he would have good success. So this is the first factor we have to take into account: our task is not to say what we think or what others think, but to let people know what God has to say.

When I was Vicar of Christ Church, Cockfosters, where we had to have two evening services on Sundays in order to get everyone in, one of the big London evening newspapers ran a series of articles about those churches in the capital which were very well attended. The question they were asking was, 'Why are these churches so full when so many are so empty?' When they came to my church and asked me this question I replied, 'Well, I believe that people want to know what God has to say. My task is to find out from the word of God what he has to say and then say it.' The words of Holy Scripture must be the source of all our preaching and the final authority behind what we say.

The second source of material that the preacher will use I will call *the works of godly men*. In addition to the Bible, which of course comes first and holds the supreme place in all our study and thinking, there are other books which will be helpful. We may need to use several commentaries explaining the meaning of scriptural passages. However, I would throw in one word of warning here: we need to make sure that the commentaries we study are written by people who accept the authority of the word of God.

In addition to the commentaries there are the books of doctrine of theology. These will, of course, help us, but usually they are written by men who have spent their lives in colleges and universities, so their vocabulary is not the vocabulary of ordinary people. They are helpful in making us find out exactly what the Bible has to say, but we need to remember that the language of the scholar is not necessarily the language of the pulpit!

There are, of course, biographies too. These can be very helpful, and very rich in spiritual insights. Finally there are books of sermons. Sadly, these are not popular today. It seems strange to me that we should not study these books and become familiar with the sermons of men who have made their mark by their preaching ability. When surgeons are trained in our universities and hospitals, part of their training is to watch men who are expert at the job. Unfortunately most theological students do not get the opportunity to study preachers of the past during their training. The emphasis seems to be put on passing exams.

The preacher's third source of material is *the world of human need*. There is a strange attitude in existence today which denigrates the pastoral side of the ministry. I think this is a monumental blunder. The preacher has to get to know his people and they have to get to know him. There has to be built up a relationship of confidence based upon knowledge and trust between preacher and people. The world of human need among our own congregations can only be understood through faithful, diligent and careful pastoral work.

So these are the sources that a preacher will use: *the words of Holy Scripture*: *the works of godly men* and the *world of human need*. The first two mean that, in all probability, his mornings will be spent in his study and the third means that during some of the rest of the day he will be found among his people.

I should add that the preacher must not neglect his family. He has a responsibility towards them and should set some time aside every day when he can be with his wife and children. The high incidence of problems among clergy families today may in part be due to neglect by the fathers.

The Structure of the Message

Let us now consider the structure of the message the preacher will give. It is often the case that as the preacher studies the word of God during the week it begins to speak to him, and as Sunday draws near, the Spirit of God, who promises to guide us into all truth, lays upon the preacher's heart a text, a parable or a character that will be the subject for his sermon.

When I was asked to contribute to a book called *My Way of Preaching* I had to try and work out what my way of preaching really was. I had never really given it much thought. It seemed to me that there were three things I did when preparing a sermon. The first was to *analyse the text* – in other words, to find out exactly what the passage, parable or miracle had to teach. So I would break the text into bits and pieces, finding out everything that seemed relevant, that

5

seemed to speak to the needs of my heart and of the hearts of my people.

The second thing I tried to do was to *crystallise the truth* – that is, to gather the bits and pieces into groups or headings. (I prefer three, simply because that's about as much as most people can cope with!) The bits and pieces in the groups had to hang together and say something distinctive. Then my task was to find some words that would briefly sum up what those bits and pieces had to say.

Take, for instance, a simple text like Philippians 1.21, where Paul writes 'To me to live is Christ.' I would entitle that, 'What it meant to Paul to be a Christian.' There are only six words in the text and they fall into three little phrases. The first is 'To me'. This means that to Paul being a Christian meant something *personal*. In what way would it be personal? Personal in his acceptance of Christ? Personal in his allegiance to Christ?

The next two words are 'to live'. That suggests that for Paul being a Christian was something *practical*, that it had to do with living. This means that every moment of his life was spent with Christ, and so every matter in his life was shared with him.

The final words, 'is Christ', mean that being a Christian is something *possible*, because the sort of life Paul had is available to all in Christ and attainable by all through Christ.

Now that is a very simple text of just six words, broken down and put back together in a form which people can understand and remember. That brings us to the third thing I do when preparing a sermon: I *humanise the telling*. As I have said before, the vocabulary of the study is not necessarily the vocabulary of the pulpit. There are a few pulpits where academic language is acceptable. In university cities there are often churches which cater for the student mind. However, while students are used to coping with words they don't understand, ordinary people are not. Much of our preaching tends to use a vocabulary that our people don't begin to understand. The language we use must be that of the ordinary person.

We should speak not simply to the head but to the heart. The marginal readings in the words from Isaiah, 'Speak ye comfortably to Jerusalem' are 'speak to the heart'. This is one of the weaknesses of a great deal of our preaching: it is all aimed at the head, at the mind. It never comes from the heart and never reaches the heart. It is a purely intellectual exercise.

If we examine the teaching of Jesus, who was surely the best of all preachers, we find that everything he had to say was concerned with real human life and human need. His teaching was full of illustrations and parables and they were all taken from ordinary life. Yet today there is a tendency to neglect illustrations, and we find some preachers who never use them at all. They never seem to relate the message of their preaching to the lives and the needs of the ordinary people in their congregations. So the people go away with plenty of information but very little application or inspiration.

The Spirit in the Ministry

So we have thought about the sources of the material the preacher will use and the structure of the message he will give. Finally, we must consider the work of the Holy Spirit in the ministry the preacher will have. Ultimately it is not what the preacher says that achieves anything. The promise of power given to the early Church is tied up with the work of the person of the Holy Spirit. The Holy Spirit is the power, and if he is not able to work in and through the preacher, the people will go away unblessed.

The central importance of the Holy Spirit has implications first of all for *the matter of the preacher*. If he deviates from the truth of the word of God, he deviates from the blessing of the Spirit of God. A sermon may be brilliant, entertaining and informative, but it will be destitute of any spiritual power unless the Holy Spirit is saying 'Amen' to what the preacher is saying. That means that all he says must be true to the word of God. In some churches the word of God is not preached. That is why those churches are in reality dead, even though they may be very happy family gatherings or social clubs. They are not meeting the desperate spiritual needs of their members or of their neighbourhood. The matter of the preaching is vitally important. We are to preach the pure word of God.

There is also the question of *the manner of our preaching*. In his Gospel the Apostle John says that Jesus 'was made flesh, and dwelt among us, and we beheld his glory, the glory as of the only begotten of the Father, *full of grace and truth.*' Elsewhere it is said of Jesus: 'They wondered and marvelled at the *gracious* words that he said.' So we can learn from this that *how* we preach is as important as *what* we preach. There are some men who preach what is called the gospel, the good news, as if it were the worst of news. I remember one occasion when I preached in a certain church, and after the service an elder of the fellowship came up to me and thanked me. He went on to say that he had seen something in the pulpit that evening that he hadn't seen there for years. 'What was that?' I asked with curiosity; 'A smile,' he replied. It is sad that some preachers seem so preoccupied with the greatness, majesty and sovereignty of God – all of which are of course an essential part of the whole truth about God – that they seem to have forgotten that the glory of God that was revealed in Jesus Christ was the glory of his grace!

A third important factor is *the motive of the preacher*. The Holy Spirit's task is not to glorify me, the preacher, but to glorify Christ. If I preach wanting supremely to please my people or achieve popularity, then as far as God is concerned I'm a write-off. The one thing that matters is that through the preaching of the word people may be made to think more worthily of Christ. That is why preaching is so important in a service of worship. In some churches the sermon is almost a non-event – ten minutes is enough for it. (Of course, ten minutes of some preachers is more than enough!) But what is the purpose of worship? It is 'to give God his worth in my life' – not merely to sing about it but to really give it. So if through the preaching of the word God's mind has been made known more clearly, and if the hearer has responded in faith and obedience so that at the end of the sermon he is giving God more fully his worth in his life, then that is the highest point of worship. I believe the final hymn in a service ought to be a response to the truth which has just been heard, so that in that hymn we are worshipping our God more truly than before.

So there we have my concept of the preacher's task. As I write now, I find myself looking back over fifty years of ministry. During that time God, in his mercy and grace, and through the faithfulness of his praying people, has blessed my preaching of the word so that individuals and congregations have been built up, to his praise and glory.

What a privilege it is, and what a responsibility. Every preacher will one day have to stand before the judgment seat of God to give an account of his preaching of God's word.

Preach the word. What a privilege, what a responsibility – what a joy!

Chapter 2: The Message of the Preacher

I am not ashamed of the gospel of Christ, for it is the power of God unto salvation to everyone that believeth (Rom. 1.16).

It is surely essential that the preacher should be convinced of the relevance of the message he is to proclaim. Leslie Weatherhead, the well-known Methodist preacher, tells in one of his sermons of the visit he paid to a young doctor engaged in cancer research. Weatherhead asked him, 'If you found a cure for cancer, what would you do?' The doctor's face lit up and he said, 'Sir, if I found a cure for cancer I would tell the world!' Having been in the ministry for over 50 years, I'm all too aware of the terrible hurt that cancer causes. But I am also certain that there is one thing that causes even more trouble, hurt, distress and death than cancer. It is what the Bible calls sin – human sin. And because the gospel of Jesus Christ deals with that problem I'm convinced of its supreme relevance and importance for the world today.

At the time of writing, Scotland is celebrating the current year as the Year of the Bible. In that connection I have been asked frequently to speak at annual meetings of the Bible societies. Why is the Bible important? Why does the gospel matter? These are the questions I try to answer.

A condition which baffles the minds of men

First of all, I believe the message of the gospel is supremely relevant because it deals with a condition which baffles the minds of men. Some years ago the letters page of a leading daily newspaper (I believe it was the *Times*) was dominated by the subject, 'what is wrong with the world?' The well-known writer and thinker G. K. Chesterton made a memorable contribution to this debate. In what was probably the shortest letter ever written to any daily newspaper, he answered the question thus:

Dear Sir,
  I am.
Yours truly,
G. K. Chesterton

Chesterton was saying that what was wrong with his world was himself. In other words at the heart of every human problem we find people. This is why the Bible is so relevant, and why the gospel is such a wonderful message to proclaim.

First of all, *the Bible exposes the true nature of man.* When a baby is born, adoring parents, grandparents and other relatives come to see him or her, and so often they say something like, 'Isn't he a perfect little angel?' But unfortunately that just isn't true. We are not born perfect little angels. The Bible says quite frankly that we are born with something wrong with us.

A seven-year-old girl in my Sunday school at Cockfosters discovered this. One night, after she had had her bath, and had said her prayers and had been tucked up in bed, she suddenly asked one of those questions young children ask which grown-ups find difficult to answer: 'Mummy, why is there something inside me that likes being naughty?' That little girl at the age of seven had put her finger on the heart of the problem that baffles the mind of man. It is the problem of man himself.

Malcolm Muggeridge, who became a Christian in his middle sixties, was asked to preach at a university chapel on the subject, 'Christianity and World Problems'. His conclusion was that 'There are no world problems. There is just *one* world problem and that problem is man.'

Some years ago a man named Dr D. R. Davies wrote a book entitled *The Secular Illusion or Christian Realism*. Davies had found spiritual truth in the Christian faith after trying many others. The 'secular illusion' he wrote about was, and is, that man is born good. On the other hand, 'Christian realism' says that man is not born good. He is born with a nature that has already been affected by human sin. In his introduction to the book, Dr William Temple, then Archbishop of York, wrote, 'This book goes to the root of the trouble of the modern world. Essentially this is none other than the root of the world's trouble, the sinfulness of man.'

That is why the Bible is relevant and why the gospel is good news. I know there are other voices that speak very differently. It's not all that long ago that a bishop of the Church of England wrote a book called *Honest to God*. In it he made some extraordinary statements. He claimed that 'man has come of age.' He wrote of men being 'like gods'. I believe that before he died he changed his position! The evidence was against him. Men are not like gods. They are more like devils.

So the Bible exposes the true nature of man. When David wrote, 'In sin did my mother conceive me', he didn't mean there was anything sinful about his birth; he did mean there was something sinful about him when he was born. So the Bible goes to the root of the problem that baffles the minds of men, the problem of man himself.

Indeed, the Bible goes further than this and *explains the failure of man*. What are the remedies with which modern man seeks to solve the problems that baffle him? I suppose there are two main remedies. First, we find an emphasis upon education. Nobody but a fool would deny the value of education, provided it is of the right kind. But there is a great fallacy behind this remedy, and that is the assumption that because someone knows what is right he will want to *do* what is right. One doesn't need much experience of life to realise that this is just not true. All you need is an alarm clock and a very cold morning. The alarm clock wakes you up and tells you the right thing to do – to get up out of bed! Your problem is that although you know the right course of action, you don't want to do it.

The other remedy has to do with trying to solve problems like poverty, unemployment and homelessness. All these are, of course, real social evils, and we should try to end them. However, again there is a basic weakness behind the remedy. If it were really true that solving these problems would cure all the ills of mankind, we would then find the most unselfish, upright, honest, kind and loving of people living in the biggest houses with the biggest incomes. Of course, that is not the case!

One of my former curates was at one time the chaplain at a very expensive public school. When on one occasion I visited him he told me that they had recently had a 'flu epidemic at the school and that his wife had been helping the matron to notify the parents of the boys who were ill. The big problem was deciding whom they should contact, since about a third of the boys in that school came from broken homes. Their parents had plenty of money, but they were not happy.

When I was studying moral philosophy at Edinburgh University I had the privilege of being taught by Professor A. E. Taylor, who had one of the most brilliant minds in Europe. He had made a spiritual pilgrimage from agnosticism as a student to orthodox Christianity as a mature thinker. In the middle of one of his lectures he paused, looked up at us and said: 'Ladies and gentlemen please remember this: there *must* have been an Adam.' He was simply stating that there must have been a time when man first sinned. Whether or not we literally accept the form in which that fact is stated in the Bible, the fact remains that 'there must have been an Adam.' We are familiar with the idea of heredity in the physical and mental realm of the human personality. The Bible shows that we are also affected by a spiritual heredity. We are not born as 'perfect little angels' but, on the contrary, we come into the world with an heredity of sin which has infected human nature at its very source!

A provision which meets the needs of men

The Bible goes on to speak of a provision that will meet the needs of men. That is why the gospel is good news – God has provided a way out of our sinful condition. The Bible speaks of this provision in two ways. First of all it speaks of *a new relationship with God that is possible*. We're all familiar with the fact that relationships constitute a major problem in life – relationships between husbands and wives, between parents and children, between teachers and pupils, between employers and employees, between race and race, between governments and governed. The Christian gospel goes one step further and says that there is a fundamental relationship which has to be put right before the others can be sorted out, and that is the relationship between man and God. The cross on which Christ died was the way in which God made it possible for that relationship to be put right.

Dr Howard Guiness once wrote about a man who was brought up for trial, having committed a serious offence. When the judge entered the court to try his case the man was appalled to see that he was in fact someone he knew. They hadn't seen each other for years, but they had gone to the same school and had been the closest of friends! The judge, of course, recognised the prisoner too. As the case went on it was quite obvious that the man was going to be found guilty. The judge summed up the evidence very fairly, and then the jury went out to consider their verdict. Somehow the nature of the relationship between the judge and the prisoner had leaked out during the course of the trial, and when the jury came back you could have heard a pin drop in the court. Everyone wondered what would happen. The verdict, as expected was 'guilty'. All that remained was for the judge to pronounce sentence. How would he handle the case of his former very good friend? He passed the heaviest sentence that the law would allow, and the court was shocked at the severity of it. The prisoner had the choice of either paying a massive fine (which he couldn't possibly afford) or serving a long term of imprisonment. It looked as if he was going to go to jail. Then the court witnessed something amazing. The judge stepped down from his seat, went up to the dock where the prisoner was standing and quietly said to him, 'I'll pay that fine for you.' Then he turned and left the courtroom. The law was satisfied and so was love.

In a similar way, in a mystery beyond all our understanding, God took upon himself the penalty of the sins of the whole world when Jesus Christ died on the cross. That is surely what lies behind that cry of agony, torn as it were from the very heart of the Saviour, 'My God, my God why didst thou forsake me?' At the cross something happened beyond all human comprehension and calculation, something that is conveyed by the words of the Old Testament prophecy: 'All we like sheep have gone astray; we have turned everyone to his own way; and the Lord hath laid on him the iniquity of us all.'

So a new relationship between man and God is now possible because the keeping of the Law, which was impossible, has been replaced by faith in Jesus Christ, who bore the penalty of our sins on our behalf. Through Christ sinful man can now look up into the face of a holy, righteous and loving God who has done everything necessary to put the relationship right, if only man is prepared to accept it on God's terms.

As well as a new relationship with God the good news speaks of *the new resources that are available in Christ*. Man needs much more than forgiveness: he needs something or someone to deal with what that little girl called 'the thing inside me that likes being naughty.' And so the promise of God is that the living Christ will come and dwell in our hearts if we put our faith in him. The Holy Spirit will live in us, bringing new resources into our lives. The change can be so dramatic that Paul describes it in these words: 'If any man be in Christ [and Christ be in him] he is a new creature.' This is the fulfilment of what our Lord meant when he told Nicodemus, 'Ye must be born again.' In other words, man needs not just forgiveness, but also the power to live a new life. Man is not wise enough, but Christ is. Man is not loving enough, but Christ is. Man is not strong enough, but Christ is. Man is not caring enough, but Christ is. Man is not patient enough, but Christ is. All that man is not, Christ is, and when Christ comes into our hearts and lives in us by his Spirit we have new resources, adequate to meet our every need.

If a pauper married a millionaire there would obviously be a drastic change in the pauper's life. Someone becoming a Christian is just like a pauper marrying a millionaire. The pauper wouldn't own an ordinary car but would instead drive around in a Rolls Royce! His style of life would be different because his resources would be different. That is the transformation which man desperately needs – he needs the resources of God in order to live to please God. He needs someone to control the sinful nature which he has inherited, which inclines him to do what is wrong and makes him fail to do what is right.

A decision which changes the lives of men

So we come to the third point of the gospel, the good news. It calls for a decision which changes the lives of men. Here we face an extraordinary inconsistency and irrationality in human nature. People are prepared to make decisions about many things in life – about which car to buy, which clothes to wear, which foods to eat, which place to go for their holidays. However, when people are asked to make a decision about God, their hackles are immediately raised! And yet we do have to make a decision. How else could it be? Would God ram salvation down man's throat whether he wanted it or not? God has respect for the integrity of the human personality that he has created. So there is a decision to be made, and it has to be a simple one, so that children as well as adults can understand it and make it.

What is the nature of that decision? First of all there is *an acceptance of Christ that we must make personally*. If the gift of God is eternal life, that gift has to be received. Possibly the most well-known picture of Jesus Christ is Holman Hunt's *Christ the Light of the World*. One of the two originals hangs in Saint Paul's Cathedral in London. It is based on Revelation 3.20, where Christ likens himself to someone standing outside a door knocking, wishing to enter. The words are: 'Behold, I stand at the door and knock: if any man hears my voice and opens the door, I will come in to him.' How should I respond to this? The answer is simple. If I want Christ to enter my life, all I have to do is open the door. All I have to do is ask him in, and he will come in! This verse in Revelation helped me to become a Christian. I was a minister's son, born on the mission field, baptised as a baby. I went to church every Sunday once I was old enough, read my Bible, said my prayers (when I remembered)* and tried my best. However, I came to realise that none of these things actually made me a Christian. Only receiving Christ into my life could do it, so that's what I did. Just as simply as we would welcome a friend into our home, so we can welcome Christ into our lives.

How can we know that he has come in? Will we feel anything? Perhaps we will, perhaps we won't. But the reason we can be sure he will come in is because he said he would:

'If any man hears my voice and opens the door, *I will* come in.' And when he comes into our lives, he comes to stay.

But if we look closely at Holman Hunt's picture, we notice that Christ is wearing a crown. This means that he is not only our Saviour but he is also our Lord and King. So the other crucial part of the decision we have to make is *an allegiance that we must give to Christ*. This, I think, is where the rub comes. This is why people resist the Christian gospel.

How do most people live? If they are not Christians they are in reality like those people at Ephesus to whom Paul wrote. He showed them that before they were Christians they based their lives upon two principles. First, they 'walked according to the course of this world.' In other words, they did what everybody else did. And that, of course, is the principle that determines the conduct of so many people. They say, 'Everybody does it.' But how do we know that everybody is right? Someone once said cynically that 'the majority is generally wrong.' So what everybody does is not necessarily right. Paul went on to say that if the Ephesians were not doing what everybody else was doing, they were doing what they wanted to do – they were 'Fulfilling the desires of the flesh and of the mind.' So that's the other principle – I do what I want!

In one of the parishes in which I worked, a mother, father and daughter started coming to church regularly. One day I called at their home, and the father and I had a chat. He wasn't young – his hair was white. After a while he said, 'Mr Duncan, I want to be frank with you. For thirty years I didn't darken the door of a church, and for thirty years I was wrong!' He felt that he had wasted a great deal of time, a great deal of life. Malcolm Muggeridge made the same mistake, and when he wrote his autobiography, after becoming a Christian in his sixties, he entitled it *Chronicles of Wasted Time*.

We must accept Jesus Christ as Saviour and we must also give our allegiance to him as our Lord. 'Lord, what wilt thou have me to do?' was the question Saul of Tarsus asked Jesus on the road to Damascus. From then on he did Christ's will, and so was able to say towards the end of his life, 'I was not disobedient.'

I don't watch a great deal of television I'm afraid, maybe I should watch more just to see what other people are watching, but there's one programme that I always find fascinating, the Paul Daniels Show where with illusion after illusion he simply does the most incredible things. I always wonder how on earth he does it. Big boards are put up on the platform, they form a box and are there for a minute and then taken away – and there's an elephant, a live elephant!! However did that happen? When I was in my teens there were two men named Maskeleyne and Devant who became famous for performing illusions. In one of their most celebrated illusions the curtain went up to reveal an artist sitting in a chair in front of a painting he had just finished. It was a painting of his dead wife sitting on a swing in a garden. As the artist sat and looked at the canvas on the easel in front of him he dropped off to sleep. While he slept, the audience suddenly saw the figure of his wife on the canvas rise up, step out of the painting, move towards her husband and touch him lovingly. Then she went back, climbed up into the canvas and sat on the swing again. Then the artist awoke. He rose up and, taking the canvas off the easel, carried it away. It was just a picture! I cannot begin to understand how they did that illusion.

There are so many people for whom Christ is just a picture painted on the canvas of history. But he is far more than that. He is a living reality, and he wants to step down from that painting and enter our lives. He wants to bring us into a new relationship with God and give us new resources to cope with that thing inside us that 'likes being naughty'. How relevant the message of the Christian gospel is, and how thrilling for the preacher to have such a message to preach!

John Wesley travelled the length and breadth of this land of ours, and historians agree that in all probability he saved

England from bloody revolution. At the end of a day's preaching he would write in his journal, 'I came to such and such a place and I offered them Christ.' The preacher's message is Christ, who died for us on the cross and wants to live in us by his Spirit and bring about such a transformation that, as Paul said, we become new creations.

Chapter 3: What Should We Expect a Sermon To Do?

Unto me . . . is this grace given, that I should preach among the Gentiles the unsearchable riches of Christ (Eph. 3.8).

One of the things which disturbs me about the overall state of the Church of today is how the sermon – which at one time, certainly in Scotland, held a very distinguished place in its life – now seems to be discredited and demoted. In Helmut Thielicke's book, *The Trouble with the Church*, the first chapter is entitled 'The Plight of Preaching'. There he writes, 'Anybody who keeps in mind the goal which the Reformation once had for itself would be appalled at what has happened in the Church of Luther and Calvin to the very thing that their fathers regarded as the source and spring of Christian faith and life, namely preaching.' In the hectic bustle of today's ecclesiastical routine it appears to be relegated more and more to the margin of things. We seem to have lost the sort of abiding sense of wonder which Paul expressed when he wrote to the church at Ephesus: 'Unto me, who am less than the least of all saints, is this grace given, that I should preach among the Gentiles the unsearchable riches of Christ' (Eph. 3.8).

In tune with the mind of Paul is the mind of that famous and distinguished preacher of the Church of Scotland, Professor James S. Stewart. In his book, *Heralds of God* he has written:

'Do not listen to the foolish talk that suggests that in the 20th century the preaching of the Word is an anachronism and the pulpit, having served its purpose, must now be displaced by the Press, radio or discussion group . . . and finally vanish from the scene. As long as God sets his image upon the soul . . . so long will the Preacher's voice be heard and his task persist through all the clamour of the world.'

It may be that Paul Althaus is very near the mark when he says, 'People today are not tired of preaching but they may be tired of our preaching.' That may be the kind of preaching of which Luther said, 'It would not entice a dog from beside a warm fire.'

With all this in mind I want to ask this question: 'What should we expect a sermon to do?' It may well be that we have been disappointed by the preaching we have heard in the past because we have had wrong expectations of it. To guide our thinking I want to turn to what was possibly the greatest sermon ever preached – that of Simon Peter on the Day of Pentecost, recorded in Acts 2.14–47. This sermon was so effective that on that day three thousand souls were added to the Church! We can see what this sermon did among the people by studying the concluding verses of this passage.

A sermon should disturb

First, we should expect that the preaching of the word will disturb us: 'When they heard [Peter's sermon] they were pricked in their heart, and said . . . "What shall we do?"' Unfortunately many people don't want to be disturbed, particularly middle-aged people who may be comfortable and content and set in their ways.

I once read a little booklet called *Comfy Christians* written by that famous and wonderful missionary, Amy Wilson Carmichael. She told the story of a little girl who was going to a party. Her mother gave her the usual words of advice: 'See that you're a good girl.' When the little girl came back from the party her mother asked her, 'Have you been a good girl?' The girl replied, 'Mummy, I haven't been very good, I haven't been very naughty. I've just been comfy!' I suppose that is the tragedy of so many of us who call ourselves Christians. We aren't outstandingly good or bad – we're somewhere in the middle. We are comfy, and we don't want to be disturbed. We may be a little bit like Moses, who while in the wilderness was called by God. We read that he was reluctant to obey God's call because he was 'content to dwell with his father-in-law'. He had settled down and was quite happy to spend his life as a shepherd. But God wanted him to deliver a nation!

I want to ask two questions about the way a good sermon disturbs us. First, what is *the reason for this disturbance*? It is quite simple. In Psalm 119 v.130 we are told, 'The entrance of thy words giveth light' – and light can be disturbing. People do things in the dark which they would not do in the light. The light of God's word may be the light of God's truth or it may be the light of God's holiness, but in whichever way it shines upon us, it can disturb us. The action it calls for may be negative – perhaps there is something which has got to go out of our lives; or the action it calls for may be positive – there may be something which has got to come into our lives. Change is the last thing that most people want. They are quite content as they are. But unless we regard ourselves as perfect (and who, with any degree of honesty, can do that?) we should expect to have to change – we should not resent it. It is as stupid to resent disturbance by God's word as to resent the diagnosis of a doctor or a dentist. All of this applies to the believer as much as to the unbeliever, and surely neither has grounds for complacency.

The second question is, what is *the response to this disturbance*? The people in Acts chapter 2 said, 'What shall we do?' Their minds had been awakened to a need for action. When we face God's truth, action is always the next step. We should be not only hearers of the word, but doers of the word as well. Here we come up against a dangerous trend in modern preaching, the influence of which has spread even into Evangelical circles and into contemporary evangelism. This trend is towards cutting out the appeal for decision and action. But such an appeal, which is neglected in so much preaching today, seems to me to be quite in order. Many modern preachers ask people to discuss, but they do not challenge them to act. I find again and again that this call to act is very evident in the New Testament. There it is made quite plain that we need to 'obey the gospel'. Those people who heard Peter on the day of Pentecost were quite right. When truth is understood it calls for action and their question – 'What shall we do?' is a question that everyone sitting under the authority of God and under the ministry of the Holy Spirit should be prepared to ask. It is the 'doing' that completes the disturbance caused by God.

Responding to the disturbance may affect the pattern of my life, it may change my relationships with people. Perhaps I will go one way and they will go another. I should expect the preaching of the word to disturb my life. Although he had been content, Moses was certainly deeply disturbed by God. Excuse after excuse fell from his lips, but God answered them all and called on him to act and become the leader of a nation.

A sermon should direct

I believe the second thing we should expect the preaching of the word to do is to direct. Acts 2.38 says, 'Then Peter said unto them, Repent, and be baptised every one of you in the name of Jesus Christ for the remission of sins, and ye shall receive the gift of the Holy Ghost.' They had been disturbed, and now they must be directed. Action was called for, but what action? Peter now showed them that they needed to repent and be baptised. One bit of advice given by the great Scottish preacher, Dr Alexander Whyte of St George's, Edinburgh, was this: 'Never forget to tell them how.' It's not enough to tell folk what; we should also tell them how.

There are two things we should note about Peter's words

in verse 38. First, there is *the clarity of what he said*. It can be summed up in two words: repent and receive. Or, if you like, 'admit your need and accept God's gift.' But neither of these things is easy for a proud man to do. It's not easy for a satisfied, self-righteous man to admit his need and receive salvation. But whether or not he acts upon the direction of Peter and preachers like him, he must at least hear it; he must understand what he is expected to do. That is why clarity is so important.

I remember hearing of two people who were discussing the sermon they had just heard as they left church one Sunday. 'That was deep – very deep,' said one of them. The other replied, 'No, it wasn't deep – it was just muddy!' Bishop Taylor Smith once pointed out to me that the most profound statements that Jesus ever uttered were very often made in short sentences composed, in English translation, of one-syllable words. Consider this sentence, for example: 'I am come to seek and to save that which was lost.' How differently some preachers present the word today. Their language is the language of the theologian, not that of the common people who, we are told, 'heard Jesus gladly'.

Jesus presented truths in picture form, drawing his pictures from the everyday experience of his hearers. A distinguished Christian teacher of our day has denigrated the use of illustrations, describing the book entitled *The Art and Craft of Sermon Illustration* by that distinguished Methodist Preacher, Dr Sangster, as 'an abomination'. But to criticise Sangster on this issue is to criticise the Saviour, because he made great use of illustrations. I think I know what Sangster's critic meant. If a sermon is all illustration – just one big collection of stories – then it is, of course, irrelevant and useless. But illustrations are very worthwhile if they are being used to bring to life the truth of the word of God.

Someone once remarked that there are two kinds of sermons. One kind is all door and no house. That's true of a great deal of Evangelical preaching, which tends to show people how to be saved without describing what Christian living is like. Another kind is all house and no door. A picture of Christianity is painted, but the way in isn't explained. That's what a lot of liberal preaching is like. I'd like to add a third kind. Some sermons have a door and a house but no windows! It is the windows – the illustrations – which let in the light. I prefer to follow the example of my Saviour, whose teaching was full of illustrations and parables from ordinary life.

The second thing we need to note about the words of Peter is *the certainty of what he said*. He promised the people, 'You shall receive,' not 'You may receive.' Peter was certain about what he was saying because his message rested upon the word of God, upon the promises of God. If we are true preachers, we are not moving in the realm of human speculation but in the realm of divine revelation. We are not moving in the realm of theological reasoning – of what men think, even if they are thinking of spiritual things – but in the realm of what God has said. When we stand on the ground of the word of God, we can preach with certainty. Of course, some people feel that it is presumptuous of us to be sure of what we preach. If the grounds of our assurance were merely in ourselves, then, of course, we would be guilty of presumption. But if those grounds are in our Lord and in his work and word, it is not presumptuous to be certain.

I was sure that he would come into my life, because he had promised that he would. In his first epistle John writes, 'These things have I written unto you that believe on the name of the Son of God; that ye may know that ye have eternal life.' We are not merely to hope that we have eternal life – we are to know. We can be sure that we can know, because God has promised that we can.

I remember hearing the first Christmas radio broadcast by King George V when I was a child. He was speaking not only as King but also as a father, so he had a special word for the children. He made it perfectly clear that he wanted to speak to us by saying, 'Children, *the King* is speaking to you.' When we preach the word of God we are preaching the word of the heavenly King. So that word has authority and certainty.

A sermon should divide

The third thing we should expect of the preaching of the word is that it will divide. In Acts 2.40 Peter speaks of the people's need to save themselves from 'this untoward [crooked, perverse] generation'. In verse 41 we read of those who 'gladly received his word'. Every hearer adopted one of just two attitudes. First of all, there was *the attitude of reception*. I am struck by the fact that they received the word 'gladly'. There's nothing miserable about obedience to the truth. How the Church today needs to grasp the truth that the Gospel is Good News! It is not the path to misery but the path to liberty, to a new relationship with God and man, to a life filled with new resources, wisdom and power.

That famous verse, John 3.16, has been described as 'The gospel in a nutshell'. It speaks of God's love as a giving love: 'For God so loved the world, that he *gave* his only begotten Son, that whosoever believeth in him should not perish, but have everlasting life.' God did not stop giving when he gave Jesus to us, to die for us upon the cross. He goes on giving forever. Many of us know and love this poem by John Oxenham:

Love ever gives
Forgives, outlives
And ever stands with open hands
And while it lives it gives
For this is love's prerogative
To give, and give, and give.

Jesus said, 'I am come that they might have life, and that they might have it more abundantly.' 'These things write we unto you,' said the apostle John, 'that your joy might be full.' God's love is a giving love, and it is his will to give us abundant life and joy through Christ, if we will receive them.

The alternative to this attitude of reception is *an attitude of rejection*. Scripture says that a man who deliberately rejects and turns away from God's truth is crooked. Such a man is in rebellion against God. This attitude has its source in what the Bible calls the carnal mind, which is at enmity with God. If our argument is with the preacher of a sermon, that's all right, but if it is with his message that's all wrong! We have the right to disagree with what the preacher thinks, but if we are disagreeing with the preacher's Master, we're on dangerous ground and taking a disastrous course. To prefer our way to God's way is indeed presumption.

In Acts 5.29 Peter is on his feet again and declares that 'We ought to obey God rather than men.' It is not enough to be sincere in rejecting God's truth, for such sincerity is wrong. The Bible says, 'There is a way that seemeth right unto a man, but the end thereof is the way of death.'

So preaching divides. Every time God speaks through his word congregations are divided into those whose attitude is one of reception and those whose attitude is one of rejection. Let us remember that when the word of God is being preached, 'The King is speaking to us.' When we respond to it in obedience and faith, we are truly worshipping him.

Chapter 4: The Preacher as Pastor

Feed the flock of God (1 Pet. 5.2).

In the tenth chapter of John's Gospel the Lord has a great deal to say about the good shepherd. Of course, primarily he is referring to himself, but there are aspects of good shepherding which any good pastor will share with Jesus. In this chapter our Lord mentions five specific things about the good shepherd: in verses 14 and 27 he speaks of 'my sheep'; in verses 16 and 27 he speaks of 'my voice'; in verses 15 and 17 he speaks of 'my life'; in verse 28 he speaks of 'my hand'; and in verses 17, 18, 25 and 29 he speaks of 'my Father'. Each of these words seems to throw light upon the task of the one who is to be a good shepherd of the flock of God.

Let's examine each in turn and see what we can learn. The importance of shepherding needs to be reaffirmed today because there are those who denigrate the pastoral side of the ministry. This attitude is based in part upon Acts chapter 6 where, due to the growth of the church, the apostles appointed men to take on some leadership tasks while they devoted themselves entirely to prayer and preaching the word. I don't believe in basing a doctrine upon a single verse, and it seems to me that to apply that kind of approach to the work of the minister can be dangerous. In the first place we're not apostles, and in the second place the task confronting ministers today is generally not of the magnitude of that which faced them. Their task was a unique one, ours is not.

'My sheep'

So let us look at these words that our Lord used to describe what it meant to him to be a good shepherd. He calls the

29

sheep 'my sheep'. So there is *a responsibility that must be assessed* by the shepherd as he looks after his sheep. Each of us will have a flock for which we are responsible before God. It may be a congregation, it may be a Sunday school class or it may be a Bible study group, but we have the same responsibility to care and provide for these sheep. So Peter urges the elders of the church to which he is writing in his first letter to 'Feed the flock of God.' We also need to assess competing responsibilities carefully. We not only have a spiritual responsibility but a natural one too. We may have a big flock in church, but we also have a small flock at home – our own family. Both flocks need to be cared for.

There is also *a relationship that must be achieved* between the shepherd and the sheep. In John 10.14 Jesus says, 'I know my sheep, and am known of mine.' In verse 3 the Good Shepherd calls his sheep by name. He knows his sheep, so that he may provide for them. We cannot know the needs of our people just by looking at them from the pulpit. We need to know them, and not simply when they are sick or in trouble, but in every situation in life. So the good shepherd will constantly be found among his people.

The relationship is, of course, a mutual one. Not only do we get to know our people, but they get to know us. This should lead them to trust us – provided, of course, that we are worthy of their trust! They cannot get to know us merely by looking at us in the pulpit. We need to spend time with them, and that time is never wasted. Tom Rees, one of Britain's great evangelists of this century, said, 'You won't get people to trust your Saviour until they trust you.' So this relationship should be a high priority in the preacher's timetable. We must know our sheep and they must know us.

'My voice'

Jesus speaks of himself as the good shepherd and then speaks of 'my voice'. In verse 27 he says, 'My sheep hear my voice, and I know them, and they follow me.' In the ancient East the shepherd was always ahead of the flock – he always led them, he didn't drive them. This fact contains *a subtle note of challenge* for us, since it implies that we who shepherd the flock must also be ahead of them. We must be ahead of them in our understanding of the word of God and the ways of God, ahead of them in our experience of the sufficiency of the grace of God. We are not to guide them to an experience of which we ourselves know nothing, but to that which we have already gone through ourselves. Also, our sheep must be within range of our voice. We must not use language which is too far ahead of where they are.

In verse 4 Jesus says, 'The sheep follow him.' There is *a subtle danger* that the sheep may follow the shepherd blindly and that their loyalty will be attached chiefly to him and not to the One under whose service he works. We need to be careful lest we attract people to ourselves rather than to the Master whom we seek to serve.

'My hand'

In verse 28 Jesus says, 'Neither shall any man pluck them out of my hand.' He is thinking of *the existence of dangers* when in verse 10 he speaks of 'the thief [that] cometh not, but for to steal, and to kill, and to destroy'. We should always remember that there are influences at work which are hostile to the well-being of the flock. There are spiritual forces. We must never forget the enemy of souls. There is also the world and, alas, there are misguided believers. We are living in days when some would seem to wish to take sheep from other pastors' flocks and put them in their own. This is known as 'sheep stealing'.

So the existence of danger is a very real factor in the life of the shepherd. But there is also *the endurance of devotion*, the strength of the shepherd's hold on the sheep in the flock. He won't let them go easily. Jesus won't, and neither should the shepherd. Many people love that hymn by George Matteson which begins, 'Oh love that wilt not let me go.' The shepherd's grip upon his sheep must be strong. We mustn't let people slip away unnoticed and disappear from the membership and fellowship of the church, as if they were unwanted. We need to keep a careful record of our members and their families and of the visits we pay them, because if people do slip away it may be because they have been neglected.

'My life'

Jesus says in verse 15, 'I lay down my life for the sheep,' and in verse 17, 'Therefore doth the Father love me, because I lay down my life.' For Jesus, of course, that included a literal laying down of his life in death. It may mean that for some of us today, but usually it means laying down our lives in sacrificial service.

In the East the shepherd lived with the sheep. His work and his life were the same thing. This shows us that the pastor's work is *a service from which there is no release*. He lays down his life – his is quite literally a full-time job from which there is never any retirement. And yet, having said that, we have to be careful. The pastor should have one day's rest, just like anybody else. The good book says, 'Six days shalt thou labour,' not seven, and it is most important that the pastor himself should obey that command as well as expect his people to do so. The only way to do that is to mark a day in your diary and put a line right through it – that's your day off! It could be Monday, Wednesday, Thursday – any day except Sunday, becaue you are working that day. Once you have put a line through that rest day, don't accept any engagements for that day which may come your way. You can say, quite truthfully, 'I'm sorry, but that day is already booked in my diary.' That's the day when you can rest and spend time with your family.

The pastor's work also entails *sacrifice to which there is no limit* – sacrifice even to the point of death. The service of the shepherd is costly. That great Scottish preacher Professor A. J. Gossip recalls in one of his sermons how doubting Thomas faced the believing disciples after the resurrection of Jesus. He hadn't been with them when Jesus had come to them, and when they were together again later he said, 'Except I shall see in his hands the print of the nails, I will not believe.' The disciples were full of the joy, excitement and wonder of the fact that Christ was alive, but they faced an unbelieving man in Thomas. Gossip, in a dramatic switch of thought, takes those words of Thomas and remarks that the church today is facing an equally unbelieving world which is saying what Thomas said: 'Except I see in your hands the print of the nails, I won't believe.' The world wants to see evidence that our serving Christ is costly to us.

'My Father'

So Jesus has spoken of 'my sheep', 'my voice', 'my hands' and 'my life', and finally he speaks of 'my Father'. We have to think of **the trust** that has been placed in us. We are responsible to the One who himself knew what it was to be a shepherd and who has given us the task of caring for his sheep. **The task** has been designed and suited to our own personalities, capabilities and gifts. We are called to it by God. We didn't go to this or that church because we liked it, because it had a nice congregation, because the vicarage or the manse was a beautiful house in a lovely town. We went there because God called us to go. We didn't go because of the money we would be paid, but simply because we wanted to do his will. God has entrusted us with a job to do. Now the responsibility is ours to justify God's trust in us. Jesus said, 'Therefore doth my Father love me, because I lay down my life.' The Father will love us in the same way if we lay down our lives. Surely the ultimate reward we have in the ministry, in the pastoring of the flock, is knowing that if we have been found faithful, a time will one day come when the Father will say to us, 'Well done, good and faithful servant. Enter thou into the joy of thy Lord.'

My father was a great cricketer, both at school and university. He used to say that the greatest satisfaction and pleasure he got out of it was not the applause of the spectators but the praise of his aged father. When a match was over he would always go and see him. His father would say, 'Well, how did you get on today, John?' and my father would be able to tell him of his success. One day you and I will face our heavenly Father, and what great joy will be ours when we hear him say, 'Well done.'

Chapter 5: Pitfalls which the Preacher Must Avoid

Woe unto you, Pharisees! (Luke 11.42).

I believe there are certain dangers and areas of potential weakness which are peculiar to those involved in the ministry and spiritual leadership. In chapter 11 of Luke's Gospel, where Jesus attacks the hypocrisy of the Pharisees, he pinpoints six of these dangers with words of warning preceded by the little phrase, 'Woe unto you.' We are not concerned with the exact content of each warning, but with the principle that it reveals.

Stressing the unimportant

Let's look first at verse 42: 'Ye tithe mint and rue and all manner of herbs, and pass over judgment and the love of God.' Here is the temptation of stressing the unimportant, a sin of which some of us may well be guilty. The Americans have a delightful phrase to describe this: they talk about people who 'major in minors', who make big issues out of little things. That fine American preacher, Dr S. D. Gordon, remarks that it is possible to block out the light of the sun with a sixpence if you hold it close enough to your eye!

There are two sides to what our Lord is saying in this verse. First, there is *the importance which is attached to some minor issues*, to some details of little significance . . . The details may be to do with belief, or conduct or assessment of character. We may have some little pet idea of our own and demand that others agree with us. It may be that someone has an irritating personal weakness or habit which looms so large in our thinking that we can't see that person's good points. Now,

35

our Lord is not setting aside the importance of minor matters, but he is warning us against treating them as if they were of supreme significance.

The other aspect of what Jesus is saying in this verse is concerned with *the indifference which is shown towards some major issues* such as the love of God and the holiness of God. These are the great priorities to which we should attach the most importance.

Seeking the unmerited

Another warning which Jesus gives us is against seeking the unmerited or the undeserved. In verse 43 he says, 'ye love the uppermost seats in the synagogues, and greetings in the markets,' and the implication is, 'You don't deserve them!' So here Jesus is speaking of *the prominence they love* among the people of God and among the community. There are those who want prominence, who want position, who want recognition by and deference from others. In 3 John verse 9 the apostle writes of someone called Diotrephes, 'who loveth to have the pre-eminence among them,' who liked to put himself first.

After many years in the ministry I can say that one of the most common problems in churches is people who want position and power. Dr Paul Rees writes of a minister he knew who when dying said, 'I'm not ready to die. I see it all so clearly now. I have used the offices of the Church as stepping stones to gratify my own ambition!' How subtle is the temptation to seek position, prominence and the praise of men. If my experience is anything to go by, sometimes it is those who find themselves to be failures in what they are doing who seek prominence in some other sphere.

Our Lord speaks of the prominence such people love, and he also indicates *the experience they lack*. They want something for which they are neither fit nor ready. They want the place but they are not willing to pay the price – the price of spiritual maturity with all that it involves, such as intimacy with God and integrity of life. I remember very clearly a young preacher of great ability telling me there were only two pulpits he wanted to preach from. One of them happened to be the most important and famous pulpit in London and the other the most important and famous pulpit in Edinburgh. He got neither of them. Instead he spent his life ministering to a mere handful of people.

The Keswick speaker Dr Donald Barnhouse once said, 'The way up is down.' Of course, Jesus said the same thing in John Chapter 12: 'Except a corn of wheat fall into the ground and die, it abideth alone.' The mother of Jesus' disciples James and John had big plans for them. Sometimes parents can be dangerously ambitious. Doubtless at her instigation they asked the Master, 'Grant unto us that we may sit, one on thy right hand, the other on thy left hand, in thy glory.' To which Jesus replied, 'Ye know not what ye ask: can ye drink of the cup that I drink of and be baptised with the baptism that I am baptised with? . . . Whosoever of you will be the chiefest, shall be servant of all' (Mark 10:37–44). James and John had not begun to understand that 'the way up is down.'

Concealing the unworthy

In verse 44 Jesus warns us about concealing the unworthy: 'Ye are as graves which appear not, and the men that walk over them are not aware of them.' Some people may appear beautiful on the outside, but inside they are full of dead men's bones and uncleanness! I believe that our Lord is here speaking firstly of *a deception which is deliberate*. The word of God says, 'If we say we have no sin, we deceive ourselves, and the truth is not in us' (1 John 1.8). We may deceive ourselves but we don't deceive God. I sometimes come across people who claim that if a person is a Christian, his or her sinful nature within has been eradicated. I don't find that in my Bible. In Romans 7.18 Paul says, 'I know that in me (that is, in my flesh), dwelleth no good thing.' However, the person Jesus is talking about in Luke 11.44 is trying to ignore these facts – they are deliberately condoning and concealing their sin. They are pretending it's not there!

Behind this lie there is also *a presumption which is dangerous*. Such people are presuming upon the grace of God. In Psalm 19.13 the psalmist prays, 'Keep thou thy servant from presumptuous sins.' Paul asks, 'Shall we continue in sin that grace may abound?' The answer, of course, is 'no'. Sometimes we can be so familiar with failure that we cease to feel it to be so. 'Familiarity breeds contempt,' we are told. But we are dealing with One 'to whom all hearts are open, all desires are known and from whom no secrets are hid.'

Also involved is a presuming upon the gullibility of men. Jesus says, 'The men that walk over them are not aware of them.' While we may deceive some of the people some of the time, we cannot deceive all people all the time. A brilliant pianist once said, 'If I miss my eight hours of practice for one day, I know it. If I miss it for two days, the critics know it. If I miss it for three days, the public knows it!'

Proclaiming the unfulfilled

Another pitfall which Jesus warns us about is that of proclaiming the unfulfilled. In verse 46 he says of the Pharisees 'Ye lade men with burdens grievous to be borne, and ye yourselves touch not the burdens with one of your fingers.' There are two thoughts here. First, *the obligation which they are ready to lay upon others*. There are obligations in the Christian life. They may be to do with obedience. The Christian's initial obedience is to obey the gospel and receive Christ as Saviour and Lord. But this leads on to a continual obedience, a continual reverencing of Jesus as Lord. We now stand in the grace of God, but that does not mean that we no longer have to be obedient.

Christians also have an obligation to pray. 'Men ought to pray,' says Luke 18.1. There is an obligation to be holy. The command still stands, 'Be ye holy as I am holy.' And we need to remember that not only is there a negative side to holiness but a positive one too. Holiness basically means separation from sin and separation to God. Furthermore, there are obligations to witness and to study the word of God.

These are all obligations which we leaders are ready to lay on our people, and rightly so. But what our Lord is saying in the case of the Pharisees is that these are *obligations which they are happy to leave to others*. 'Ye yourselves touch not the burdens with one of your fingers.' Is the same thing true of us today? It's easier to preach truth than to practise it. It's much easier to preach obedience than to be obedient, to preach on prayer than to pray, to preach holiness than to be holy, to preach witnessing than to witness. It's much easier to preach on the importance of the word of God in our lives than to really give it that importance. So what our Lord is saying here is – 'Be careful that you are not preaching and proclaiming the unfulfilled' – that which has not yet been fulfilled in your own life. Preaching has been described as 'truth through personality'. I believe that this is profoundly true. If we are not practising what we preach, how can the Holy Spirit set his seal upon the truth we proclaim? How can the truth reach the minds and hearts of the people if it has not first been accepted and obeyed in the life of the preacher?

Reverencing the unwanted

In verse 47 we find our Lord speaking about another potential area of danger. I call it reverencing the unwanted. Jesus says, 'Ye build the sepulchres of the prophets, and your fathers killed them.' In other words he is saying, 'You would kill the prophets too if they were here now.' They are very willing to pay lip service to the past, but if the past were to appear again in the present, it would be a very different story. So we see here *the demands of orthodoxy which they are prepared to meet*. Not to reverence the prophets would in their eyes be completely unacceptable – indeed, it would be almost blasphemy. So they are not afraid to pay lip service to the facts of history – to the fact that these men had been the mouthpieces of God. Similarly, sometimes churches are made famous by the great ministries which go on within their walls, and in later years those ministries are piously remembered and the men at the heart of them are honoured.

However, even though the Pharisees are prepared to meet the demands of orthodoxy, we should also notice *the distance from reality which they are glad to maintain*. The prophets lived long ago, but if they were to come now they would be too disturbing, too demanding! It's a lovely thing that these men lived the way they did and did the good that they did, but it's a mercy that they don't live now! That great ministry which made the church famous is respected, but if that same ministry were to come back, would it be welcome? We pay lip service to the need for revival, but when revival does come it's often the last thing that people really want. As long as it's remote, in the past and not touching them they are prepared to give it the honour and respect due to it.

Hindering the unenlightened

The final pitfall that Jesus deals with is to be found in verse 52. I call it hindering the unenlightened: 'Ye have taken away the key of knowledge: ye entered not in yourselves, and them that were entering in ye hindered.' There is *an assumption made here by Christ* when he speaks of 'them that were entering in'. There are those, then, who are seeking the light; there are those who are looking for the warmth of the love of God. We need to remember that man is never at ease, never at home away from God. Augustine, one of the great saints of the Church, wrote: 'Our hearts are restless until they find their rest in thee.' There *are* those trying to enter in.

A survey made about churchgoing some years ago showed that 17 per cent of people in England were then going to church, and that another 12 per cent were wanting to go. What was keeping them from going? The answer was rather a shattering one. It was the 17 per cent who were already going to church who were discouraging the 12 per cent! We may infer from this that there are many looking wistfully and wonderingly to Christ, but what they see of his Church is not impressing them!

When the Rev G. R. Harding was Vicar of Holy Trinity Church, Hampstead, he once went to one of the wealthy homes in the area to visit one of the servants there who was a member of his church. As a matter of courtesy he first spoke to the master of the house, who was a very rich young man. They sat and chatted for a while and then Harding asked him, 'Do you mind if I ask you a personal question?'

'No, what is it?' replied the young man.

'Are you a Christian?'

The young man looked at him seriously and said, 'Why do you ask that?'

'Well, I suppose it's my job,' replied Harding. 'I'm a vicar!'

'That's not the point. But listen – I want to tell you something. I'm not a religious man. I never go to church, I never read the Bible and I never pray. But recently I was on a business trip in a cathedral city. I had time on my hands, so I went into the cathedral because I had nothing else to do. I sat down. Suddenly an urge came upon me to pray. I don't normally pray as I said, but for some reason I knelt anyway. How long I knelt I don't know, but while I was kneeling a voice seemed to say to me, as clearly as any audible human voice, "Go home at once and I'll send someone to talk to you."' Then he looked at Harding and said, 'That was three days ago, and I've been waiting!' I wonder how many people are waiting, wanting to enter in. As well as an assumption made by Christ there is here also *an assertion made by Christ* – an assertion that those people find the road blocked. They cannot enter in because 'ye have taken away the key of knowledge; ye entered not in yourselves and them that were [wanting to enter in] ye hindered.' What stops people in their search for Christ? Sometimes it is Christians who have failed to enter into the fulness that is theirs in Christ, who are failing to live the quality of life that Jesus has made possible, who are not revealing the grace and love of the God who loves the world. In Luke 11.33 Jesus likens the Christian to a lighted candle or lamp. He says, 'No man, when he hath lighted a candle, putteth it in a secret place, neither under a bushel, but on a candlestick, that they [which are entering in] may see the light.' Every Christian should be a welcoming, guiding light. But sometimes we fail in that and instead offer a path which is blocked. The way is made difficult just because we are what we are. Sometimes this is, sadly, true even of some of us ministers. In some pulpits the word of God, the truth of God and the grace of God are not being preached. The preacher has taken away the key of knowledge, he has not entered in himself and he is blocking the way for those trying to enter in.

How much we need to pray the prayer with which the Communion Service in the Church of England always opens: 'Oh God to whom all hearts be open, all desires known and from whom no secrets are hid, cleanse the thoughts of our hearts by the inspiration of thy Holy Spirit, that we may perfectly love thee and worthily magnify thy holy name for Jesus' sake. Amen.'

Chapter 6: Expectancy

But [Jesus,] after he had offered one sacrifice for sins for ever, sat down on the right hand of God; from henceforth expecting till his enemies be made his footstool. (Heb. 10.13).

What should be the distinctive characteristic of the life of the Church? In Scripture it is described as 'the body of Christ', a body of which Christ himself is the Head. So I think we are justified in assuming that the characteristic disposition of the mind of Christ should also be that of the Church. Here in this verse we have what is perhaps the predominant characteristic of Christ: 'expectancy.' He is portrayed as seated, having finished his work of redemption, 'from henceforth expecting'. He is seated, but I believe he is also leaning forward, looking outward expectantly! I want us to look at this quality of expectancy which I believe should mark the life of the Church of Jesus Christ. To do this I want to ask three questions.

What do the members have a right to expect of their minister?

First, what do the members have a right to expect of their minister? He has a two-fold relationship with his people. First, *he is a preacher*. He has been ordained to the ministry of the word. 'Preach the word' was Paul's order to Timothy. Members of a church have a right to expect their minister to do just that; to come to them from the presence of God with a message which is the word of God. He will not come to tell them what he thinks, but what God has to say. They have a right to demand that the proclaimed word, like the living

Word, the Lord Jesus, will be 'full of grace and truth'. So both in the matter and the manner of his preaching the word of God will come through to their hearts. Every time the members come into the church they should be, they must be, expecting that to happen.

A word similar to 'expectant' which is often found on the lips of Christians today is the word 'excitement'. But expectancy has a deeper undertone than mere excitement.

There is something else the members of a church have a right to expect, for the minister is not simply a preacher. *He is a pastor* too. If as a preacher his task is to proclaim the word of God, as a pastor he is surely meant to portray the mind, ways and grace of God – a God who is both light and love. The commissioning word of Christ to his disciples was, 'As the Father has sent me, even so send I you.' The purpose for which the Father sent the Son was a three-fold one. It was a redeeming purpose which, of course, took him to the cross. It was also a revealing purpose; that was why Jesus claimed that 'He that hath seen me hath seen the Father.' And it was a renewing purpose; it was God's will that men born in sin might be made new and be born again of the Spirit.

We need to think over that second purpose, the revealing purpose. Jesus wonderfully revealed through his life the mind of God – a blending of light and love, of grace and truth. That same mind of the Father should also be revealed by the life of the pastor. He faces the same challenge as the little girl who once sat down and started trying to draw God. Her mother asked her what she was doing.

'I'm drawing God,' she replied.

'But you can't draw God,' said her mother. 'You don't know what he looks like. Nobody knows what he looks like!'

'They will know what he looks like when I've finished drawing him!' declared the little girl.

Is it any wonder that the work of the ministry is one from which all true servants of God shrink? The minister must be 'full of grace and truth'. This will affect not only what he says but also how he says it and how he shows it in his life day by day. There was a time in my own life when I needed to learn that lesson. I could honestly say that I was chock full of truth when I preached, but I don't think there was much grace in the way I preached!

What has the minister a right to expect from his members?

Here's the second question: What has the minister a right to expect from his members? As a minister prepares for a church service he is expectant. And what has he a right to expect? First of all, he has the right to expect *the presence of his people* – that his people will be there. In Galatians 4.20 Paul describes the Church as 'the mother of us all'. That is a very suggestive concept of the Church. Part of a mother's work is, of course, to provide meals for the children, the good food that will help them to grow. But in the life of the ordinary family nothing is more discouraging for the mother than to prepare the meals and then to find that the members of the family don't turn up to eat them at mealtimes!

How pathetic are the excuses which people make for their non-attendance at church! Turning up at church isn't that much of an effort to make, is it? Isn't it strange how casually and lightly people treat their Christian obligations and duties? However, thankfully there are many faithful church members. I remember that on one very wet Sunday, as I was shaking hands with my congregation as they went out, I said to one lady, 'You deserve a medal for coming out on a day like this.' She replied, 'I won't get a medal tomorrow if it's a day like this and I go to work!' I think it was Lindsay Glegg who fondly remembered one of his church members who was nick-named 'Ever Faithful, Ever Sure' because whatever the weather, he always turned up, not only at the Sunday services but also at the mid-week fellowship meetings.

So I believe the minister has a right to expect the presence of his people. I also believe he has a right to expect *the prayers of his people* in the light of the immensity of his task and the intensity of the pressures he faces. This is what a minister needs above everything else. Again and again in Paul's writings comes the cry, 'Pray for me.' Private prayer is supremely important, but corporate prayer is also vital. We find that in the Bible prayer is sometimes talked of as a very private matter: Jesus said, 'When you pray, shut the door and pray in secret.' We also read in the Bible of people praying together. In Acts Chapter 12 at the house of Mary 'many were gathered together praying.' Jesus made a special promise about corporate prayer: 'If two of you shall agree on earth as touching any thing that they shall ask, it shall be done.' (Matt. 18.19).

When I was growing up my parents always attended a prayer meeting on Thursday nights. Thursday night was always Prayer Meeting night. For some reason or other we always had macaroni and cheese for tea, so macaroni and cheese and prayer meetings are bound up inseparably in my thinking, and 'what God hath joined together let no man put asunder!'

I believe the most important meeting of the week in any church is the prayer meeting. It has to be fixed at a time which is convenient for people. The minister must not make unreasonable demands. His people have other responsibilities. Some of them may have other Christian commitments which make demands upon their time. In my church the mid-week Bible study and the prayer meeting were combined so that people didn't have to come out more than once or twice a week. This gave them plenty of time for their families and for their other forms of work, Christian or otherwise. However, the minister has a right to expect that his people will be there to pray. I can understand that not all Christians can *always* come to the prayer meeting, but it is sad that it is usually the smallest meeting of the week. Why do so many *never* come? That I simply cannot understand.

What does the Master have the right to expect from us all?

The last question is this: What does the Master have the right to expect from us all – from ministers and members alike? For, after all, it is his Church. He said, 'Upon this rock [the rock of his own deity confessed by Peter] I will build *my* Church.' The Church is neither the minister's nor the people's. It is Christ's Church.

A building has a design. It is important that we make certain that the design of the Church is his design. We also need to be sure that what is in the Church is there because he wants it there. If there is something he does not want, we must be willing to remove it from the Church.

A building that is being built will be marked by development – there will be growth, there will be progress. So we should see these things in the life of the Church. Sadly, there are many churches where growth is absent. Sunday by Sunday just the same faithful few turn up.

A building has a destiny. When we see it being built we ask, 'What is it for?' It could be intended for use as a hospital, a school, a factory or a home. It is bound to have a purpose, a design and a destiny. What is the purpose of the Church? Paul says 'It is built for an habitation of God.' In other words, when people come to the Church they should find God there!

So what does Christ expect? I believe he expects *a worship that will enthrone him*. We talk about going to church to worship the Lord, we call our services 'services of worship'. But what do we mean by 'worship'? Do we mean singing hymns? Saying prayers? Listening to a sermon? Receiving of the Sacrament? What *does* worship really mean? As I understand worship, it means giving God his worth in my life. The very word used to read 'worthship'. Jesus said, 'They that worship the Father *must* [note that there is no option here] worship him in spirit and in truth.' We must know him truly, we must relate to him wholly. Every part of our lives must be brought under his authority. Some people seem to think that all God asks is that they should be converted. Not a bit of it. Getting right with God is, of course, the beginning, but no more than that. After new birth comes growth. I believe that this is why some Christians do not seem to like a full Bible ministry, a ministry that relates the truth of God to the lives of Christians as well as to those of the unconverted. They love to hear about salvation because, having been converted, they are no longer in the target area of that part of God's truth. But they don't want to hear what Paul loves to call the 'whole counsel of God', because when that is preached they find themselves once again in the target area! But God will not have it any other way.

Paul, in the first chapter of his letter to the Colossians, speaks of Christ as the Head of the Church and describes the Church's purpose as that of ensuring that 'in all things he might have the pre-eminence.' Doctor Stuart Holden, a well-known Keswick speaker, used to say there were three kinds of Christians. Some give Christ a place in their lives. They are Christians – they have received Jesus. Others give him a prominent place in their lives, and that is good. But still others give him the pre-eminent place in their lives. They worship him from their hearts. He is not only their Saviour, but also their Lord.

So the Master expects a worship from his people which will enthrone him. But the Christian life is to be lived outside the church building as well as inside it, so I believe that Christ also expects of us *a witness through our lives which exalts him*. A witness to what? Surely a witness to the reality of Christ and of his power to save! For it was said at his birth, 'Thou shalt call his name Jesus, for he shall save his people from their sins.' We need to remember that Christ said that the promise of the power of the Holy Spirit given on the Ascension Mount in Acts 1.8 was made so that we could be witnesses to him, witnesses who would speak of him with their lips and through their lives – not only their personal, individual lives but also their corporate life as a fellowship. For sin not only separates man from God but also separates men from one another. So part of the witness of the Church lies in the solving of relationships, in providing the answer to the conflicts and alienations which bedevil all areas of social life.

In our Lord's great prayer in John chapter 17 he asked God that 'they may all be one in us [Christ and the Father], that the world may believe that thou hast sent me.' In other words Christ was saying that authentic evidence of an authentic experience of God's grace among his people would convince the watching world. Oneness in Christ, unity and harmony in the Spirit – that is something which people notice. It is not always to be found, but when it is found it is beautiful. It makes people wonder how it is that these Christians 'love one another'.

A worship which enthrones Christ in our hearts, a witness through our lives which exalts him. This is what the Master expects from his people. It is, indeed, what the world expects from the Church. If there is anything less than that, they might as well close the doors of our churches and let them remain closed forever.

Chapter 7: The Challenge of the Spirit

Tarry until ye be endued with power from on high (Luke 24.49).
You shall receive power . . . you shall be witnesses (Acts 1.8).

These two verses indicate that the success of the work to which the apostles and indeed the Church were called would be dependent upon the presence and the power of the Holy Spirit. Jesus had said, 'without me ye can do nothing.' It is essential, then, that we think through the nature of the person and work of the Holy Spirit. It is hard to believe, but fifty years ago a well-known missionary wrote, 'The Holy Spirit is largely unknown, ignored and unnoticed in the Church today.' However, in recent years that situation has changed dramatically. The Church has rediscovered the Person of the Holy Spirit. Because of that there has been a significant advance. But in spiritual warfare, whenever there is an advance there is always a counter-attack. The devil is not foolish enough to deny the reality of the Holy Spirit. His tactics have been more subtle than that. He has in many areas diverted the Church from the main purpose for which the Holy Spirit has been given, and that is not primarily the blessing of believers but rather the equipping of the Church with power to reach effectively unbelievers.

I needed this adjustment in my own thinking and received it when sharing in the ministry of the Gulf Coast Keswick held in Houston, Texas some years ago. One of the speakers quoted Acts 1.8, where Jesus says to the disciples after his resurrection, 'Ye shall receive power, after that the Holy Ghost is come upon you: and ye shall be witnesses unto me both in Jerusalem, and in all Judaea, and in Samaria, and unto the uttermost part of the earth.' The speaker went on to say that he hoped we had noticed that the promise of power was linked with the task of witnessing to the world. In other words, the Holy Spirit was not given to us only for ourselves, but rather so that through us his power might change the lives of others. I found, to my profound interest, that this truth runs right through the teaching of the New Testament. Take the words of our Lord spoken in the Temple: 'If any man thirst, let him come unto me, and drink . . . out of his belly [inner being] shall flow [to others] rivers of living water.' In 1 Corinthians chapter 12, we read of the gifts of the Spirit, and we notice that they were given 'for the edifying of the church' – for others. In Paul's letter to the Galatians we read of the fruit of the Spirit. The fruit does not exist for the tree but for others. Some people today say we are living in an exciting era of church growth, and church planting. It may be true that we have hundreds of new churches, but do we have hundreds of new Christians? The answer to that question is very largely 'no'. Is the power of the Holy Spirit really the characteristic of the Church today? I very much doubt it. So let us face the challenge of the Spirit in those words of Christ in Acts 1.8 – the last words he spoke on earth. Last words are always important words, and there are none which the Church today more urgently needs to think through.

The challenge of a programme

I want us first to note that in Acts 1.8 the apostles (and therefore we today) faced the challenge of a programme. It was a threefold challenge. The first part of it lay in *what they were to be*. They were to be witnesses: 'Ye shall be witnesses unto me.' While serving as a minister in Glasgow I was asked from time to time to lead the opening prayers in the High Court, so I became familiar with the function of witnesses. I found that they were there to do either one or both of two things. Primarily they were to speak. They were there to say what they knew about the case being heard. Similarly, one of the functions or ministries of the Holy Spirit, as Jesus said, is to testify of him. I used to think that that meant that the Spirit's role was to let me know more of Jesus, that the Spirit would testify to me about Christ. That was true, of course, but later I came to realise that the Spirit wanted not only to testify *to* me, but *through* me to others. We hear a great deal about the gift of speaking in tongues, and I believe that there is such a gift – though it is not an important one, according to Paul, who said he would rather speak five words in a known tongue than ten thousand in an unknown tongue. He also made it quite clear that not every one has that gift. But every one is called to be a witness and speak for Christ and about Christ in a tongue that every one can understand. The other thing a witness sometimes has to do is to show something, such as the scars from an injury they have received. Similarly, the Christian has to show through his life what Christ can do.

The second challenge for the apostles lay in *what they were to do*. At the end of Matthew's Gospel Jesus said they were to 'make disciples' and to 'teach all nations'. Fruitfulness in the New Testament has two meanings. In Galatians Paul talks of the 'fruit of the Spirit', and that refers to character. In John chapter 15 Jesus refers to fruit, meaning the results of service. All life is reproductive. God said to Adam and Eve, 'be fruitful and multiply.' The fruit of a cat is a kitten, so the fruit of a Christian is another Christian. The Holy Spirit working through us wants to see more people being brought to new life in Christ. Someone has calculated that in Britain today it takes 1,500 Christians twelve months to produce one new Christian. Not a very high rate of reproduction!

The third challenge lay in *where they were to go*. They were to go everywhere, to 'the uttermost part of the earth'. The Christian is committed to the doing of the will of God. Every time we pray the family prayer and say the words, 'Thy will be done,' we don't mean that the will of God is something that is to be done to us by God (and that something not usually pleasant!), but we mean that the will of God is to be done by us and through us. And what is that will? Paul tells us that 'God will have all men to be saved and come to the knowledge of the truth.' Peter confirms the words of Paul when he writes that 'God is not willing that any should perish but that all men should come to repentance.'

But how are we to go 'to the uttermost part of the earth'? Of course, in one sense every time we go out of our front door we are going into the world. But we can also go through our giving, through our praying, through our writing, through our sending people. There was a time when I thought that my church was doing pretty well in the sending business, since quite a number had gone into full-time service either as ministers of the gospel or as missionaries, until I went to a church in Lancaster, Pennsylvania. It was not a big church by American standards – the membership was then 1,200 – but they had sent out 120 missionaries. One for every ten members!

The late Geoffrey King defined the task of the Church as 'the offering of the Whole Christ, for the Whole Man, by the Whole Church, to the Whole World.' I know of no definition more comprehensively biblical than that. That task is to be carried out in the power of the Holy Spirit.

The challenge of a presence

Now we need to look at a second aspect of the challenge of the Spirit, which we will call the challenge of a presence. The thinking of so many Christians on this subject is inadequate. I find myself recalling the title of a book by J. B. Phillips, *Your God is Too Small*. The understanding of so many Christians is so limited and so confused! When I hear the word 'confused' I remember a story told by the late Lindsay Glegg at Filey about a visit he once paid to the USA. At that time the ties worn by the men were very colourful and also very large. He met one man whose tie was different. It was absolutely plain apart from four letters embroidered across it: B. A. I. K. Lindsay's curiosity was aroused and so he spoke to the man, saying that he was intrigued by the tie. 'What do the letters mean?' he asked. 'That's no problem,' the man replied. 'They stand for "Boy Am I Confused".' Lindsay looked again at the letters and said 'But you don't spell "Confused" with a "K".' The man replied, 'You don't know how confused I am!' I sometimes feel that a lot of Christian men could wear ties like that, and many ladies could go around with handbags bearing those letters too! There is so much confusion around today about the Holy Spirit. I want to suggest that three very simple concepts would clear up most of the confusion, if we started thinking about the challenge of the presence of the Holy Spirit in our lives. His presence is challenging just as the presence of another person can be challenging in someone's life. A newly married couple can find it a challenge living with each other, and parents can find a baby challenging.

We need to think first of *the life the Holy Spirit wants to live in our lives*. The life he wants to live in us is *His* life. He is a Person, albeit a divine person. Paul said to the Christians at Corinth, 'Do you not know that your body is the temple of the Holy Spirit, who dwells in you?' The kind of life he will want to live in your life and mine will be determined by his character. And what are the attributes of the divine character that are revealed in Scripture? John, in his first epistle, names two: 'God is light' and 'God is love'. Light speaks of truth and holiness, and those aspects of the divine character will determine what the Holy Spirit will want in our lives or want out of our lives.

Paul, writing to the Romans, told them that 'the love of God has been shed abroad in our hearts by the Holy Spirit who has been given to us.' That means that we don't need to ask for that love, because when the new life came in, the new love came in too. So John tells us that 'we know we have passed from death unto life because we love.'

However, this word 'love' needs to be defined accurately. It is a word tossed around very freely today, without any real understanding of the nature of the love of God. I was helped enormously when I read in the IVF Bible Dictionary about the meaning of the word the early Church chose to describe God's love. They rejected the Greek word *eros*, which denoted sensual love and from which we get our word 'erotic'. They also rejected the word *phileo*, used to describe the love of a parent for a child, of a husband for a wife, of a friend for a friend. It is a word that entails fondness and affection. The word the Christians chose to describe the love of God was *agape*. The Bible Dictionary said 'It was very seldom used in classical Greek and when it was used it was always used as meaning something infinitely precious.' The definition of God's love given by Dr Paul Rees says it has within it 'a minimum of emotion and a maximum of evaluation'. So if the Holy Spirit is free to live his life in us, he will produce the fruit of the Spirit, which is 'love, joy, peace, longsuffering, gentleness, goodness, faithfulness, meekness and self-control'.

The second concept which we need to think about is that *there are gifts the Holy Spirit wants to give to us*. These gifts are functional and are for the edifying of the Church, which is the body of Christ. Paul likens the gifts to the various members of the body. They are listed in 1 Corinthians chapter 12, Romans chapter 12 and Ephesians chapter 4. Some Christians believe that some of the gifts may have ceased, others believe that the list is not exhaustive and there may be other gifts. But there are two important things to note about the gifts of the Spirit. The first is that it is the Spirit who determines who is going to have which gift. In 1 Corinthians 12.11 we read of the Holy Spirit 'dividing to each man severally *as he will*'. That means that no Christian has the right to tell any other Christian that they ought to have this or that gift. It also makes it nonsense to describe some Christians or pastors or churches as 'charismatic'. The word 'charismatic' comes from the Greek word *charisma* which means 'gift'. So since the Scripture states that every Christian has a gift, then every Christian is a 'charismatic' Christian! The mis-use of this word has divided the Christian Church, whereas one of the functions of the Spirit is to bind Christians together. The task of each Christian, then, is to find out what gift the Holy Spirit may have given him or her, and to make certain that that gift is being put to good use.

But there is still more to be said about the challenge of the presence of the Holy Spirit in the life of the believer. We now need to think about *the things he wants to do in us*. We could call these things the ministries of the Holy Spirit. One of the vital questions that every Christian ought to ask is 'what has the Holy Spirit been given to do in my life?' The difference between a ministry of the Spirit and a gift of the Spirit is that a ministry is a thing which he wants to do in *every* Christian's life, while different gifts are given to each individual.

Here are some of the ministries of the Spirit. First, there is a teaching ministry (see John 16.13). In order to receive this ministry from him, we need to spend time with the Bible, so that the Holy Spirit can teach us through it. There is also the praying ministry (Rom. 8.26). There is the sealing ministry (Eph. 1.13). There is the Christ-glorifying ministry (John 16.14). There is the caring ministry (Rom. 5.5) and many other ministries too.

A saintly man of God once answered the question, 'how do we grieve the Holy Spirit?' with the words 'we grieve the Holy Spirit when we fail to allow him to do in us that for which he has been given.' And Sister Eva of Friedenshort speaks of 'the Christians in whose lives the Holy Spirit is a prisoner without power'. The New Testament warns us that the Spirit can be grieved and quenched and that the gifts of the Spirit can be neglected. So after discovering what the Holy Spirit wants to do in my life, I then have to exercise a discipline that ensures that he is free to do those things. That is why the one positive command to do with the Holy Spirit is a present tense command which really means, 'Be ye continually being filled with the Holy Spirit.' This calls for a sustained discipline. This may begin at any moment, but it has to be maintained. Incidentally, it is worth noting that nowhere in the New Testament are believers commanded to be baptised with or in the Spirit. That phrase is always within the context of either a promise, and a promise to all, or of something which has happened, and happened to all – never to some and not to others.

There is one more aspect of the challenge of the Spirit, and it is to be found in that scene on the Ascension Mount. It is **the challenge of a prospect**. The prospect was that of the return of the Christ, which had been promised by the angels in Acts 1.11: 'this same Jesus shall come as ye have seen him go.' In other words, 'You had better get busy, since you don't know how long you may have!' The promise of Jesus' return still has the same implications for us today. Whether he will come for us in what we call death or whether he returns before we die, there is still a limit to the time we have in which to carry out the commission he has given us.

What meaning, then, does the coming of Christ hold for us? To me it speaks of *the certainty of judgment*. There is a judgment day for Christians. This has nothing to do with our sin, but everything to do with our service. It will be a time of evaluation and of reward. (See Matt. 25.19; 1 Cor. 3.9–15 and Rom. 14.10). This great hope of Christ's return therefore also calls for *an urgency in my service*. Jesus speaks of servants waiting for the return of their Lord with 'girded loins and burning lights'. John indicates that this hope will lead to *a sanctity in my living*: 'Every man that hath this hope in him purifieth himself, even as he [Jesus] is pure' (1 John 3.3). We want not only to be busy when he comes, but holy too!

I wonder whether J. B. Phillips' words, *Your God is Too Small*, could justifiably be said about the Church today. If the challenge of the Holy Spirit were truly faced, the result would be the power of God being released in and through the Church, so that the world would be changed. Just after the start of World War II, I visited Lanercost Vicarage in Cumbria. It was a lovely house in a beautiful setting, but I knew that some of these old vicarages were not comfortable to live in because of a lack of modern facilities. However, when I entered I saw that it had obviously been modernised. Electric light and the conveniences that go with electricity were there. I congratulated the vicar. He gave me a wry smile. He said that the work had been completed just before the outbreak of the war. Everything had been done except one thing – the cable connecting the house with the grid had not been laid. When war was declared that kind of work was stopped, and so the house had everything except power! I find myself wondering how many churches and Christians who have rediscovered the Person of the Holy Spirit nevertheless seem to have everything except the power.

Chapter 8: Spreading the Load

They shall bear the burden with thee (Exod. 18.23).

How amazingly up-to-date the Bible is with its message, and how perennial are the strains and stresses involved in serving God. This eighteenth chapter of Exodus could have been written at any time about almost any kind of Christian work in which the burdens carried by the few were too great. It was written thousands of years ago, but it reads as if it might have been written today. The passage poses a question which we should face and that is: Are the burdens which some men bear too heavy? The work of the ministry can either mean overwork or underwork. Ministers can either become exhausted or lazy. It might benefit many men who are kept busy – perhaps too busy – to read through this chapter from the book of Exodus and note the lessons which can be learned.

The limits which should be sensed

First of all we see here the limits which should be sensed in the work of God. Someone once asked, which is the greater man, the man who can do the work of ten men or the man who can get ten men to do the work? The problem with the man who can do the work of ten men is that when he goes, the work may collapse! However, the man who can get ten men to do the work may ensure thereby that the work goes on. In the ministry there is all the difference between drawing a crowd and building a congregation. The man who simply draws a crowd has done a work which may not last. When the man goes, the crowd goes. But building a congregation means building a closely knit fellowship of those committed to the work of God.

There is obviously a limit to what one man can do. This is what Jethro, the father-in-law of Moses, sensed when he came to see him (Exod. 18.5). First of all there is *a limit to time*. Moses was not only his people's leader, but was their judge as well. Jethro noticed that 'the people stand by [Moses] from morning unto evening' (verse 14). The task of administering justice remained unfinished because it was so vast. It is a simple fact that there is a limit to what one person with one pair of hands can do, even if he gives all the time he can to the job. This truth applies in any area of life – in the business world, in the home, in a church. There is a limited amount of time, the need is so great, there is so much to do and not nearly enough time in which to do it all. Two friends of mine in the ministry have told me that they only have four hours of sleep a night! The limit to time has to be accepted.

Then there is also *a limit to strength*. Jethro said to Moses, 'The thing thou doest is not good. Thou wilt surely wear away,' (verse 17). Again, it is a simple fact that there is a physical limit to what one person can do. Today great numbers of people are dying in middle age. Not so long ago medical science was predicting that people would in the future live much longer lives. Some, of course, do, but others are living much shorter lives. One insurance company's annual report has stated that 50 per cent of deaths of people over the age of forty are due to heart trouble. We seem to be living in days when many of us are overtaxing our reserves of strength, both physical and mental.

Activities seem to be increasing. Sunday is no longer a day of rest – it's become a day of activity. Anxieties are increasing too. We may live in an age of wonder because of the discoveries of science, but we also live in an age of worry. Life in our modern society is full of pressures, temptations, and stresses which stretch a person in mind, body and soul.

The loads which must be shared

Secondly, we read in this passage in Exodus of loads which must be shared. Jethro said, 'this thing is too heavy for thee; thou art not able to perform it thyself alone' (verse 18). The job is too much for one man. It is a load too heavy for one pair of shoulders, and should be shared with others. We need to think first of *the size of the task*. Moses had led the people safely out of Egypt. In one sense that was a comparatively simple thing to do. But it was not the end of his task – it was only the beginning! To then look after so many people was a gigantic undertaking, far too great for one man alone. We have a similar situation in the Church of Jesus Christ. If the Church is really doing its job, its workload is massive. The Church must seek the lost, comfort the despondent, encourage the defeated, instruct the children, shepherd the young people, strengthen the faith and fellowship of the mature, visit the sick, comfort the bereaved, welcome the stranger, guide the bewildered, care for the lonely, pray for the needy, arrange the programme, conduct the meetings and services, prepare the sermons and addresses, write the letters, plan the policy, conduct the weddings and funerals, maintain the building, look after the money and support the missionaries!

The words of Winston Churchill about the Battle of Britain are true, not only of that battle but also of the spiritual battle which the Church has to fight: 'Never was so much owed by so many to so few.' We could alter that slightly: 'Never was so much left by so many to so few'!

Next we need to think about *the sharing of the task*. Jethro advised Moses, 'Thou shalt provide out of all the people able men . . . they shall bear the burden with thee' (verse 21). It is a true saying that 'many hands make light work.' Trying to carry the burden alone can be exhausting. If there are others to share the burden with, the task becomes so much easier. My friend Alan Redpath used to say that every Christian is either a missionary or a mission field – they are either part of the burden or under the burden. There are, of course, some things which cannot be shared. In verse 19 Jethro makes that clear, saying, 'Be thou for the people to God-ward,' or, in other words, 'be the people's representative before God.' Moses could not delegate his responsibility as their spiritual leader. The apostles came to the same conclusion when the growing Church found itself facing administrative problems. They felt that others could handle the day-to-day running of things, while they would devote themselves 'continually to prayer, and to the ministry of the word' (Acts 6.4). So there are some things which cannot be shared, while there is much that could and should be shared. However, as Jethro and the apostles realised, the people to whom responsibilities were to be delegated had to have the right spiritual qualities. Jethro said they must be 'men such as fear God, men of truth' (verse 21). In Acts chapter 6 they had to be 'men of honest report, full of the Holy Ghost and wisdom'. Spiritual qualities are always needed in the work of the Church of Jesus Christ. Christian work needs Christian people. It needs men and women who will work in the name of Christ, for the sake of Christ, in the power of Christ and for the glory of Christ. People who seek power and position in the Church for their own glory are always more trouble than they are worth.

The lives which could be saved

Finally, we read in this passage of the lives which could be saved. Jethro said: 'If thou shalt do this thing . . . then thou shalt be able to endure, and all this people shall also go to their place in peace' (verse 23). He was thinking first of *the tragedy which would be avoided*. 'Thou shalt be able to endure' – Moses could avoid dying prematurely through strain. It is so sad when a life is shortened through overwork and a person's work for God is abruptly ended. One of the famous chaplains of World War One was the Rev G. A. Studdart-Kennedy, known more familiarly as Woodbine Willie. When

I read the story of his life I was surprised to find how young he was when he died – just thirty-six! It was said of him that 'He was worn out but not worked out.' He could have achieved so much more if he had lived longer. Sadly, in God's work there are men who die young. Sometimes one asks, 'Is it necessary?' No doubt sometimes, in the purpose of God, the answer is 'Yes'. But not always. Christians need to ask themselves whether they are adding to the burden or whether they are under the burden. So often there are many who could be under the burden but are not.

Jethro was also thinking of *the efficiency which would be achieved*: 'All this people shall also go to their place in peace.' If Moses were to follow his advice, the work could be done, the needs could be met, hearts could be blessed.

So let's keep in mind the importance of spreading the load in the work of the Church. The task is so great and the need so urgent that we must make certain that the work is being done adequately and efficiently. It is beyond the resources, ability and strength of a mere few. We need to get more and more people involved in the work of God. We need to encourage people to get under the burden through their prayers, through their loyalty, through the willing giving of their time, through their commitment to do the work they are asked to do, and above all through their devotion to Christ and his Church.

Chapter 9: Reaching the Preacher's Objective

But Jerusalem which is above is free, which is the mother of us all (Gal. 4.26).

The objective of the preacher is surely to build the Church of Jesus Christ, or rather to allow Christ to build his Church through the ministry of the word and sacraments. The New Testament describes the Church in a number of different ways. Sometimes it is called 'the body of Christ'. That is a very meaningful term, since it suggests that the Church possesses the life of Christ, that it is submitted to the will of Christ and that it expresses the mind of Christ. Elsewhere the Church is called 'the Bride of Christ'. This name speaks of a loveliness which the Bridegroom will want to see in his Bride, of a lavishness which he will want to shower upon her and of a loneliness which he will want to share with her.

Another name for the Church is 'the Building of Christ'. As we have already mentioned in an earlier chapter, the Church, like any other building, will have its design, its development and its destiny or purpose. The name which is for me the most relevant today is the one Paul uses in Galatians 4.20–26, where he describes the Church or the heavenly Jerusalem as 'the mother of us all'. Calvin makes this comment: 'There is no other way of entering life unless we are conceived by her and born of her. We must be nourished at her breast and continually preserved under her care and government till ye are divested of this mortal flesh and become like angels.'

Protestants are a little nervous of the name 'Mother Church' because of the claims of the Roman Catholic Church to be the true 'Mother Church'. But it is a very suggestive analogy. It speaks of one of the deepest and strongest of human relationships, that between a mother and her child. We need to experience a similar bond in the spiritual dimension of our lives, with the same strength and depth of affection and loyalty as exists between a mother and a child. The Church in South Korea, which is growing so fast as to be literally exploding, lays great stress upon this loyalty. In fact they go so far as to say that every Christian needs to be converted twice – first to Christ, then to his Church.

The cost to the mother of the birth of her child

I want to suggest that there are three lessons which we can learn by thinking of the Church as the 'mother of us all'. First, there is what the birth of her child costs the mother. Under this heading there are two things to be considered. To begin with we need to think about *the magnitude of the cost*. While there is nothing which causes more excitement and delight than the news that a baby is expected, the parents-to-be are only too aware of how costly parenthood will be. The pregnancy and birth will be costly to the mother. She will get tired carrying the child and she will be in pain during labour. There is even the possibility that she will die giving birth, although, thankfully, that very rarely happens these days.

Looking after a baby is costly, too, in terms of money. A pram, a cot and clothes will be needed. When I sometimes used to go into the local branch of Mothercare with my wife I was always horrified by the price of the things sold there! Parenthood is also costly, of course, in terms of time, thought and strength. Is the birth of a soul into the family of God going to be any less costly? Surely not. In fact, it will be infinitely more costly. In physical and spiritual terms it was costly for the Son of God because he had to die upon the cross to save the soul. The birth will also be costly for many others: costly for those who pray, for those who preach, for those who give financially to the Church and so provide a spiritual home for the Christian, with all the facilities which are needed so that he or she can be cared for. The spiritual birth will be costly in terms of time, toil and thought.

The second thing we need to think about is *the attitude to the cost*. We are bound to adopt one of two attitudes: either one of acceptance of the cost or avoidance of it. There is a close parallel here between the birth of a child into a family and the birth of a soul into the family of God. We need to ask ourselves whether we are willing to accept the cost of the new birth, which is bound to disrupt the normal pattern of our lives. When my son Henry and his wife Anna had their first baby, Andrew, their lives went on fairly normally. He knew that night-time was the time to sleep and daytime was the time to be awake. But their second child, Richard, seemed not to understand that! He thought daytime was the time to be asleep and night-time was the time to be awake!

One of the biggest thrills in my ministry has been the many young people whom I have had in my churches. Of course there have been plenty of weddings! After the joy of the wedding there then comes the arrival of the first baby. I often say to the young couples, 'You know, this baby is going to make prisoners of you. You'll no longer be able to do all the things you used to do.' A baby curbs the freedom of a couple. They can no longer do things together unless someone can babysit for them. Their lives are restricted because that helpless little baby needs constant care and attention.

I find that some Christians are not willing to accept this curbing of their freedom. At one stage one of my churches was not in a very healthy state, and so prayer was a priority. One lady member of the church refused to come to the prayer meetings because a radio programme called *ITMA* clashed with them. The programme was more important to her than prayer.

Parenthood entails cutting down our spending on ourselves

so that we may have the money to spend on our children. My father was a clergyman, and in his day ministers were not all that well paid. In winter time he used to wear a coat when he was in his study so that he didn't need to put on the electric fire. As a result he saved money which he could spend on the children.

The well-known American preacher, Dr Sam Shoemaker, on one occasion attended a women's meeting at which a lady talked about setting up what she called a 'church pantry' – we might call it a bring and buy stall. The idea was that the ladies should bring their jams and jellies to be sold in order to raise money for charities. Later that same day Shoemaker had lunch with the lady who had spoken at the meeting and asked if any ladies she knew were doing anything for the street women in the notorious part of that city close to the church. She replied: 'It's curious, you know. There are several of those girls in hospital just now, and yesterday I called up fourteen of our ladies to see if some of them would go down and visit them. But they all declined.' Shoemaker commented on this story: 'Orange marmalade is a good deal easier to make than Christians.'

The care of the mother for the health of her child

The second lesson which we can learn by thinking of the Church as the 'mother of us all' concerns the care of the mother for the health of her child. Every mother knows that the birth of a child is only the beginning. It has to be followed by growth, health and happiness. These are the constant concern of a mother. How essential and vital it is that the Church, the spiritual mother, should be fully alert to this responsibility. While spiritual birth is a cause for thanksgiving and joy, there will be cause for sadness if it is not followed by growth. I remember once visiting a mentally retarded lady who lived in a nursing home. I knocked at the door of her room and went in, and found her sitting happily at her desk drawing with crayons, surrounded by her dolls and teddy bears. She was in her thirties, yet she had the mind of a child of four. Her birth had not been followed by growth.

We need to remember *how varied the needs of the children are.* People are made up of soul, spirit, mind and body. One of the weaknesses of a great deal of church thinking, particularly among those of us who call ourselves evangelical, is that it deals simply in terms of spiritual needs and neglects the rest of the human personality. In our Bibles we find that God is concerned about the whole person. We find that Jesus was moved to compassion when he saw people who were physically hungry or physically sick, as well as when he saw them spiritually lost. I believe that the life of the Church ought to provide for the whole needs of the whole person. That is what the world needs to see. I very vividly remember being rebuked by a young person in one of my churches. She wasn't a Christian and had a number of problems in her life – practical as well as spiritual. She challenged me when she said, 'The trouble with you folk in this church is, you're only interested in my soul. You only want to see me converted.' But, of course, God wasn't interested just in her soul – he was concerned for her as an entire person. The Church should have the same concern for her children.

We also need to remember *how vital the role of the mother is.* We need to take this role seriously, particularly in today's world which is such a difficult place for many people. Both the young and the old can be vulnerable to loneliness, and they need the support of the Church. They not only need fellowship in church meetings – they need to relax and have fun with other people. For example, when I lost my wife Catherine, somebody said to me, 'Why don't you go for a holiday?' To which I replied: 'Who with?' There are lots of people who haven't got anybody to go on holiday with. Can the local church step in and do something? In my churches that is just what we have done. We have arranged coach holidays, pilgrimages to the Holy Land, trips up in the Highlands of Scotland and house parties at Keswick and Filey. These activities give church members who otherwise would have no-one to go with the opportunity to enjoy a holiday in the company of other Christians.

Sometimes it's the little extra things that will make all the difference. I remember the story of a little girl who had been given a doll. She was very thrilled with it and was examining it very carefully. 'Mummy, it's got two pockets!' she called out excitedly. That wasn't all that unusual, but it was still nice that there were pockets in the dress. She examined the doll even more carefully, and then with even greater excitement announced, 'Mummy, it's got two pockets *and a hanky*!' Never before in her life had she seen a doll with a tiny little hanky in its dress. It was that extra, unexpected little touch which made the gift all the more wonderful to her. I like to call this sort of thing 'the hanky touch'. Jesus called it 'going the second mile'. Unexpected, unrequested gifts are the most memorable.

Easter is a wonderful day, a festival day. I well remember my first Easter Sunday as a curate at Broadwater Church. As I walked into the church in the morning, I was delighted to discover that the building was ablaze with daffodils. They perfectly expressed the joy of Easter. Ever since then I've always had my churches decorated cheerfully at Easter. The spring flowers speak of the Resurrection, don't they?

But Easter can be a sad time for those who have been bereaved. Their sense of loss is then particularly acute. My church in Glasgow had a big congregation, so every year there were quite a number of families who lost loved ones. When Easter Sunday came I would make a special note of the names and addresses of these families and after the evening service I would give cards bearing a message of love to elders of the church, who would take a plant to each of the homes of the bereaved. There was one family which had been virtually wiped out by alcohol. First the father died, then the mother, and then the thirty-six year-old daughter. The only member left was an aunt of the daughter, and she was a Roman Catholic. I took a card and an attractive potted plant to her myself. Later she wrote to me, thanking me for the plant. She added, 'Never in all my life have I received such kindness from my Church.'

Have you ever stopped to think about what the Bible calls 'the kindness of God'? One way of expressing it is by doing those little extra things – the posy of flowers for Mum on Mothering Sunday, the hanky touch, going the second mile, doing the unexpected.

The claims of the mother on the strength of her child

The third lesson we can learn by thinking about motherhood concerns the claims of a mother on the strength of her child. To begin with everything is done for the child by the mother. *How great is the debt of the child*! Everything is done for it without complaint, without payment, just out of love. But when the child gets older he or she is able to do things to help the mother in return.

I always remember the story of a little boy who watched his mother as she opened the mail at the breakfast table. He noticed that she put aside some letters and opened the others. 'What are those letters you're putting aside, Mummy?' he asked. 'Oh, they're bills,' she replied. 'When people like the electrician or the plumber do something for me, I have to pay them afterwards.' The little boy said nothing. The next day, when his mother came down to breakfast, there was a little note beside her place at the table. It read:

For running errands	5p
For clearing up my room	5p

For getting the
newspapers   5p
TOTAL: 15p

Johnny.

The next morning, when he came down for breakfast, there was a note beside his place:

For washing your
clothes   0p
For cooking three
meals for you   0p
For buying what you
need   0p
TOTAL: 0p

Mummy.

How great the debt is. Sometimes it's not appreciated or paid by children. I once had a neighbour who was a physiotherapist. I asked her one Christmas how she was getting on. 'Well,' she said, 'it's been very mixed. A lot of my patients are elderly and lonely and I feel so sorry for them. Today one of them said to me, "You know, I haven't even had a Christmas card from my children."' The debt had not been paid.

I think there has only been one thing which has really hurt me during my career as a minister, and that was those times when somebody who owed their new life in Christ under God to the preaching of the word in my church, to the prayers of God's people and to the loving concern of us all – would suddenly, for no reason at all, just walk out! The debt they owed was unpaid. This sort of thing is still happening today. Many who owe their salvation under God to a fellowship which is alive and real suddenly disappear, and join another one which they think will be more fun. Such behaviour is deeply ungrateful.

Some time after my father died I was talking with my sister, and she made a remark which she meant to be helpful but which in fact made me ashamed: 'George,' she said, 'Daddy lived for your letters.' That hurt. I'm afraid I could have written to him much more often than I did. In that respect I did not fully pay my debt to him.

Finally, I think *how glad the heart of the mother should be*. However, there are also many grateful children about. I once visited an old lady who lived alone in a flat in Glasgow. 'How are you getting on?' I asked her. 'Oh, fine,' she said. 'I have a wonderful daughter. Every day she calls to see how I am and what she can do for me.' The debt of that child had been paid. I thank God for those children of the Church who remember the debt they owe her and who give back generously to the life of the fellowship in which they were born.

Part II
Sermon Outlines

Introduction to the Sermon Outlines

It is important that whatever text or passage has been laid on the heart of the preacher should first of all be studied thoroughly and meditated upon with what Dr Sangster calls 'prayer thought'. The outlines are designed simply to provide the pegs upon which the preacher can hang his own clothes. They are not designed to be the whole message, but rather to give a structure around which the message can be built. What is built around each heading or subheading will amplify the truth which it enshrines. Each heading or subheading should be supported by at least one illustration which will help the preacher to relate its truth to ordinary life.

The outlines are a selection only, but my hope and prayer is that preachers, teachers and speakers will find in them stimulus and inspiration which will help them to handle other passages not included in this book.

Genesis to Deuteronomy

Genesis

Beginnings

Genesis 1.1: 'In the beginning God . . . '

   A.   *At the beginning of each new year*
(a) The place which God claims in our lives.
(b) The price which man pays if he yields.

   B.   *At the beginning of each new week*
(a) How that day belongs to God.
(b) What that day becomes to us.

   C.   *At the beginning of each new day*
(a) The practice which is difficult.
(b) The purpose which is determined.

The garden of our lives

Genesis 2.8: 'The Lord God planted a garden'
'Thou shalt be like a watered garden' (Isa. 58.11)

   A.   *There are flowers in a garden – so our lives should be attractive*
(a) Think of the intention which God has.
(b) Think of the perfection which God seeks.

   B.   *There is fragrance in a garden – so our lives should be distinctive*
(a) We should be recognisable.
(b) We should be pleasurable.

   C.   *There is fruit in a garden – so our lives should be productive*
(a) The good which fruit does.
(b) The seed which fruit has.

An address for the weddings of Christian leaders

Genesis 2.18: 'It is not good that the man should be alone'

    A. *The basis you have found for your faith*
(a) The Saviour you have made your Lord.
(b) The Scripture you must make your guide.

    B. *The burdens you will share in your work*
(a) The spiritual burdens.
(b) The practical burdens.

    C. *The blessing you will be through your lives*
(a) The prayers which will secure this.
(b) The praise which will complete this.

The tactics of the tempter

Genesis 3.1–15 'Hath God said, Ye shall not . . . ?'

    A. *The element of doubt*
(a) He tries to get us to doubt the goodness of God.
(b) He tries to get us to doubt the guilt of sin.

    B. *The element of denial*
(a) It was a denial which was blatant: 'Ye shall not surely die.'
(b) It was a denial which was believed.

    C. *The element of deceit*: 'Ye shall be as gods'
(a) How attractive sin was made to look – 'pleasant to the eyes'.
(b) How deceptive sin was found to be – 'they hid themselves'

Hiding from God

Genesis 3.9–10: 'The Lord God called . . . ' Adam said, 'I heard thy voice . . . and I was afraid . . . and I hid myself'

A. *The facts which men must face*: God does speak – 'I heard thy voice'
(a) What words reveal.
(b) What words require.

B. *The fears which men may have*: 'And I was afraid'
(a) Afraid of the liberty they may lose.
(b) Afraid of the poverty they may find.

C. *The fools which men can be*: 'And I hid myself'
(a) Where they will hide.
(b) What they will miss.

Avoiding social responsibility

Genesis 4.9: 'Am I my brother's keeper?'

A. *How inconsistent some people can be*
(a) Some implications they accept.
(b) Some implications they avoid.

B. *How intolerant some people can be*
(a) The compulsion they would impose.
(b) The conclusion we can deduce.

C. *How indifferent some people can be*
(a) The liberty they claim for themselves.
(b) The misery they cause for others.

A couple's first child

Genesis 5.22: 'Enoch walked with God after he begat Methuselah'

A. *The new world entered*
(a) There are new relationships.
(b) There are new responsibilities.

B. *The new walk enjoyed*
(a) The direction of the walk.
(b) The duration of the walk.

C. *The new wealth experienced*
(a) The abundance which will satisfy our needs.
(b) The assurance which will pacify our fears.

What is the measure of our obedience?

Genesis 12.1–13 and 13: 'So Abram departed, as the Lord had spoken unto him; and Lot went with him'

A. *The revelation given to Abram*
(a) It was a revelation of the person of God (cf. Acts 7.2).
(b) It was a revelation of the purpose of God: 12.1–3.

B. *The reservation made by Abram*: 'and Lot went with him'
(a) The reservation was deliberate.
(b) The reservation proved disastrous.

C. *The restoration found by Abram*
(a) Note the way in which we find God working in his life: 13.5–7.
(b) Note the word for which we find God waiting from his lips: 'Separate thyself.'

Blessed to bless

Genesis 12.2: 'I will bless thee . . . and thou shalt be a blessing'

    A. *The sphere of my influence*
    (a) Those to whom I am naturally related.
    (b) Those with whom I am spiritually involved.

    B. *The source of my influence*
    (a) My dependence on the Spirit.
    (b) My difference from society.

    C. *The scale of my influence*
    (a) The range of it.
    (b) The reward for it.

Sarah, who had greatness thrust upon her

Genesis 12.5.

    A. *The fact which changed her life: her marriage to Abram*
    (a) The vision through which her husband was called.
    (b) The venture to which her husband was committed.

    B. *The fears which filled her heart*
    (a) Did she dislike this life?
    (b) Did she distrust his Lord?

    C. *The faith which crowned her end*: Heb. 11.11
    (a) The promise which was repeated.
    (b) The purpose which was completed.

Lot's choice

Genesis 13.11: 'Then Lot chose'

A. *The promise he showed*
(a) Was he attracted by the spiritual faith of Abram?
(b) Was he infected by the initial weakness of Abram?

B. *The pathway he took*
(a) The crisis of change.
(b) The crisis of choice.

C. *The problem he was*
(a) The summons for help: Gen. 14.
(b) The sequel of harm.

God is no man's debtor

Genesis 15.1: 'Fear not . . . I am thy shield, and thy exceeding great reward'

A. *The obedience he had given*
(a) The reservation he had made at the first: Gen. 12.
(b) The consecration he now gave in the end: Gen. 13.9.

B. *The consequences he had feared*
(a) What he lacked.
(b) What he lost.

C. *The assurance he now received*
(a) The presence of his Lord.
(b) The purpose for his life.

Availability and flexibility

Genesis 22.1, 11: 'Here am I'

   A. *Available for testing: Abraham*
(a) The purpose which God desired.
(b) The price which God required.

   B. *Available for talking: Samuel (1 Sam. 3.4)*
(a) A love which meant much to Samuel.
(b) A loyalty which meant more to Samuel.

   C. *Available for trusting: David (2 Sam. 15.26)*
(a) The shattered world of David.
(b) The submissive will of David.

   D. *Available for toiling: Isaiah (Isa. 6.8)*
(a) The loss which was crushing.
(b) The Lord who was calling.

When God tests us

Genesis 22.1–19: 'God did tempt [test] Abraham'

   A. *The request God made*
(a) How definite were the instructions.
(b) How desperate were the implications.

   B. *The response God met*
(a) The form his response took.
(b) The faith his response showed.

   C. *The reward God gave*
(a) The grounds on which this reward was based.
(b) The gain to which this reward led.

Marriage

Genesis 24.1–67: 'Wilt thou go with this man?'

   A.   *The wealth with which love approaches*
   (a) The desire of love to enrich.
   (b) The display of love to entice.

   B.   *The word for which love asks*
   (a) The authority which was sensed.
   (b) The urgency which was shown.

   C.   *The welcome with which love awaits*
   (a) The prayerful expectancy with which love looks.
   (b) The privileged intimacy to which love leads.

The battle for the wells

Genesis 26.18–19: 'Isaac digged again the wells of water, which they had digged in the days of Abraham his father'

   A.   *The memory of the wells*
   (a) The need for the wells recalled.
   (b) The names of the wells remembered.

   B.   *The tragedy of the wells*
   (a) The presence of an enemy.
   (b) The purpose of the enemy.

   C.   *The victory of the wells -*
   (a) The determination shown.
   (b) The satisfaction found.

The furnishings of faith

Genesis 26.25: 'An altar . . . a tent . . . a well'

A. *A dedication to the will of God: 'he built an altar there'*
(a) The altar was erected.
(b) Was the altar neglected (this is the only mention of it in Isaac's story).

B. *A detachment from the ways of men: 'he pitched his tent there'*
(a) A detachment from the pleasures of the world.
(b) A detachment from the praises of the world.

C. *A dependence on the word of life: 'and there he digged a well'*
(a) The difficulty they found in digging the well.
(b) The necessity they faced in digging the well.

A place of vision

Genesis 28.19: 'He called the name of that place Bethel'

A. *Bethel was the place of a vision*
(a) Jacob had a vision of his life.
(b) Jacob had a vision of his Lord.

B. *Bethel was the place of a voice*
(a) God spoke of his presence.
(b) God spoke of his purpose.

C. *Bethel was the place of a vow*
(a) The reasons for the vow.
(b) The recording of the vow.

Wrestling with God

Genesis 32.24–32: 'Jacob was left alone; and there wrestled a man with him until the breaking of the day'

A. *The solitude of a deserted place*
(a) The silence which had fallen.
(b) The struggle which had followed.

B. *The surrender of a defeated man*
(a) How the struggle was prolonged.
(b) How the surrender was procured.

C. *The splendour of a different name*
(a) The desperation of Jacob.
(b) The transformation of Jacob.

Where and when does God bless us? (1)

Genesis 32.29: 'He blessed him there'

A. *A place was found*
(a) A time when he was aware of his need.
(b) A place where he was alone with his God.

B. *A price was paid*
(a) God needed honesty before he could bless him.
(b) God needed humility before he could bless him.

C. *A prince was born*
(a) The termination of the struggle.
(b) The transformation of the sinner.

Where and when does God bless us? (2)

Genesis 32.29: 'He blessed him there'

  A. *Where did God bless this man?*
(a) The man was alone with his God.
(b) The man was afraid for himself.

  B. *When did God bless this man?*
(a) When an intensity came into his praying.
(b) When an integrity came into his thinking.

  C. *How did God bless this man?*
(a) Note what God said to him.
(b) Note what God said of him.

The way on is the way back

Genesis 35.1: 'Arise, go up to Bethel, and dwell there'

  A. *The discovery which was challenging to the will of God: that Jacob was living in Shechem*
(a) Material prosperity marked his life there.
(b) Spiritual disloyalty marred his life there.

  B. *The memory which was cherished in the heart of God: God had not forgotten Bethel*
(a) The confrontation he had had with Jacob.
(b) The dedication he had won from Jacob.

  C. *The sovereignty which was claimed by the words of God*
(a) The command which was given by God.
(b) The consent which was given to God.

What is God doing when we are up against it?

Genesis 42.36: 'All these things are against me'

A. *There is bitterness here*
(a) The reasons for his bitterness were understandable.
(b) The results of his bitterness were unforeseeable.

B. *There is blindness here*
(a) Many things were being concealed from Jacob.
(b) Everything was being controlled by God.

C. *There is blessedness here*
(a) Note the new integrity God was wanting to secure in his family.
(b) Note the new prosperity God was planning to create for his family.

The unseen hand of God at work in our lives

Genesis 45.8: 'Not you . . . but God'

A. *The people that God had fitted into his life*
(a) How different the lives they had lived.
(b) How decisive the links they had forged.

B. *The pathway that God had mapped out for his life*
(a) How unbearable the circumstances suffered by him.
(b) How unbreakable the endurance shown by him.

C. *The purposes that God had worked out through his life*
(a) The dreams through which the purposes of God were revealed.
(b) The days in which the purposes of God were fulfilled.

The life of Joseph

Genesis 49.22: 'Joseph is a fruitful bough, even a fruitful bough by a well; whose branches run over the wall'

A. *There was a well in Joseph's life*
(a) The well speaks of a hidden source of strength.
(b) The well speaks of a hidden sphere of strife.

B. *There was a wall in Joseph's life*
(a) There is a protection which God gives to his servants.
(b) There is an intention which God has for his servants.

C. *There was a wealth in Joseph's life*
(a) There was a fulfilment of God's purpose in him.
(b) There was an enrichment of others through him.

Exodus

The birth of Moses

Exodus 2.1 ff

A. *The mother he had*
(a) Her fears for her child.
(b) Her faith in her God.

B. *The miracle he was*
(a) His preservation from his enemies.
(b) His preparation for his destiny.

C. *The man he became*
(a) The fellowship he enjoyed with his God.
(b) The leadership he exercised with his people.

Moses' childhood

Exodus 2.9: 'Take this child'

   A. *How perilous were the times in which he was born*
   (a) How rampant was the sin of God's enemies.
   (b) How wretched was the state of God's people.

   B. *How courageous were the hearts by which he was loved*
   (a) How determined they were in their love.
   (b) How dependent they were on their Lord.

   C. *How glorious was the work to which he was called*
   (a) The foundations for his life they were able to lay.
   (b) The fulfilment of their hopes they were never to see.

The God who revealed himself to Moses

Exodus 3.6: 'I am the God of thy father, the God of Abraham, the God of Isaac, and the God of Jacob'

   A. *The God of the individual heart*
   (a) There is comfort here.
   (b) There is challenge here.

   B. *The God of differing temperaments*
   (a) The adaptability of the grace of God.
   (b) The availability of the grace of God.

   C. *The God of succeeding generations*
   (a) The inheritance bestowed on each generation.
   (b) The inheritance bequeathed by each generation.
(With acknowledgements to the late Dr George Morrison.)

God calls Moses
Exodus Chapters 3 and 4

    A.   *His contentment (2.21)*
    (a) The passing of the years.
    (b) The pattern of his life.

    B.   *His amazement*
    (a) The vision he saw.
    (b) The voice he heard.

    C.   *His encouragement*
    (a) The protests he made.
    (b) The promises he got.

    D.   *His achievement*
    (a) The authentic stamp of the presence of God.
    (b) The majestic sweep of the purpose of God.

For Mothering Sunday
Exodus 10.23: 'all the children of Israel had light in their dwellings'

    A.   *The happiness brought by Christ*
    (a) The people who can spoil the happiness in our homes.
    (b) The presence which can save the happiness in our homes.

    B.   *The obedience sought by Christ*
    (a) Obedience must be learned.
    (b) Obedience will be loved.

    C.   *The thoughtfulness blessed by Christ*
    (a) The life the mother leads in the home.
    (b) The love a mother needs in a home.

    D.   *The emptiness filled by Christ*
    (a) The parting which is coming.
    (b) The promise which will comfort.

The blood of the Lamb (1)

Exodus 12.13: 'When I see the blood, I will pass over you'

A. *The shedding of the blood of the lamb*
(a) The sovereignty which is here.
(b) The sufficiency which is here.

B. *The sprinkling of the blood of the lamb*
(a) A token of where their faith lay.
(b) A token of where their faith led.

C. *The seeing of the blood of the lamb*
(a) What the Lord was able to see.
(b) What the Lord was able to say.

The blood of the Lamb (2)

Exodus 12.13: 'When I see the blood, I will pass over you'

A. *The type which is seen here*
(a) The Person of Christ.
(b) The passion of Christ.

B. *The truth which is sensed here*
(a) The liberation purposed by God.
(b) The liberation planned by God.

C. *The trust which is shown here*
(a) The conditions to be fulfilled.
(b) The consequences to be enjoyed.

A communion address (1)

Exodus 12.26 'What mean ye by this service?'

    A.   *We have here a deliverance which comes in God's way*
    (a) The plan which was revealed by God.
    (b) The price which was required by God.

    B.   *We have here an obedience which yields to God's will*
    (a) A submission which obedience entails.
    (b) A salvation which obedience enjoys.

    C.   *We have here an assurance which rests on God's word*
    (a) The word they were told.
    (b) The word they must trust.

A communion address (2)

Exodus 12.26

    A.   *It is a service of worship*
    (a) The Person of Christ is central here.
    (b) The passion of Christ is central here.

    B.   *It is a service of witness*
    (a) To the new relationship we have found with God.
    (b) To the new relationship we have found with one another.

    C.   *It is a service of wonder*
    (a) When we think of the guests who are present at the Table.
    (b) When we think of the Host who will preside at the Table.

A communion address (3)

Exodus 12.26

    A.   *The presence which should be sensed here*
    (a) Christ is the Host who presides at the Lord's Supper.
    (b) Christ's are the hands which provide at the Lord's Supper.

    B.   *The purpose which should be served at the Lord's Supper*
    (a) The acceptance we recall.
    (b) The assurance we receive.

    C.   *The praises which should be sung here*
    (a) Grateful for the simplicity of our salvation.
    (b) Thankful for the sufficiency of our salvation.

Avoiding short-cuts

Exodus 13.17: 'God led them not through the way of the land of the Philistines, although that was near'

    A.   *The existence of a purpose*
    (a) The enslavement God would end.
    (b) The enrichment God would bring.

    B.   *The avoidance of a pathway*
    (a) How attractive the short-cuts in life can seem.
    (b) How deceptive the short-cuts in life can prove.

    C.   *The emergence of a people*
    (a) What they had to learn.
    (b) What they had to lose.

The crisis of faith

Exodus 14.10–22

A. *The deliverance which faith had known*
(a) The divine provision.
(b) The divine promise.
(c) The divine purpose: 'Brought out . . . brought in.'

B. *The dilemmas which faith may face*
(a) The enemies who pursued them.
(b) The environment which perplexed them.
(c) The emotions which perturbed them.

C. *The decision which faith must make*
(a) The faith which was daring.
(b) The fears which were dispelled.
(c) The foes who were dispersed.

A time for rest

Exodus 15.27: 'They came to Elim'

A. *The path the pilgrim treads*
(a) The distance they had come.
(b) The dangers they had faced.

B. *The rest the pilgrim needs*
(a) The refreshment they received at Elim.
(b) The renewal they obtained at Elim.

C. *The goal the pilgrim seeks*
(a) The further progress they must make.
(b) The fulfilled purpose they would see.

Daily Bread

Exodus Chapter 16, Matthew 6.11: 'Give us this day our daily bread'

A. *The manna was provided daily*
(a) The effort they had to make.
(b) The lesson which some had to learn.

B. *The manna was provided early*
(a) The reason for this diligence.
(b) The results of any negligence.

C. *The manna was provided surely*
(a) The supplies never failed.
(b) The hungry never lacked.

Prayer – the secret of victory

Exodus 17.8–16

A. *The hands which got weary*
(a) The task which prayer is.
(b) The time which prayer takes.

B. *The hands which were welcome*
(a) The principle which others had seen.
(b) The problem which others could solve.

C. *The hands which ensured victory*
(a) The stability which marked the prayers on the Mount.
(b) The victory which crowned the prayers on the Mount.

Prayer and action

Exodus 17.8–16: 'And it came to pass, when Moses held up his hand, that Israel prevailed'

A. *We note that there is conflict here*
(a) How desperate the engagement can be.
(b) How different the involvement can be.

B. *We note that there is contrast here*
(a) There is a contrast here numerically.
(b) There is a contrast here physically.

C. *We note that there is conquest here*
(a) The power of God which was experienced.
(b) The praise of God which was expressed.

Sharing the burdens in Christian work

Exodus 18.1–27

A. *The limits which should be sensed*
(a) There is the limit imposed by time.
(b) There is the limit imposed by strength.

B. *The loads which must be shared*
(a) Think of the size of the task.
(b) Think of the sharing of the task.

C. *The lives which could be saved*
(a) The tragedy which could be avoided.
(b) The efficiency which would be achieved.

The Ten Commandments

Exodus 20.1–17: 'And God said . . . Thou shalt . . . Thou shalt not'

A. *The making of the rules which is wise*
(a) Why are the rules made?
(b) What do the rules say?

B. *The breaking of the rules which is bad*
(a) The reasons why people break the rules.
(b) The results when people break the rules.

C. *The keeping of the rules which is right*
(a) The importance of the One who controls the game.
(b) The obedience to the One who controls the world.

For Mothering Sunday

Exodus 20.12: 'Honour thy mother'

A. *Think of a mother's hands*
(a) Her hands are working hands, doing everything for us when we are small.
(b) Her hands are waiting hands, waiting for the time when we can help her.

B. *Think of a mother's heart*
(a) What a mother keeps in her heart.
(b) How a mother cares for her child.

C. *Think of a mother's hopes*
(a) The heights she hopes her children will reach in their lives.
(b) The help she knows her children will need from her Lord.

Love is glad to serve

Exodus 21.1–6: 'I love my Master . . . I will not go out free'

A. *The motive of love's consecration: 'I love my Master'*
(a) What the years might reveal.
(b) How the heart would respond.

B. *The meaning of love's consecration*
(a) The acceptance of the Master's authority.
(b) The permanence of the Master's authority.

C. *The moment of love's consecration*
(a) The decision was to be recorded personally.
(b) The decision was to be revealed publicly.

The treatment of strangers

Exodus 23.9: 'Thou shalt not oppress a stranger: for ye know the heart of a stranger, seeing ye were strangers in the land of Egypt'

A. *The memories these instructions would awake*
(a) The recollection of their own experience.
(b) Its repetition in the experience of others.

B. *The sympathies these instructions would arouse*
(a) The affinity which sympathy enjoys.
(b) The attraction which sympathy creates.

C. *The tragedies these instructions would avoid*
(a) The discouragements a stranger can feel.
(b) The enrichment a stranger can bring.

Where God meets us

Exodus 25.22: 'There I will meet with thee'

    A.   *Where peace is found: Exod. 25.22*
    (a) The grace revealed there.
    (b) The guilt removed there.

    B. .*Where proof is seen: Exod. 29.42*
    (a) The obedience love must give.
    (b) The experience love will have.

    C.   *Where prayer is made: Exod. 30.35*
    (a) The expectancy with which I enter the Presence.
    (b) The certainty with which I leave the Presence.

The testing of faith

Exodus Chapter 32

    A.   *The test of ordinariness: nothing seemed to be happening – a test for the people*
    (a) What the test revealed.
    (b) Where the people's thoughts returned.

    B.   *The test of loneliness: for Aaron*
    (a) The sinful desires of the greater number.
    (b) The secret desires of the smaller number: that Aaron would stand firm.

    C.   *The test of bitterness: for Moses*
    (a) The plan of God which was nearly lost.
    (b) The place of Moses which was grimly held.

Meeting with God

Exodus 33.7–11: 'And the Lord spake unto Moses face to face, as a man speaketh unto his friend'

A. *A seeking of the face of the Lord*
(a) The eagerness in his love.
(b) The openness with his Lord.

B. *A spending of his time with the Lord*
(a) How we must find the time.
(b) How we will fill the time.

C. *A sharing of his joy in the Lord*
(a) I find a younger man going with Moses.
(b) I find a younger man learning from Moses.

The influence of a holy life

Exodus 34.29: 'Moses wist not that the skin of his face shone'

A. *An impression which was unmistakeable*
(a) A recognition which was immediate.
(b) A respect which was instinctive.

B. *An intimacy which was unclouded*
(a) The effort which secured it.
(b) The effect which sprang from it.

C. *An influence which was unconscious*
(a) Moses was quite unaware of what was happening.
(b) People were quite unable to ignore what was happening.

Leviticus
The day of atonement

Leviticus Chapter 16

   A. *Here we have a picture of the Redeemer*
   (a) In his purity.
   (b) In his identity.
   (c) In his humility.

   B. *Here we see the price of our redemption*
   (a) The offering slain.
   (b) The blood sprinkled.
   (c) The Law satisfied.

   C. *Here we see the peace of the redeemed*
   (a) The confession of sin.
   (b) The completeness of forgiveness.
   (c) The consecration of love.

The unreaped corner

Leviticus 19.9–10: 'And when ye reap the harvest of your land, thou shalt not wholly reap the corners of thy field ... thou shalt leave them for the poor and the stranger'

   A. *I must not claim all I possess*
   (a) We do well to leave something for others.
   (b) We do well to leave something for God.

   B. *I will not reap all I sow*
   (a) There is comfort here for me.
   (b) There is caution here for me.

   C. *I must not judge by all I see*
   (a) There is something here to avoid in my judgement of others.
   (b) There is something here to anticipate in my treatment by others.

101

Numbers

Lessons to be learned from humble lives: a study of Miriam

Numbers Chapter 12

A. *The home she shared with Moses*
(a) The part she played in his survival.
(b) The pride she took in his success.

B. *The help she was to him*
(a) The fellowship she had with him.
(b) The leadership she shared with him.

C. *The harm she brought to him*
(a) What were the reasons?
(b) What were the results?

The need for wholeheartedness

Numbers Chapter 13 and Joshua Chapter 14

A. *The discouragement Caleb faced*
(a) The size of the problem.
(b) The mood of the people.

B. *The commitment Caleb made*
(a) A dedication that was personal.
(b) A dedication that was perfect.

C. *The fulfilment Caleb saw*
(a) The principle of his life was unchanged.
(b) The progress in his life was unchecked.

Harvest Festival

Numbers Chapters 13 and 14

   A.   *There were grapes in the land: its delights*
   (a) How rich the land was.
   (b) How real the fruits were.

   B.   *There were giants in the land: its dangers*
   (a) How big the men were.
   (b) How bad the news was.

   C.   *There was God on their side: a deliverer*
   (a) How sure they had been of God's presence.
   (b) How safe they would be through God's power.
(With acknowledgements to the late Canon Guy King for the three main headings.)

The secret of Moses' influence

Numbers 20.6: 'And Moses . . . went from the presence of the assembly unto the door of the tabernacle of the congregation . . . and the glory of the Lord appeared unto them'

   A.   *The people by whom he was continually provoked*
   (a) Their inconsistencies.
   (b) Their ingratitude.

   B.   *The place to which he instinctively turned*
   (a) Where he went.
   (b) How he went.

   C.   *The person to whom he was ultimately responsible*
   (a) The privileged intimacy he enjoyed.
   (b) The precise instructions he received.

Incomplete consecration: a study of Balaam

Numbers Chapters 22–24

A. *Think of the reputation of the man*
(a) A reputation for effectiveness: he was worth sending for.
(b) A reputation for eloquence: he was worth listening to.

B. *Think of the reservation of the man*
(a) Consider what he wanted besides the will of God (cf. 2 Pet 2.15).
(b) Consider how the Lord warned him to hold him to the will of God.

C. *Think of the ruination of the man*
(a) Note the insincerity which gradually became apparent.
(b) Note the tragedy that finally was accomplished.

Deuteronomy

Facets of forgetfulness

Deuteronomy 6.12: 'Beware lest thou forget'

A. *There is a forgetfulness which can be dangerous*
(a) What the danger is.
(b) When the danger comes.

B. *There is a forgetfulness which should be discerning (cf Phil. 3.13)*
(a) Think of Paul's estimation of the past behind him.
(b) Think of Paul's expectations about the path before him.

C. *There is a forgetfulness which must be determined (cf Ps. 51.3)*
(a) When we face the problem of guilt.
(b) When we face the promises of grace.

Ups and downs in the Christian life

Deuteronomy 11.11: 'A land of hills and valleys'

A. *The differences they would see*
(a) There would be liberty in the land.
(b) There would be loveliness in the land.

B. *The dependence they must show*
(a) They must remember the source of their prosperity.
(b) They must remember the secret of their prosperity.

C. *The disobedience they must shun*
(a) The temptations they would face in the land.
(b) The tragedy they should fear in the land.

The ministry of memory

Deuteronomy 16.3: 'That thou mayest remember the day'
'In remembrance of me' (1 Cor. 11.24)

A. *Memory enriches our lives*
(a) Memories of different days.
(b) Memories of divine dealings.

B. *Memory strengthens our faith*
(a) Days when all seemed dark.
(b) Days when God drew near.

C. *Memory quickens our sympathy*
(a) Days when we underwent sore trials.
(b) Days when we understood more people.

D. *Memory humbles our pride*
(a) Days of failure.
(b) Days of forgiveness.

When God shuts the door

Deuteronomy 17.16: 'Ye shall henceforth return no more that way'

A. *There can be a measure of relief*
(a) Experiences which were distressing to my mind.
(b) Experiences which were dishonouring to my Master.

B. *There can be a matter of regret*
(a) Think of the enjoyment the past may have brought.
(b) Think of the achievements the past may have held.

C. *There can be a moment of resolve*
(a) Think what I must leave in the past.
(b) Think what I have learned from my Lord.

God's dealings with men

Deuteronomy 29.29: 'The secret things belong unto the Lord our God: but those things which are revealed belong unto us and to our children for ever, that we may do all the words of this law'

A. *There is a limit which God sets in his dealings with men*
(a) There is a privacy which God maintains.
(b) There is a mystery which faith accepts.

B. *There is a love which God shows in his dealings with men*
(a) There will be a simplicity which we must expect.
(b) There will be a finality which we must respect.

C. *There is a life which God seeks in his dealings with men*
(a) Think of the sequel of obedience which God desires.
(b) Think of the standard of obedience which God demands.

From discipleship to leadership

Deuteronomy 31.14: 'Moses and Joshua went, and presented themselves in the tabernacle of the congregation'

A.   *Think of the encouragement which experience can provide*
(a) They had been together in the service of God.
(b) They had been together in the presence of God.

B.   *Think of the adjustments which experience can suggest*
(a) There was the devotion which Joshua had revealed.
(b) There was the correction which Joshua would receive.

C.   *Think of the fulfilment which experience would desire*
(a) There were the matters which had been faced.
(b) There was the moment which had now come.

Blessings in Christ

Deuteronomy 33.29: 'Happy art thou, O Israel: who is like unto thee, O people saved by the Lord?'

A.   *The surprise which I get here*
(a) Consider the blessings I can have in Christ.
(b) Consider the blunders that men can make about Christ.

B.   *The secrets which I learn here*
(a) I have an adjusted relationship with God in Christ.
(b) I have the adequate resources I need in Christ.

C.   *The Saviour which I find here*
(a) My life will be controlled by his presence.
(b) My life will be conformed to his purposes.

The ministry of Moses (1)

Deuteronomy 34.10: 'There arose not a prophet since in Israel like unto Moses, whom the Lord knew face to face'

A. *The place which he had filled in the purposes of God*
(a) The reluctance of his acceptance of that place.
(b) The result of his acceptance of that place.

B. *The punishment which he had deserved as a servant of God*
(a) The tragedy which marred his life.
(b) The dignity which rewarded his love.

C. *The provision which was made for the work of God*
(a) The person who was chosen.
(b) The power which was given.

D. *The picture which was remembered of the prophet of God*
(a) The fellowship he had enjoyed with God.
(b) The fear he had inspired among men.

The ministry of Moses (2)

Deuteronomy 34.10: 'Moses, whom the Lord knew face to face'

A. *The place of appointment (Exod. 33.11)*
(a) Think of the discipline required to secure it.
(b) Think of the discoveries revealed by securing it.

B. *The place of achievement (17.8–15)*
(a) The distance at which the prayer was offered.
(b) The difference which the prayer made.

C. *The place of adornment (34.29–35)*
(a) There is a cleansing to be found there.
(b) There are changes to be wrought there.

Joshua to Esther

Joshua

The death of Moses

Joshua 1.5: 'As I was with Moses, so I will be with thee'

A. *The purpose that was unchanged*
(a) The intention of God re-stated.
(b) The initiative of man required.

B. *The presence that was unchanged*
(a) The assurance that Presence would bring.
(b) The obedience that Presence would ask.

C. *The pattern that was unchanged*
(a) The leadership for which the people would look.
(b) The loyalty for which the future would ask.

Making the most of the Bible

Joshua 1.7–9

A. *I must fit it in*
(a) The battle I must win.
(b) The blessing I will know.

B. *I must read it through*
(a) I must read it carefully.
(b) I must read it prayerfully.

C. *I must write it down*
(a) Its relevance should be defined.
(b) Its permanence will be secured.

D. *I must live it out*
(a) The illustration my life will provide.
(b) The communication my life should achieve.

E. *I must pass it on*
(a) The responsibility I cannot evade.
(b) The opportunity I must exploit.

The art of meditation

Joshua 1.8: 'Thou shalt meditate therein day and night'

A. *The tools to get*
(a) The equipment which must be provided by me.
(b) The enlightenment which has been promised by God.

B. *The time to give*
(a) Time in which God can reveal his thoughts to my heart.
(b) Time in which I can relate God's truth to my life.

C. *The truths to glean*
(a) It is good to keep a record of what I have learned.
(b) It is good to show the results of what I have learned.

Coping with bereavement

Joshua 1.1: 'Now after the death of Moses the servant of the Lord it came to pass, that the Lord spake unto Joshua'

A. *The loss from which he was asked to turn*
(a) The sorrow which must have shattered him.
(b) The summons which must have startled him.

B. *The Law from which he was asked to learn*
(a) His ignorance of the Law must be dispelled.
(b) His obedience to the Law must be complete.

C. *The Lord in whom he was asked to trust*
(a) The danger of fear.
(b) The demand for faith.

The power of the word

Joshua 1.8: 'Then thou shalt make thy way prosperous, and then thou shalt have good success'

A. *It will give me food for my soul: 1 Peter 2.2*
(a) The existence of a real threat.
(b) The importance of the right food.
(c) The insistence on regular meals.

B. *It will keep me clean in my mind: Psalm 119.11*
(a) The perils which dirt can bring.
(b) The places where dirt will lodge.
(c) The power which dirt will need.

C. *It will give me light on my path: Psalm 119.105*
(a) The mistakes we can make.
(b) The misery we can know.
(c) The ministry we can have.

D. *It will give me hope when I fall*
(a) The attacks we should expect.
(b) The attitude we can adopt.
(c) The action we must take.

Why is the Bible important?

Joshua 1.8

A. *It deals with a condition which baffles the minds of men*
(a) It exposes the nature of man.
(b) It explains the failure of man.

B. *It speaks of a provision which meets the needs of man*
(a) The new relationship with the living God.
(b) The new resources in the risen Christ.

C. *It calls for a decision which can change the lives of men*
(a) I must make a personal acceptance of Christ.
(b) I must give a personal allegiance to Christ.

Rahab – an example of faith

Joshua 2.1–21, 6.22–25; Hebrews 11.31

A. *The heart in which faith was born*
(a) The marring of life that was there.
(b) The marvel of love that was there.

B. *The truth on which faith was based*
(a) The reports faith heard.
(b) The response faith made.

C. *The life to which faith was brought*
(a) The community in which faith would now live.
(b) The eternity to which faith was now linked.

Entering the promised land

Joshua Chapters 3 and 4

A. *The place at which faith tarries: 3.1*
(a) The place of promise.
(b) The place of preparation.

B. *The prospect at which faith trembles: 3.6: 'right against Jericho'*
(a) The foe which would oppose them.
(b) The fears which could possess them.

C. *The power in which faith trusts: 3.17: 'they passed over on dry ground'*
(a) God's power which had been tested.
(b) God's power which must be trusted.

D. *The past from which faith turns: 3.17: 'passed clean over Jordan'*
(a) The tragedy of the desert years.
(b) The termination of the desert years.

Overcoming Jericho

Joshua 5.13—6.5: 'And it came to pass, when Joshua was by Jericho, that he lifted up his eyes and looked, and, behold, there stood a man'

A. *The reassessment of his task*
(a) The problem which concerned him.
(b) The presence which confronted him.

B. *The readjustment in his life*
(a) The area of God's concern.
(b) The assent to God's control.

C. *The reassurance from his Lord*
(a) The divine intention of victory.
(b) The divine instruction for victory.

Continuing the struggle

Joshua 13.1: 'There remaineth yet very much land to be possessed'

A. *The distance they had come*
(a) The enemies encountered.
(b) The energies expended.

B. *The danger they were in*
(a) A relaxation of their involvement.
(b) A satisfaction with their achievement.

C. *The demands they must face*
(a) The will to be fulfilled.
(b) The wars to be fought.

The character of Caleb

Joshua 14.12: 'Give me this mountain'

A. *The promise recalled*
(a) When the promise had been made to him.
(b) What the promise had meant to him.

B. *The prospects reviewed*
(a) The land he had waited so patiently to take.
(b) The Lord he was willing so perfectly to trust.

C. *The progress resumed*
(a) How much time had been lost.
(b) How truly he could now live.

A time of change, a time for choice

Joshua 24.15: 'Choose you this day whom ye will serve'

A. *The urgency which could be sensed in his words*
(a) There was something of which he was aware.
(b) There was something of which he was afraid.

B. *The loyalty which had been shown in his life*
(a) The loss he had suffered.
(b) The Lord he had served.

C. *The destiny for his people which must be saved*
(a) The blessing which God had planned through his people.
(b) The burden which God had placed on Joshua's shoulders.

Judges
What happened when the people offered themselves willingly

Judges Chapters 4 and 5

A. *The initiative which was demanded*
(a) The person chosen (4.6).
(b) The promise given (4.7).

B. *The illusion which was dispelled*
(a) How strong was the enemy (4.1–3).
(b) How slender were their resources (5.8).

C. *The inaction which was despised*
(a) How considerable were their numbers.
(b) How contemptible were their reasons.

D. *The impact which was divine*
(a) The distance over which the impact was felt.
(b) The duration through which the blessing lasted.

115

The story of Gideon

Judges 6.12: 'The Lord is with thee, thou mighty man of valour'

A. *His concern for the glory of God*
(a) He lived in a troubled land.
(b) He lived with a troubled mind.

B. *His consent to the purpose of God*
(a) What we find God telling him.
(b) How we find God testing him.

C. *His control by the Spirit of God*
(a) The power received by him.
(b) The power released through him.

Chosen for service

Judges Chapter 7

A. *The fear in many hearts*
(a) How they had responded.
(b) Why they were rejected.

B. *The fact about many hearts*
(a) They were distracted easily.
(b) They were discarded early.

C. *The faith in some hearts*
(a) Their eagerness to meet the foe.
(b) Their readiness to trust their Lord.

Samson, the man whom God used

Judges Chapters 13–16

A. *He was dedicated*
(a) Think of the parents God gave to him.
(b) Think of the purpose God had for him.

B. *He was discontented*
(a) The restrictions that encircled his life.
(b) The resentments that inflamed his heart.

C. *He was disobedient*
(a) The decision he made.
(b) The dangers he met.

D. *He was delivered*
(a) The secret of his deliverance.
(b) The sequel to his deliverance.

How victory returned to Samson's life: A story in four chapters

Judges Chapters 13–16

A. *Chapter One: Destiny*
(a) The intention made known.
(b) The conditions laid down.

B. *Chapter Two: Ministry*
(a) The record of what he had achieved.
(b) The record of how he was attacked.

C. *Chapter Three: Tragedy*
(a) What he allowed to happen.
(b) What he attempted to do.

D. *Chapter Four: Victory*
(a) Penitence moved him.
(b) Omnipotence mastered him.

Ruth

Playing the second fiddle

The Book of Ruth: a study in Naomi's influence on Ruth

A. *How testing were the events in her life*
(a) Think of the difficulty of her surroundings.
(b) Think of the intensity of her sufferings.

B. *How telling was her witness to her Lord*
(a) How close was the relationship between them.
(b) How clear was the reality before them.

C. *How thrilling was the outcome for the world*
(a) The immediate result for Naomi.
(b) The ultimate result for us – David (4.17).

1 Samuel

Hannah, the mother of Samuel

1 Samuel Chapter 1

A. *She had her problems*
(a) In her home.
(b) In her heart.

B. *She said her prayers*
(a) The desire she expressed.
(b) The delay she experienced.

C. *She kept her promises*
(a) The resolve she kept.
(b) The reward she got.

The barrenness of an over-busy life: the story of Eli

1 Samuel 1.1—4.18

A. *The life of sin which reproached his home*
(a) There was no instruction in their lives (2.12).
(b) There was no influence from their father (3.13).

B. *The lack of spirituality which ruined Eli's work*
(a) The closed heaven (3.1).
(b) The clumsy hand (1.12–14).

C. *The love of Samuel which redeemed his name*
(a) The popularity of Samuel.
(b) The humility of Eli.

Mothering Sunday

1 Samuel 1.20

A. *Samuel was born*
(a) His mother's prayers.
(b) His mother's promise.

B. *Samuel was brought*
(a) A love for the things of God which was born.
(b) A life which was busy in the house of God.

C. *Samuel was blessed*
(a) He discovered God's purpose for his life.
(b) He delighted in God's presence in his life.

Sunset glory – old age

1 Samuel 8.1: 'And it came to pass, when Samuel was old . . .'

A. *The shadows of the sunset*
(a) The work which seemed to have been forgotten.
(b) The ways which seemed to have been forsaken.

B. *The serenity of the sunset*
(a) The ministry of intercession.
(b) The ministry of instruction.

C. *The splendour of the sunset*
(a) The intimacy of his walk with God.
(b) The quality of his work for God.

The sin of prayerlessness

1 Samuel 12.23: 'God forbid that I should sin against the Lord in ceasing to pray for you'

A. *Prayerlessness involves despising the cross of Christ*
(a) Think of the untold price.
(b) Think of the untrod path.

B. *Prayerlessness involves defrauding the Church of Christ*
(a) Think of the encouragements to prayerfulness.
(b) Think of the impoverishment caused by prayerlessness.

C. *Prayerlessness involves defeating the cause of Christ*
(a) The warfare in which the Christian is engaged.
(b) The weapon with which the Christian is equipped.

The need for leadership in the work of God

1 Samuel Chapters 13–14

A. *Here we read of the impoverishment of a people*
(a) Their wealth was threatened.
(b) Their weapons were taken.

B. *Here we read of the impatience of a man*
(a) The courage he had.
(b) The companion he found.

C. *Here we read of the intervention of the Lord*
(a) The illusion which was dispelled.
(b) The inspiration which was given.

God working through a man

1 Samuel 14.45: 'Jonathan . . . who wrought with God'

A. *Note the inaction of man*
(a) The enemy without: 13.5.
(b) The lethargy within: 14.2.

B. *The infection of faith*
(a) The resolve formed by faith.
(b) The response found by faith.

C. *The intrusion of God*
(a) God waiting for a man.
(b) God working through a man.

The sin of envy or jealousy

1 Samuel Chapters 15–31: 'who is able to stand before envy?'
(Prov. 27.4) King Saul's jealousy of David

A. *The sin of the older man against the younger man*
(a) Note the condition of the older man.
(b) Note the conduct of the younger man.

B. *The sin of the stronger man against the weaker man*
(a) How influential was the position of Saul.
(b) How irrational was the behaviour of Saul.

C. *The sin of the smaller man against the bigger man*
(a) How dominated Saul was by self.
(b) How dedicated David was to God.

Facing contempt

1 Samuel 17.42: 'When the Philistine looked about, and saw
David, he disdained him'

A. *The form of contempt is varied*
(a) It was undisguised: 17.42.
(b) It was undeserved: 25.10.
(c) It was unexpected: 2 Sam. 6.20.

B. *The facing of contempt is vital*
(a) The faith David had.
(b) The forgiveness he owed.
(c) The fellowship he knew.

C. *The fruit of contempt is victory*
(a) A victory was procured.
(b) A testimony was preserved.
(c) A humility was proved.

David and Goliath: a triple victory

1 Samuel Chapter 17

A. *The mastery he displayed (over himself)*
(a) The charge which could have roused his temper.
(b) The concern which must have ruled his actions.

B. *The society he defied (personified by King Saul)*
(a) The importance of King Saul.
(b) The indifference of David.

C. *The enemy he destroyed*
(a) The strength of the enemy.
(b) The secret of the victory.

The blunder which David made in his marriage

1 Samuel 18.20: 'Michal, Saul's daughter, loved David'

A. *The happy beginning*
(a) The circumstances which led to the marriage.
(b) The differences which existed in the marriage.

B. *The hidden blemish: 1 Sam. 19.11–13*
(a) The test which Michal faced.
(b) The test which Michal failed.

C. *The hated bond: 2 Sam. chapter 6: a wonderful day for David which ended in tragedy*
(a) How David delighted in his God.
(b) How David was despised in his home.

2 Samuel

The friendship between David and Jonathan

2 Samuel 1.26: 'Thy love to me was wonderful'

A. *The presence which friendship desires*
(a) The harmony sensed.
(b) The privacy sought.

B. *The pressures which friendship endures*
(a) The hostility which was undeserved.
(b) The fidelity which was undismayed.

C. *The prospect which friendship secures*
(a) The strain which nearly broke David: 2 Sam. 23.14.
(b) The strength which clearly blessed David.

David's enthronement

2 Samuel Chapters 3, 17 and 18: 'Ye sought for David in times past to be king over you, now then do it'

A. *Disillusionment*
(a) The expectancy with which the reign of Saul had begun.
(b) The perplexity with which the reign of Saul was marked.

B. *Postponement*
(a) The direction of their thoughts.
(b) The diffidence in their hearts.

C. *Enthronement*
(a) The man they wanted as king.
(b) The moment they made him their king.

A message for leaders

2 Samuel 6.9: ' How shall the ark of the Lord come to me?'

    A.   *The purpose formed*
(a) How worthy the purpose was.
(b) How costly the planning proved.

    B.   *The problem faced*
(a) The situation which displeased David.
(b) The information which disturbed David.

    C.   *The pattern found*
(a) What he did.
(b) When he danced.

The pathway to life's purpose

2 Samuel 7.8–9: 'I took thee . . . I was with thee . . . I made thee'

    A.   *The trysting place of David's soul: 'I took thee from the sheepcote'*
(a) The place remembered.
(b) The person revered.
(c) The power received.

    B.   *The trusted presence of his God: 'I was with thee'*
(a) Through the delays.
(b) Through the dangers.
(c) Through the delights.

    C.   *The transformed pattern of his life: 'I have made thee'*
(a) The responsibility on his shoulders.
(b) The range of his influence.
(c) The reputation of his name.

Bringing back the king

2 Samuel 19.10

A. *The rebel who brought strife to the people of God*
(a) He was attractive in his person.
(b) He was deceptive in his purpose.

B. *The revolt which meant hurt to the people of God*
(a) The success he had.
(b) The sadness he brought.

C. *The return which spelt hope for the people of God*
(a) The appeal to the past.
(b) The address to the king.

A piece of ground full of lentils

2 Samuel 23.11–12

A. *The retreat in which Shammah would not share*
(a) The forces which menaced them.
(b) The forces which mastered them.

B. *The resolve from which he would not move*
(a) The attackers who could have swamped him.
(b) The arguments which could have swayed him.

C. *The result of which he had not dreamed*
(a) How seemingly unimportant the scene of the conflict.
(b) How surprisingly unexpected the scale of the victory.

Sacrificial love

2 Samuel 24.24: 'Neither will I offer . . . unto the Lord my God of that which doth cost me nothing'

A. *How love speaks*
(a) How possessive love is.
(b) How exclusive love is.

B. *Why love serves*
(a) The desire love has to give.
(b) The delight love finds in giving.

C. *What love spurns*
(a) The offer he had received.
(b) The answer he returned.

1 Kings

David and Adonijah

1 Kings 1.20: 'Who shall sit on the throne?'

A. *The rival to the throne*
(a) The indulgence which David had always shown to Adonijah.
(b) The intention which David had never sensed in Adonijah.

B. *The reproach on a name*
(a) The perplexity which surrounded him.
(b) The fidelity which served him.

C. *The resolve of the king.*
(a) The urgency revealed by him.
(b) The sovereignty renounced by him.

127

A peril of spiritual maturity

1 Kings 13.11: 'Now there dwelt an old prophet in Bethel'

    A.   *The lethargy which stamped his service*
    (a) The inaction into which he had settled.
    (b) The intrusion by which he was startled.

    B.   *The animosity which seared his spirit*
    (a) The pride which would not be humbled.
    (b) The plan which would not be halted.

    C.   *The tragedy which sealed his success*
    (a) The weapon the old prophet used.
    (b) The wreckage the old prophet saw.

The school of obedience

1 Kings Chapters 17 and 18.

    A.   *How positive Elijah's obedience was seen to be*
    (a) There must be a discernment of the will of God.
    (b) There must be a commitment to the will of God.
    (c) There will be an enjoyment of the will of God.

    B.   *How progressive his obedience was found to be*
    (a) A matter of which he was personally aware.
    (b) An action which might be socially awkward.
    (c) A result for which he could be publicly attacked.

    C.   *How productive his obedience was proved to be*
    (a) The enemies of the Lord were defeated.
    (b) The reality of the Lord was revealed.
    (c) The sovereignty of the Lord was acclaimed.

Elijah's dark hour of the soul

1 Kings Chapter 19

A. *By whom this was experienced*
(a) By such a man.
(b) At such a moment.
(c) Over such a matter.

B. *How it happened*
(a) His sinfulness in the sight of God.
(b) His loneliness in the will of God.
(c) His weariness in the work of God.

C. *How it was faced*
(a) There was a practical ministry.
(b) There was a personal message.
(c) There was a productive mission.

The calling of Elisha

1 Kings 19.19–21

A. *A clear call*
(a) It was unmistakeable.
(b) It was unexpected.

B. *A clean break*
(a) A costly decision.
(b) A complete devotion.

C. *A close walk*
(a) He shared the loneliness of Elijah.
(b) He showed a likeness to Elijah.

The tragedy of illegitimate desire
1 Kings 21.1–29

A. *An obsession Ahab never controlled*
(a) The smallness of it.
(b) The nearness of it.
(c) The bigness of it.

B. *The transgression he never intended*
(a) How reasonably he began.
(b) How deceitfully he continued.
(c) How tragically it ended.

C. *The possession he never enjoyed*
(a) The disturbing voice.
(b) The distorted values.
(c) The divine verdict.

2 Kings

'Make this valley full of ditches'
2 Kings 3.16

A. *The objective these kings had*
(a) The rebellion which faced them.
(b) The resources which failed them.

B. *The directive the kings sought*
(a) The wisdom which turned to the Lord.
(b) The witness which spoke of the Lord.

C. *The initiative the kings took*
(a) The instructions which meant obedience.
(b) The intervention which brought deliverance.

What God can do with what we have already got

2 Kings 4.1–7

    A.   *This woman was in need of help*
    (a) The demands which she could not meet.
    (b) The disgrace which she could not bear.

    B.   *This woman was in touch with God*
    (a) How searching were the words of God.
    (b) How simple are the ways of God.

    C.   *This woman was in earnest with herself*
    (a) The hiddenness of her obedience.
    (b) The thoroughness of her obedience.

Naaman – a man who needed God's help more than anything else

2 Kings Chapter 5

    A.   *The problem which baffled him*
    (a) His success.
    (b) His secret.

    B.   *The pride which hindered him*
    (a) The faithfulness of a maid.
    (b) The foolishness of a man.

    C.   *The power which healed him*
    (a) He was stopped as he went away.
    (b) He was saved as he went God's way.

Three angry men

2 Kings 5.12

A. *The angry sinner: 2 Kings 5.12*
(a) What were the reasons for his anger?
(b) What was the result of his anger?

B. *The angry son: Luke 15.28*
(a) The laughter which jarred him.
(b) The anger which stirred him.

C. *The angry servant: Jonah 4.1*
(a) The limit which he had set to his concern for men.
(b) The lesson which he must learn about his concern for men.

A miracle of recovery

2 Kings 6.1–7

A. *A leadership in the work of God which was thrilling*
(a) The Presence in their midst.
(b) The prospects in their minds.

B. *A loss in the work of God which was tragic*
(a) It was a conscious loss.
(b) It was a confessed loss.

C. *A life in the work of God which was taken up again*
(a) The seeming impossibility of recovery.
(b) The swift immediacy of response.

The hidden sorrows in life

2 Kings 6.30: 'He had sackcloth within upon his flesh'

A. *The unexpected discoveries which life brings*
(a) The covering which may conceal the sorrows of lives.
(b) The circumstances which may reveal the sorrows of lives.

B. *The unsuspected dangers which life holds*
(a) How inadequate our knowledge sometimes is.
(b) How inaccurate our judgments often are.

C. *The unavoidable demands which life makes*
(a) The possibility of being indifferent to human need.
(b) The responsibility of being identified with human need.

The sin of silence

2 Kings 7.3–16: 'We do not well: this is a day of good tidings, and we hold our peace'

A. *These men were amazed at what they had found*
(a) The misery in which they were placed.
(b) The mystery with which they were faced.

B. *These men were absorbed by what they had got*
(a) Their sudden enrichment.
(b) Their selfish enjoyment.

C. *They were ashamed at what they had done*
(a) The sin which troubled them.
(b) The sight which thrilled them.

The servant of God

2 Kings 8.18: 'In the sight of the Lord'

A. *The affirmation the servant of God must face*
(a) The truth of the knowledge of God.
(b) The depth of the knowledge of God.

B. *The application the servant of God must make*
(a) The comfort the servant of God can derive for himself.
(b) The contempt the servant of God can display for his foes.

C. *The approbation the servant of God must seek*
(a) The pleasure of the One loved for which love will strive.
(b) The presence of the One loved in which love will stand.

1 Chronicles

Wanting the impossible

1 Chronicles 11.17, 2 Samuel 23.15: 'The wells of Bethlehem'

A. *A craving which was intolerable*
(a) A longing for the innocence of the Bethlehem days.
(b) A longing for the irresponsibility of the Bethlehem days.

B. *The circumstances which seemed insurmountable*
(a) The barring of the road.
(b) The daring of the foe.

C. *The consecration which was inevitable*
(a) David's refusal to use the gift for himself.
(b) David's resolve to give it wholly to his God.

'Benaiah . . . slew a lion in a pit on a snowy day'

1 Chronicles 11.22

A. *The initiative he was prepared to take*
(a) The destruction the lion had caused.
(b) The danger the action would hold.

B. *The independence of circumstances he was prepared to show*
(a) The circumstances we so often demand.
(b) The circumstances he was ready to defy.

C. *The isolation in life he was prepared to face*
(a) The difference companionship makes.
(b) The demands loneliness brings.

Tested and trusted

1 Chronicles 12.38: 'All these men of war, that could keep rank, came with a perfect heart to Hebron, to make David King over all Israel'

A. *The test which they had passed*
(a) The ability they had displayed.
(b) The authority they had obeyed.

B. *The trust which could be placed in them*
(a) No reservation about their allegiance.
(b) No hesitation about their acceptance.

C. *The throne which was secured by them*
(a) The humiliation these men had seen.
(b) The determination these men had shown.

Worship

1 Chronicles 16.36: 'And all the people said "Amen"'

   A. *Worship involves a sharing by all*
   (a) There will be a leadership in worship.
   (b) There will be a fellowship in worship.

   B. *Worship involves a speaking by all*
   (a) There will be a place for stillness in worship.
   (b) There will be a place for witness in worship.

   C. *Worship involves a sealing by all*
   (a) Think of the response which worship involves.
   (b) Think of the result which worship includes.

2 Chronicles

Giving God the best

2 Chronicles 3.4: 'He overlaid it . . . with pure gold'
1 Corinthians 3.12

   A. *The best which love is able to afford*
   (a) The person for whom he was building.
   (b) The places in which the gold was displayed.

   B. *The cost which love is willing to accept*
   (a) The demand this would make.
   (b) The delight this would bring.

   C. *The test which love is willing to apply*
   (a) The rebuke I may merit.
   (b) The resolve I must make.

Seeking God's face

2 Chronicles 7.14: 'If my people will . . . then will I'

   A.   *The humbling required by God*
   (a) Note the people addressed.
   (b) Note the Presence approached.

   B.   *The hearing restored by God*
   (a) Note the condition we must meet.
   (b) Note the communion this will mean.

   C.   *The healing released by God*
   (a) Note the origin of this healing.
   (b) Note the outcome of this healing.

'Shields of gold . . . shields of brass'

2 Chronicles 12.9–10

   A.   *The testimony for which they were used*
   (a) The wealth of the king.
   (b) The word of God.

   B.   *The tragedy in which they were lost*
   (a) The disobedience which marked the king.
   (b) The disaster which met him.

   C.   *The travesty by which they were replaced*
   (a) How attractive the suggestion would be.
   (b) How deceptive the appearance would be.

The principle of separation: the life of Jehoshaphat

2 Chronicles Chapters 17–19

A. *His life was marked by dedication*
(a) Conscious of danger.
(b) Conditioned by obedience.
(c) Crowned with favour.

B. *His life was marked by complication*
(a) A strange intimacy.
(b) A silenced testimony.
(c) A sacrificed identity.

C. *His life was marked by liberation*
(a) The start of it.
(b) The secret of it.
(c) The song in it.

The songs in one's heart are born out of the sacrifices in one's life

2 Chronicles 29.27: 'When the offering began . . . the song of the Lord began also'

A. *A trend today which denies this*
(a) How attractive this may seem.
(b) How deceptive this can prove.

B. *A truth we will learn in our lives which will confirm this*
(a) The appeal to our memory.
(b) The attainment of our destiny.

C. *A trust we will have in our Lord which will demand this*
(a) His intention that we should sing.
(b) His insistence that we should surrender.

Ezra

The rebuilding of the temple

Ezra 6.16: 'The children of Israel . . . kept the dedication of this house of God with joy'

A. *The joy of achievement*
(a) The opportunities they had seized.
(b) The difficulties they had surmounted.

B. *The joy of involvement*
(a) A creative instinct planted by God in us.
(b) A compelling inspiration granted by God to us.

C. *The joy of commencement*
(a) The peace which was then available to them.
(b) The praise which was then ascribed to God.

Nehemiah

God works through the heart of a man

The Book of Nehemiah

A. *He took it to heart*
(a) The dishonour he faced.
(b) The distress he felt.

B. *He took it to God*
(a) The forgiveness he sought.
(b) The faithfulness he trusted.

C. *He took it in hand*
(a) How encouraged he was.
(b) How involved he was.

Work and war

The Book of Nehemiah

A. *The building*
(a) The leader required.
(b) The labour involved.

B. *The battle*
(a) The methods of the opposition.
(b) The meeting of the opposition.

C. *The blessing*
(a) The completion of the task.
(b) The conviction about the task.

The way people talk about God's work

Nehemiah 4.10,11,14

A. *The voice of doubt: 'We can't' (4.10)*
(a) The massiveness of the task.
(b) The weariness of the toilers.

B. *The voice of hate: 'You won't' (4.11)*
(a) How vicious was the way in which they talked.
(b) How various were the ways in which they worked.

C. *The voice of trust: 'God will' (4.14)*
(a) The inspiration of their faith.
(b) The vindication of their faith.

The call to courage

Nehemiah 6.11: 'Should such a man as I flee?'

A. *The danger of intrigue*
(a) It was marked with deceit.
(b) It was met with devotion.

B. *The danger of insinuation*
(a) The smear of suggestion.
(b) The stand of denial.

C. *The danger of intimidation*
(a) The consequences which were threatened.
(b) The courage which was triumphant.

Esther

Trying to turn a blind eye to reality

Esther 4.2: 'None might enter the king's gate clothed with sackcloth'

A. *The reason for this attitude*
(a) The meaning of the decree was simple.
(b) The motive behind the decree was selfish.

B. *The results of this attitude*
(a) The pleasures which life could then hold undisturbed.
(b) The pretence which life would then become.

C. *The reproach of this attitude*
(a) The reproach of ignorance.
(b) The reproach of inaction.

The challenge of God's destiny

Esther 4.14: 'Who knoweth whether thou art come to the kingdom for such a time as this?'

A. *Consider how comfortably she was living*
(a) Think of the affluence she enjoyed.
(b) Think of the ignorance she displayed.

B. *Consider how courageously she must act*
(a) Think of the charge given to her.
(b) Think of the chance taken by her.

C. *Consider how consequently she was used*
(a) Think of the signs of God's power which were seen in her life.
(b) Think of the songs of God's people which were sung in her land.

Job to the Song of Solomon

Job

Facing up to death

Job 14.14: 'If a man die, shall he live again?'

    A.   *The fact we must face*
   (a) There is a loneliness in death.
   (b) There is a helplessness in death.

    B.   *The fears we may have*
   (a) Consider the denial of such fears.
   (b) Consider the defining of such fears.

    C.   *The faith we shall need*
   (a) An assurance of a fuller life.
   (b) An acceptance of a forgiving Lord.

The most important question in the world

Job 25.4: 'How then can man be justified with God?'

A. *Where the Gospel begins: 'by grace' (Rom. 3.24).*
(a) What the blunder can be.
(b) Where the answer will lie.

B. *What the Gospel declares: 'by blood' (Rom. 5.8–9)*
(a) The necessity of the cross.
(b) The sufficiency of the cross.

C. *What the Gospel requires: 'by faith' (Rom. 5.1)*
(a) The integrity of personality which God respects.
(b) The simplicity of the faith which God requires.

D. *How the Gospel transforms: 'by works' (James 2.24)*
(a) The obedience involved in trust.
(b) The outcome revealed in time.

Psalms

'Like a tree planted by the rivers of water'

Psalm 1

A. *Here we have a life marked by faithfulness: verses 1–2*
(a) A permanence about the habit.
(b) An abundance about the supply.

B. *Here we have a life marked by fruitfulness: verse 3*
(a) A freshness which will be seen by others.
(b) A fruitfulness which will be shared with others.

C. *Here we have a life marked by foolishness: verses 4–6*
(a) The weakness of the life of the wicked.
(b) The emptiness of the life of the wicked.

Meeting with God

Psalm 5.3: 'My voice shalt thou hear in the morning'

A. *It meant getting up*
(a) The priority which he gave to prayer.
(b) The privacy which he gained for prayer.

B. *It meant speaking up*
(a) How natural it should be to speak with God.
(b) How personal it will be to speak with God.

C. *It meant looking up*
(a) The assurance received.
(b) The allegiance renewed.

Righteous living

Psalm 5.8: 'Lead me, O Lord, in thy righteousness'

A. *The inward implications to be held in view*
(a) There are conditions to be imposed.
(b) There is a connection to be observed.

B. *The outward implications to be held in view*
(a) The social influence which will restrict my freedom.
(b) The social conscience which will restrict my freedom.

C. *The upward implications to be held in view*
(a) The person God wants me to be.
(b) The purpose God wants me to serve.

'What is man?' (1)

Psalm 8.4

   A.   *There are the optimists – the Humanists*
   (a) The remedies in which they trust.
   (b) The realities through which they fail.

   B.   *There are the pessimists – the Communists*
   (a) The forms which their kind of thinking tends to take.
   (b) The facts which their kind of thinking fails to face.

   C.   *There are the realists – the Christians*
   (a) What Christianity affirms.
   (b) How Christianity answers.

'What is man?' (2)

Psalm 8.4

   A.   *The purpose of man's creation (Rev. 4.11)*
   (a) The new evaluation this claim demands of life.
   (b) The true explanation this claim brings to life.

   B.   *The problem of man's condition*
   (a) Think of man's natural hostility to God.
   (b) Think of man's spiritual heredity of sin.

   C.   *The provision for man's conversion*
   (a) The love of God revealed in the cross of Christ.
   (b) The life of Christ received into the hearts of men.

Is there a God?

Psalm 14.1: 'The fool hath said in his heart, "There is no God"'

A. *The existence of God denied by them*
(a) How conceited is the claim they make.
(b) How convenient is the creed they hold.

B. *The evidence for God they discard*
(a) The order we see in creation.
(b) The wonder we face in Christ.

C. *The experience of God they decry*
(a) The witness which men are willing to give of God.
(b) The welcome which God is waiting to get from man.

A good New Year's resolution

Psalm 16.8: 'I have set the Lord always before me'

A. *No better person: 'the Lord'*
(a) The influence people can exert.
(b) The importance people can acquire.

B. *No better place: 'before me'*
(a) A recognition which is inadequate.
(b) A resolution which is imperative.

C. *No better plan: 'set . . . always'*
(a) In every department of my life.
(b) In every decision in my life.

The sins of the servant

Psalm 19.13: 'Keep back thy servant also from presumptuous sins'

A. *A failure in relationships*
(a) His relationship to the Master of the house.
(b) His relationship to the members of the household.

B. *A failure in responsibilities*
(a) The tasks the servant is required to do.
(b) The time the servant is required to use.

C. *A failure in representation*
(a) The name of the Master he bears.
(b) The name of the Master he shames.

How faith faces the future

Psalm 23

A. *A future in which there is to be no lack: 'I shall not want'*
(a) There will be a supplying of the needs of the sheep.
(b) There will be a safeguarding of the name of the shepherd.

B. *A future in which there is to be no fear: 'I will fear no evil'*
(a) How fearful we can be.
(b) How faithful he will prove.

C. *A future in which there is to be no death: 'I will dwell in the house of the Lord for ever'*
(a) The future will hold the unfailing goodness of God.
(b) The future will hold the unfolding glory of home.

What God has prepared for us

Psalm 23.5

A. *Here we have the table prepared (Ps. 23.5)*
(a) Think of the enemies who accuse.
(b) Think of the enemies who assail.

B. *Here we have the things prepared (1 Cor. 2.9)*
(a) The perception which may be lacking.
(b) The provision which will be lavish.

C. *Here we have the throne prepared (Ps. 103.19)*
(a) The vision of the throne.
(b) The verdict from the throne.

God in our lives

Psalm 24.7–10: 'And the King of glory shall come in'

A. *A battle has been fought*
(a) The scene of his conflict.
(b) The seal of his conquest.

B. *A barrier must be raised*
(a) There must be consent from within.
(b) There will be constraint from above.

C. *A blessing will be given*
(a) The majesty of his Person.
(b) The certainty of his Presence.

The marks of the life of faith

Psalm 32: 'He that trusteth in the Lord'

A. *It will be a glad life*
(a) The burden which comes through conviction.
(b) The pardon which comes through confession.

B. *It will be a guarded life*
(a) Note the prayer on his lips.
(b) Note the power of his Lord.

C. *It will be a guided life*
(a) How sensitive we must be to the mind of God.
(b) How responsive we must be to the will of God.

The forgiveness of sins

Psalm 32.1–5

A. *It can be preceded by resistance to the Spirit*
(a) The presence of the Spirit.
(b) The silence of the sinner.

B. *It will be conditioned by a repenting by the sinner*
(a) There is a condition to be met.
(b) There is a confession to be made.

C. *It will be completed by a rejoicing in the Saviour*
(a) The forgiveness of our sins which will be received.
(b) The fellowship with our Lord which will be restored.

Looking to God

Psalm 34.5: 'They looked unto him, and were lightened'

A. *The fears with which faith must cope*
(a) The definite fact which fear is.
(b) The different forms which fear takes.

B. *The face on which faith must gaze*
(a) The assurance of love which can be discerned there.
(b) The confidence for life which can be derived there.

C. *The fight in which faith will win*
(a) The presence of the Lord on which we can rely.
(b) The praises of the Lord with which we can rejoice.

The goodness of God

Psalm 34.8: 'O taste and see that the Lord is good'

A. *The environment in which faith is born*
(a) The element of distress.
(b) The element of desire.

B. *The experiment on which faith is based*
(a) A reception which is essential.
(b) A reaction which is natural.

C. *The enjoyment with which faith is blessed*
(a) The goodness of God.
(b) The gladness of man.

The ways of God

Psalm 37.23: 'The steps of a good man are ordered by the Lord'

A. *The details of the plan of God*
(a) The wonder of this.
(b) The wisdom of this.

B. *The delights of the ways of God*
(a) How loving God is.
(b) How lavish God is.

C. *The deliverance of the child of God*
(a) The possibility of disaster.
(b) The certainty of deliverance.

The divine answer to human loneliness

Psalm 40.2: 'He took me from a lonesome pit' (Moffatt's Translation)

A. *The reality of human loneliness*
(a) The fact it is.
(b) The forms it takes.

B. *The tragedy of human loneliness*
(a) The burdens we cannot bear alone.
(b) The blessings we cannot share with others.

C. *The remedy for human loneliness*
(a) The presence of my Lord which I can have.
(b) The people he will bring into my life.

How God can put joy into our lives

Psalm 40.3: 'He hath put a new song in my mouth'

A. *God can put an end to the loneliness which silences the song in my heart*
(a) The tragedy of loneliness is real.
(b) The remedy for loneliness is Christ.

B. *God can put an end to the helplessness which silences the song in my heart*
(a) The area of our helplessness.
(b) The answer to our helplessness.

C. *God can put an end to the selfishness which silences the song in my heart*
(a) The blunder we make.
(b) The blessing we find.

Three things in which God is interested

Psalm 51.17

A. *The heart which is broken*
(a) When was it broken?
(b) Why was it brought?

B. *The reed which is bruised: Isaiah 42.3*
(a) A life which has been hurt.
(b) A life which can be healed.

C. *The bread which is brought: Matthew 14.15–21*
(a) The hunger of the crowd.
(b) The giver of the bread.

The desire for escape

Psalm 55.6: 'Oh that I had wings like a dove! for then would I fly away, and be at rest'

A. *The enchantment which escape can have for us*
(a) The burdens of which we are weary.
(b) The battles in which we are wounded.

B. *The estrangement which escape would mean for us*
(a) It would be selfish.
(b) It would be foolish.

C. *The enrichment which escape would take from us*
(a) The development of character.
(b) The achievement of success.

The meaning of faith

Psalm 62.1: 'Leave it all quietly to God, my soul' (Moffatt)

A. *The wholeness with which faith is asked to trust: 'Leave it all'*
(a) The exceptions we are so prone to make.
(b) The instructions we do well to heed.

B. *The stillness in which faith is asked to rest: 'quietly' (cf. John 4.43ff)*
(a) There may be some progressive steps which faith may have to take.
(b) There will be one final decisive step which faith will have to take.

C. *The greatness on which faith is asked to count: 'to God'*
(a) Faith remembers the Person he is.
(b) Faith remembers the people we are.

Waiting upon God

Psalm 62.5: 'My soul, wait thou only upon God; for my expectation is from Him'

A. *I am to wait upon God personally*
(a) Think of the admission of my need I will have to make.
(b) Think of the attention of my Lord I am sure to have.

B. *I am to wait upon God patiently*
(a) So that there will be time for the silence to fall.
(b) So that there will be time for the Saviour to respond.

C. *I am to wait upon God purposefully*
(a) The disclosures He will make to me.
(b) The decisions He will ask from me.

Spreading the word

Psalm 68.11: 'The Lord gave the word: great was the company of those that published it'

A. *The facts which are alarming*
(a) The soaring numbers of the world's people.
(b) The staggering needs of the world's people.

B. *The forces which are active*
(a) The political forces.
(b) The beneficial forces.

C. *The faith which is alert*
(a) The opportunities which must be seized.
(b) The responsibilities which must be shared.

What to do with the burdens of life

Psalm 68.19: 'Blessed be the Lord, who daily beareth our burdens' (RV)

A. *There are burdens to be shed*
(a) The failure we face.
(b) The future we fear.

B. *There are burdens to be shared (Gal. 6.2)*
(a) The tragedies lives can know.
(b) The sympathy love will show.

C. *There are burdens to be shouldered (Gal. 6.5)*
(a) I must assess that for which I am responsible.
(b) I must accept that I am accountable to God.

Limiting God

Psalm 78.41: 'They limited the Holy One of Israel'

A. *By the prayerlessness of our lives (James 4.2)*
(a) The abundant promises.
(b) The abandoned practice.

B. *By the sinfulness of our ways (Eph. 4.30)*
(a) The presence we have of the Holy Spirit.
(b) The problems we give to the Holy Spirit.

C. *By the faithlessness of our hearts (Matt. 13.58)*
(a) The resources which were adequate.
(b) The refusal which was adamant.

Why some churches are lovely in our eyes

Psalm 84.1: 'How lovely is thy dwelling place, O Lord of Hosts!' (RSV)

A. *There is the beauty of adornment*
(a) The beautiful things which are found there.
(b) The beautiful lives which are shaped there.

B. *There is the beauty of association*
(a) The association of happiness.
(b) The association of helpfulness.

C. *There is the beauty of affection*
(a) There is a loveliness which love sees.
(b) There is a faithfulness which love shows.

Serving God

Psalm 84.10: 'I had rather be a doorkeeper in the house of my God, than to dwell in the tents of wickedness'

A. *Think of the dignity which service confers*
(a) The privilege of serving certain people.
(b) The pride in serving certain people.

B. *Think of the qualities which service requires*
(a) There must be efficiency.
(b) There must be reliability.

C. *Think of the loyalty which service displays*
(a) The love motivating our service.
(b) The Lord vindicated through our service.

The life of peace

Psalm 84

A. *Peace is linked with the house of God*
(a) The place for which the psalmist longs.
(b) The peace with which the psalmist is blessed.

B. *Peace is linked with the power of God*
(a) The transforming power of God.
(b) The sustaining power of God.

C. *Peace is linked with the will of God*
(a) The preference which is shown for the will of God.
(b) The confidence which will rest in the will of God.

Learning wisdom

Psalm 90.12: 'Teach us to number our days, that we may apply our hearts unto wisdom'

A. *Think of the opportunities which life holds*
(a) How varied are the courses which life can take.
(b) How crucial are the choices which life can bring.

B. *Think of the brevity of life*
(a) How short it is.
(b) How best to use it.

C. *Think of the finality of life*
(a) How irrevocable life is.
(b) How irresponsible man is.

The perils of middle age

Psalm 91.5–6: 'The destruction that wasteth at noonday'

A. *These dangers are distinctive*
(a) The kind of person I have now become.
(b) The kinds of perils I must now resist.

B. *These dangers can be deceptive*
(a) Deceptive concerning their presence.
(b) Deceptive concerning their progress.

C. *These dangers may be destructive*
(a) Consider the severity of the loss which can be inflicted.
(b) Consider the security in the Lord which must be safeguarded.

An invitation to praise

Psalm 95

A. *I find here a sense of wonder*
(a) The invitation to praise that is here.
(b) The inspiration of praise that is here.

B. *I find here a call to worship*
(a) The attitude which God's greatness demands.
(b) The gratitude which God's goodness evokes.

C. *I find here a note of warning*
(a) What is central in worship.
(b) What is crucial in worship.

Breaking the silence: speaking up for God

Psalm 107.2: 'Let the redeemed of the Lord say so'

A. *The conspiracy we must break*
(a) How illogical the silence is.
(b) How insidious the silence is.

B. *The enemy we must meet*
(a) Fears which would muzzle our lips.
(b) Forces which would mould our lives.

C. *The qualities we must have*
(a) Humility.
(b) Honesty.

D. *The victories we must see*
(a) The results we hope to see.
(b) The resources we have to use.

Knowing the right way to live

Psalm 107.7: 'He led them forth by the right way'

A. *The upward look*
(a) The Person God is.
(b) The purpose God has.

B. *The outward look*
(a) Accept that we are related to one another.
(b) Accept that we are restricted by one another.

C. *The inward look*
(a) There must be no wastage in our lives.
(b) There must be no bondage in our lives.

God delivers us

Psalm 116.8: 'Thou hast delivered my soul from death, mine eyes from tears, and my feet from falling'

    A.   *Deliverance when death is faced*
(a) The aspects of death which we find disturbing.
(b) The answer to death which we find assuring.

    B.   *Deliverance when tears fall*
(a) There are times when tears can be shed.
(b) There are times when tears can be spared.

    C.   *Deliverance when strength is failing*
(a) The weariness we can know.
(b) The faithfulness we can prove.

The life of praise

Psalm 103

    A.   *In spite of the failure he has been*
(a) How grace acts.
(b) What grace adds.

    B.   *Because of the Father he has*
(a) How merciful God is to his own.
(b) How mindful he is of his own.

    C.   *In view of the future he sees*
(a) The changelessness of God which will persist.
(b) The righteousness of God which will prevail.

Trying to get our own way with God

Psalm 106.15: 'He gave them their request but he sent leanness into their souls'

A. *The insistence sensed by God*
(a) Their desire.
(b) Their delight.

B. *The reluctance shown by God*
(a) The hurt behind the gift.
(b) The hope within the act.

C. *The decadence sent by God*
(a) Something had been lost.
(b) Something could be learned.

Man's response to God's goodness

Psalm 116.12–14: 'What shall I render unto the Lord for all his benefits toward me?'

A. *My acceptance of his gift: 'I will take the cup of salvation'*
(a) To refuse is unthinkable.
(b) To receive is unavoidable.

B. *My dependence upon his love: 'I will call upon the name of the Lord'*
(a) A love which cares for me.
(b) A love which comes to me.

C. *My obedience to his will: 'I will pay my vows unto the Lord now'*
(a) The note of regret.
(b) The need for resolve.

Facing each new day with the Lord

Psalm 118.24: 'This is the day which the Lord hath made; we will rejoice and be glad in it'

A. *It will be a day shaped by him*
(a) The wisdom which will guide our steps.
(b) The wonder which will fill our heart.

B. *It will be a day shared with him*
(a) The openness which sharing requires.
(b) The happiness to which sharing leads.

C. *It will be a day spent for him*
(a) The failure which can cloud our day.
(b) The pleasure which can crown our day.

The word in my heart

Psalm 119.11: 'Thy word have I hid in mine heart, that I might not sin against thee'

A. *Note the resolve in this man's heart*
(a) The difficulty which must be overcome.
(b) The necessity which must be recognised.

B. *Note the recesses in this man's heart*
(a) The existence of the depths.
(b) The importance of the depths.

C. *Note the results in this man's life*
(a) The word will deal with the cause of the trouble.
(b) The word will provide a cure for the trouble.

A call to stop and think

Psalm 119.59–60: 'I thought on my ways, and turned my feet unto thy testimonies. I made haste, and delayed not to keep thy commandments'

  A. *There is here a call to think*
(a) Consider the sinner I am.
(b) Consider the Saviour I need.

  B. *There is here a call to turn*
(a) There is a decision to make.
(b) There is a direction to take.

  C. *There is here a call to trust*
(a) This will call for a dependence upon God.
(b) This will lead to an experience of God.

What the Bible can mean in my life

Psalm 119.103: 'How sweet are thy words unto my taste! yea, sweeter than honey to my mouth!'

  A. *The difference which the Bible makes to faith (cf. Rom. 10.17)*
(a) The basis upon which faith rests.
(b) The boldness with which faith acts.

  B. *The dynamic which the Bible brings to love*
(a) The communion where love begins.
(b) The compulsion which love becomes.

  C. *The direction which the Bible gives to life*
(a) There are decisions I must make.
(b) There is direction I can have.

Guided by the word

Psalm 119.105: 'Thy word is a lamp unto my feet, and a light unto my path'

A. *Here we have a picture of progress*
(a) My progress through time is irresistible.
(b) My progress through time is irreversible.

B. *Here we have the problem of darkness*
(a) The forms which darkness may take.
(b) The fears which darkness may bring.

C. *Here we have the promise of brightness*
(a) This light will shine permanently.
(b) This light will shine personally.

Looking towards God (1)

Psalm 121: 'I will lift up mine eyes unto the hills'

A. *How small the psalmist felt in the sight of God*
(a) The magnitude which his faith was willing to admit.
(b) The attitude which his faith was willing to adopt.

B. *How safe the psalmist felt in the hands of God*
(a) The weariness which could endanger the people's safety.
(b) The watchfulness which would ensure their progress.

C. *How sure the psalmist felt of the help of God*
(a) The ignorance which could trouble the mind.
(b) The confidence with which he could trust his Lord.

Looking towards God (2)

Psalm 123: 'Behold, as the eyes of servants look to the hand of their masters, and as the eyes of a maiden unto the hand of her mistress; so our eyes wait upon the Lord our God'

A. *How grateful the servants should be*
(a) That we should be where we are.
(b) That we should do what we do.

B. *How watchful the servants should be*
(a) Concerned with the requests of the Master.
(b) Concerned with the return of the Master.

C. *How faithful the servants should be*
(a) Faithfulness is what our Lord requires.
(b) Faithfulness is what our Lord rewards.

What the Bible has to say about laughter

Psalm 126.2: 'Then was our mouth filled with laughter'

A. *The laughter in which men should share (Ps. 126.1–3)*
(a) The deliverance by which they had been freed.
(b) The exuberance with which they had been filled.

B. *The laughter by which men could sin*
(a) Laughing at the promises of God (cf. Gen. 18.12).
(b) Laughing at the people of God (cf. Neh. 2.19).

C. *Laughter from which men should shrink (Psalm 2)*
(a) Man's insolence expressed against the Person of God.
(b) Man's impotence experienced before the power of God.

Sowing, weeping, reaping, rejoicing

Psalm 126.5–6: 'They that sow in tears shall reap in joy. He that goeth forth and weepeth, bearing precious seed, shall doubtless come again with rejoicing, bringing his sheaves with him'

A.   *The task of the servant of God*
(a) The seed is incorruptible.
(b) The store is inexhaustible.

B.   *The tears of the servant of God*
(a) The toughness of the work.
(b) The treatment by the world.

C.   *The thanks of the servant of God*
(a) The fruitfulness of our service.
(b) The faithfulness of our Saviour.

A Psalm which begins with a discovery and ends with a prayer

Psalm 139

A.   *A searching which all should be ready to expect*
(a) Think how critical love is.
(b) Think how practical love is.

B.   *A searching which some would want to evade*
(a) The possibility of escape is considered.
(b) The futility of escape is exposed.

C.   *A searching intended by love to enrich*
(a) What love will want to reveal.
(b) How love intends to reward.

Three prayers worth praying

A. *'Search me' (Psalm 139.23)*
(a) How practical the prayer is.
(b) How personal the prayer is.

B. *'Save me' (Matt. 14.30)*
(a) The condition which was the reason for it.
(b) The conviction which was the result of it.

C. *'Send me' (Isa. 6.8)*
(a) The concern in the heart of God.
(b) The consent to the will of God.

God wants to bring loveliness into living

Psalm 149.4: 'He will beautify the meek with salvation'

A. *The divine intention: 'He will beautify'*
(a) There is a love of beauty which we share with God.
(b) There is a loss of beauty which we see in life.

B. *The divine provision: 'with salvation'*
(a) Salvation is something wrapped up in a person.
(b) Salvation is something worked out in a process.

C. *The divine condition: 'the meek'*
(a) I must be humble enough to admit my need of Christ.
(b) I must be humble enough to submit my will to Christ.

Proverbs

Trusting God

Proverbs 3.5–6: 'Trust in the Lord with all thine heart; and lean not unto thine own understanding. In all thy ways acknowledge him, and he shall direct thy paths'

A. *The Person whom faith trusts*
(a) The rejection faith makes.
(b) The direction faith takes.

B. *The practice which faith forms*
(a) How inclusive this is.
(b) How decisive this is.

C. *The pathway which faith treads*
(a) The directions God will give.
(b) The corrections he will make.

Coping with our critics

Proverbs 5.12: 'My heart despised reproof'

A. *The reasons for the criticism*
(a) The motives for it.
(b) The meaning of it.

B. *The reaction to it*
(a) We can react negatively and resent it: Proverbs 5.12–13.
(b) We can react positively and receive it: 24.32.

C. *The results of it*
(a) The loss which can be sustained: 15.10, 13.18.
(b) The life which can be strengthened: 19.20, 15.32.

Grappling with gossip

Proverbs 11.13: 'A talebearer revealeth secrets'

A. *There are the people who love to spread gossip*
(a) Think of the malice they betray.
(b) Think of the menace they become.

B. *There are the people who try to stop gossip*
(a) Think of the guilt they will refuse to share with others.
(b) Think of the grace they are resolved to show to others.

C. *There are the people who never want to start gossip*
(a) The Spirit people sense in them.
(b) The secrets people are ready to share with them.
Other references to gossip in Proverbs: 6.11–19, 12.18, 16.27–28, 17.9, 18.8, 20.19, 25.23, 26.20.

The pathway to prosperity

Proverbs 11.24: 'There is that scattereth and yet increaseth; and there is that withholdeth more than is meet, but it tendeth to poverty'

A. *What developments will the future see?*
(a) The enrichment we must surely desire.
(b) The impoverishment we must surely dread.

B. *What demands will the future make?*
(a) How relentlessly demands are made.
(b) How revealingly demands are met.

C. *What disclosures will the future bring?*
(a) The surprises which some will get.
(b) The sorrow which some will know.

Where there is money there is muck

Proverbs 14.4: 'Where no oxen are, the crib is clean'

A. *An emphasis in the work of God which can be dangerous*
(a) An emphasis we can see in the life of the home.
(b) An emphasis we can see in the appearance of the countryside.
(c) An emphasis we can see in the life of the Church.

B. *An experience in the work of God which can be disastrous*
(a) Cleanliness in the home can mean there are no children.
(b) Beauty and order in the countryside can mean there is no wealth.
(c) Order in the life of the Church can mean there is no progress.

C. *An expectation in the work of God which must be obvious*
(a) In the home something may have to be lost in order for something to be gained.
(b) In the countryside prosperity may demand change.
(c) In the Church spiritual prosperity will call for sacrifice.

Sincerity is not enough

Proverbs 16.25: 'There is a way that seemeth right unto a man, but the end thereof are the ways of death'

A. *The convictions a man can hold*
(a) The existence of the mind.
(b) The importance of the mind.

B. *The direction a man will take*
(a) Think of the expectancy which hope gives to life.
(b) Think of the energy which hope imparts to life.

C. *The instruction a man will need*
(a) Think of the possibility of disillusionment.
(b) Think of the necessity of enlightenment.

What is the good of man conquering space when he cannot conquer himself?

Proverbs 16.32: 'He that ruleth his spirit [is better] than he that taketh a city'

A. *The achievements of science can be so impressive*
(a) We live in an age of wonder.
(b) We live in an age of worry.

B. *The allurements of sin are so seductive*
(a) The pressures are so fierce.
(b) The pictures are so false.

C. *The attainment of serenity is so elusive*
(a) Think of the remedies which men have tried.
(b) Think of the reality which men must face.

Friendship (1)

Proverbs 18.24: 'A man that hath friends must shew himself friendly: and there is a friend that sticketh closer than a brother'

A. *The possibility of friendship*
(a) The loneliness it ends.
(b) The happiness it holds.

B. *The necessity for friendship*
(a) The action I must take.
(b) The attitude I must show.

C. *The quality of friendship*
(a) Think of the fear of losing friends.
(b) Think of the fact of finding friends.

Friendship (2)

Proverbs 18.24

A. *The making of friendships*
(a) The efforts which friendship will ask of me.
(b) The effects which friendship will have on me.

B. *The blessings of friendships*
(a) The openness of friendship (27.9).
(b) The steadfastness of friendship (17.7).

C. *The guarding of friendships*
(a) The passing of time (27.10).
(b) The wagging of tongues (17.9).

Laziness

Proverbs 19.24: 'A slothful man hideth his hand in his bosom, and will not so much as bring it to his mouth again'

A. *His partial energy*
(a) He feels deeply (13.4).
(b) He speaks readily (26.16).
(c) He hunts successfully (12.27).

B. *His pitiful excuses*
(a) The excuse of difficulty (15.17).
(b) The excuse of danger (22.13).
(c) The excuse of delay (20.4).

C. *His pathetic end*
(a) The enjoyment he loses (12.27).
(b) The employment he lacks (10.26).
(c) The impoverishment he finds (13.4).

Bringing up the children

Proverbs 22.6: 'Train up a child in the way he should go: and when he is old, he will not depart from it'

A. *A task to perform*
(a) Think of the opportunities of parenthood.
(b) Think of the responsibilities of parenthood.

B. *A time to utilise*
(a) It is a limited time.
(b) It has a lasting effect.

C. *The truth to impart*
(a) Think of the people he will meet.
(b) Think of the pressure he will face.

Abstaining from alcohol

Proverbs 23.20–21:

A. *The effects of drink can be unpredictable*
(a) They can be destructive.
(b) They can be progressive.

B. *The extravagance which can be unwarranted*
(a) Consider the social loss.
(b) Consider the spiritual loss.

C. *The example which may be unconscious*
(a) Consider the reality of our influence.
(b) Consider the results of our influence.

175

Envy

Proverbs 27.4: 'Wrath is cruel, and anger is outrageous; but who is able to stand before envy?'

A. *The discovery of it*
(a) The frontiers of the soul demand our vigilance.
(b) The feelings of the heart betray its presence.

B. *The dangers in it*
(a) It can be dangerous to ourselves.
(b) It can be dangerous to others.

C. *The deliverance from it*
(a) The glory of love as expressed in Christ.
(b) The gift of love as experienced in Christ.

The man of vision

Proverbs 29.18: 'Where there is no vision, the people perish'

A. *The man of vision is aware of other dimensions*
(a) He is aware of greater depths in human need.
(b) He is aware of greater distances in human need.

B. *The man of vision is alert to a higher direction*
(a) He considers the authority of God.
(b) He discerns the urgency for action.

C. *The man of vision is alarmed by the possibility of utter destruction*
(a) The reality of evil is faced.
(b) The resources of grace are used.

Fettered by fear

Proverbs 29.25: 'The fear of man bringeth a snare'

    A.   *The reasons for this fear*
    (a) How powerful are the influences on us.
    (b) How natural is the instinct in us.

    B.   *The results of this fear*
    (a) It can lead to the degradation of the human personality.
    (b) It can lead to the destruction of the divine purpose.

    C.   *The release from this fear*
    (a) A concern for the rights of the Lord.
    (b) A contempt for the rest of the world.

Learning wisdom from nature

Proverbs 30.24–28

    A.   *The ants face a future for which they are prepared*
    (a) The opportunity which summer brings.
    (b) The certainty which summer ends.

    B.   *The rabbits have a fortress in which they are protected*
    (a) Think of the enemies they face.
    (b) Think of the security they find.

    C.   *The locusts share a fellowship in which they are partners*
    (a) Think of the assistance they can find in it.
    (b) Think of the allegiance which must control it.

    D.   *The spiders show a faithfulness for which they are praised*
    (a) Their work is largely unseen by the eyes of men.
    (b) They work without heeding the praise of man.

Ecclesiastes

'A threefold cord'

Ecclesiastes 4.12

A. *The Christian's adjusted relationship with his God*
(a) The fact of Jesus Christ.
(b) His faith in Jesus Christ.

B. *The Christian's adequate resources for his needs*
(a) The bankruptcy the Christian has faced.
(b) The adequacy the Christian has found.

C. *The Christian's accepted responsibility in the world*
(a) The new Master controlling his life.
(b) The new motive constraining his life.

Unkept promises

Ecclesiastes 5.1–7: 'Pay that which thou hast vowed'

A. *God's plea for restraint*
(a) The reasons for this are simple.
(b) The results of this are sound.

B. *God's preference for refusal*
(a) Consider the tragedy of not vowing.
(b) Consider the travesty of vowing and not paying.

C. *God's passion for reality*
(a) The assumption God makes.
(b) The action God wants.

A message for young people

Ecclesiastes 12.1: 'Remember now thy Creator in the days of thy youth'

A. *Because it is the better thing to do*
(a) Think of the blunders we can make.
(b) Think of the blame we can merit.

B. *Because it is the easier time to act*
(a) Postponement never makes action easier.
(b) Development never makes alternatives simpler.

C. *Because it is the wiser course to take*
(a) How deceptive life can prove.
(b) How decisive youth will prove.

The Song of Solomon

The longing of love

Song of Solomon 1.1—2.7

A. *The desire of the bride expressed: 1.2–4*
(a) The preference she declared.
(b) The privacy he desired.

B. *The dismay experienced by the bride: 1.5*
(a) The humility to which she was reduced.
(b) The intimacy on which she was resolved.

C. *The delights enjoyed by the bride*
(a) The appreciation shared.
(b) The assurance sensed.

The clouding of love

Song of Solomon 2.8—3.5

A. *How swiftly the bridegroom comes*
(a) The expectancy with which he comes.
(b) The despondency with which he waits.

B. *How simply the bridegroom speaks*
(a) The companion he would have: 2.10.
(b) The communion they would share.

C. *How sadly the bridegroom goes*
(a) We hear the words of dismissal.
(b) We see the way of discipline.

The singing of love

Song of Solomon 3.6—5.1

A. *What love shares*
(a) The resources love wants to give.
(b) The response love longs to get.

B. *What love sees: 4.1–11*
(a) The perfection he finds in his bride.
(b) The attraction he feels for his bride.

C. *What love seeks: 4.12—5.1*
(a) Fruitfulness.
(b) Readiness.

The summons of love

Song of Solomon 5.2—6.10

A. *The abundance which love bestows*
(a) The enrichment which Christ brings to life.
(b) The enjoyment which Christ plans for life.

B. *The disturbance which love creates*
(a) The nature of the Bridegroom.
(b) The need of the Bridegroom.

C. *The reluctance which love confronts*
(a) There is lethargy here.
(b) There is tragedy here.

D. *The experience which love permits*
(a) The way she was treated.
(b) The way she was troubled.

E. *The repentance which love rewards*
(a) The conviction she had reached.
(b) The companion she must have.

The testing of love

Song of Solomon 6.11—8.14

A. *The testimony evoked 6.11—7.9*
(a) The desire by which she was amazed: 6.13.
(b) The delight with which she was acclaimed: 7.1–9.

B. *The identity expressed*
(a) The sharing of love.
(b) The serving of love.

C. *The security enjoyed*
(a) The word on which assurance must rest.
(b) The work to which assurance will lead.

The heart seen as a garden

Song of Solomon 4.16: 'Let my beloved come into his garden'

A. *The intention the garden reveals*
(a) It should be attractive.
(b) It should be productive.

B. *The inspection the garden demands*
(a) The progress which should be seen.
(b) The problems which must be solved.

C. *The impression the garden creates*
(a) The delight a garden can give.
(b) The desire a garden can arouse.

Isaiah to Malachi

Isaiah

The fire of God

Isaiah 4.4: 'The spirit of burning'

A. *How fire burns through man's defences*
(a) The defences men build up.
(b) The defences fire burns through.

B. *How fire burns out sin's dross*
(a) The revealing of sin.
(b) The replacing of sin.

C. *How fire burns in God's design*
(a) How lovely in its design.
(b) How lasting in its duration.

The start of significant living

Isaiah 6.1–8: 'I saw the Lord sitting upon a throne, high and lifted up'

A. *A person was removed by God*
(a) How God can be concealed.
(b) When God can be revealed.

B. *A problem was resolved by God*
(a) The conviction which caused the problem.
(b) The provision which solved the problem.

C. *A purpose was revealed by God*
(a) The concern in the heart of God.
(b) The consent to the will of God.

The light of God's truth

Isaiah 9.2: 'The people that walked in darkness have seen a great light: they that dwell in the land of the shadow of death, upon them hath the light shined'

A. *There had been a shining of the light*
(a) This meant a dispelling of man's ignorance.
(b) This meant a revealing of man's importance.

B. *There can be a shrinking from the light*
(a) There are those who are afraid of the light.
(b) There are those who stay away from the light.

C. *There has been a spreading of the light*
(a) The source from which the light comes.
(b) The sphere in which the light shines.

The Christ has come into the world

Isaiah 9.6–7: 'Unto us a child is born [in his humanity], unto us a son is given [in his divinity] . . . and his name shall be called Wonderful Counsellor, the mighty God, the everlasting Father, the Prince of Peace'

A. *In Jesus Christ there is a guide we can have: 'Wonderful Counsellor'*
(a) How right are the directions which Christ gives.
(b) How wrong, so often, are the decisions we make.

B. *In Jesus Christ there is a strength we can use: 'the mighty God'*
(a) The freedom men claim.
(b) The freedom Christ gives.

C. *In Jesus Christ there is a love we can trust: 'the everlasting Father'*
(a) The fickleness of human love.
(b) The faithfulness of divine love.

D. *In Jesus Christ there is a peace we can know: 'the Prince of Peace'*
(a) The authority which will be acceptable to us.
(b) The adequacy which will be available to us.

'The Prince of Peace'

Isaiah 9.6–7

A. *'Wonderful Counsellor': we can have peace through the acceptance of his will*
(a) The mistakes we can make.
(b) The wisdom we can have from God.

B. *'The mighty God': we can have peace through the abundance of his grace*
(a) The weakness in our lives.
(b) The greatness in our Lord.

C. *'The everlasting Father': we can have peace through the assurance of his love*
(a) How important we are to him.
(b) How observant he is of us.

'Peace, perfect peace'

Isaiah 26.3: 'Thou wilt keep him in perfect peace, whose mind is stayed on thee: because he trusteth in thee'
A study based on the hymn, *Peace, Perfect Peace*

A. *Peace in spite of the sense of sin*
(a) The clouding of our sky.
(b) The cleansing of our sin.

B. *Peace in spite of the stress of living*
(a) The environment which can break us.
(b) The adjustment which will bless us.

C. *Peace in spite of the sorrows of life*
(a) The experiences which can hurt.
(b) The assurance which will help.

D. *Peace in spite of the separations of love*
(a) The worry which ignorance begets.
(b) The Watcher which ignorance forgets.

E. *Peace in spite of the strain of uncertainty*
(a) The fears which can shatter our peace.
(b) The facts which can strengthen our hearts.

F. *Peace in spite of the shadow of death*
(a) The loss suffered.
(b) The life entered.

Slow down and live

Isaiah 28.16: 'He that believeth shall not make haste'

A. *The ignorance begotten by haste*
(a) The impoverishment of life.
(b) The endangering of life.

B. *The indifference betrayed by haste*
(a) The time which love desires.
(b) The thought which love displays.

C. *The importance bestowed on faith*
(a) What is required for faith.
(b) What will result from faith.

New strength from God

Isaiah 40.31: 'But they that wait upon the Lord shall renew their strength; they shall mount up with wings as eagles; they shall run, and not be weary; and they shall walk, and not faint'

    A. *The exhaustion we can know*
    (a) Because of our ceaseless conflict in the service of Christ.
    (b) Because of our careless neglect of our time with God.

    B. *The exchange we can make*
    (a) The Source of our renewal.
    (b) The secret of our renewal.

    C. *The experience we can have*
    (a) The content which will be varied.
    (b) The conquest which will be vital.

God is with us

Isaiah 41.10: 'Fear thou not; for I am with thee: be not dismayed; for I am thy God: I will strengthen thee; yea, I will help thee; yea, I will uphold thee with the right hand of my righteousness'

    A. *The prospects which alarm our minds*
    (a) the strength of the enemy.
    (b) The standards of the Master.

    B. *The presence which allays our fears*
    (a) The relationship enjoyed.
    (b) The reality experienced.

    C. *The promise which assures our hearts*
    (a) He fortifies the weak.
    (b) He qualifies his word.

What God says to his own

Isaiah 43.1–7

A. *God says, 'I have'*
(a) The diversity of which God speaks.
(b) The security of which God speaks.

B. *God says, 'I will'*
(a) The prospects which could alarm our hearts.
(b) The presence which will allay our fears.

C. *God says, 'I Am'*
(a) The Person he is.
(b) The purpose he has.

Assurance of salvation

Isaiah 43.1–3: 'Fear not: I have redeemed thee, I have called thee by thy name; thou art mine'

A. *The difficulty of the way*
(a) This arises from our share in the human lot.
(b) This arises from our service in the will of God.

B. *The security of the child*
(a) The price God has paid.
(b) The possession God now claims.

C. *The intimacy of the walk*
(a) The privilege of love.
(b) The permanence of love.

Salvation is from God alone

Isaiah 45.22: 'Look unto me, and be ye saved, all the ends of the earth: for I am God, and there is none else'
Also consider Numbers 21.4–9; John 3.14–17

A. *The condemnation to which it speaks*
(a) The plight of man.
(b) The plan of God.

B. *The proclamation for which it calls*
(a) How inclusive it is.
(b) How exclusive it is.

C. *The obligation with which it comes*
(a) The direction in which we must look.
(b) The decision with which we are faced.

Lessons from the mountain paths of life

Isaiah 49.11: 'I will make all my mountains a way'

A. *The mountain path*
(a) The stillness of the hills.
(b) The steepness of the way.
(c) The sharpness of the stones.

B. *The meeting place*
(a) The mountain can become the place of instruction: Matthew 5.1–2.
(b) The mountain path can become the place of communion: Matthew 14.23.
(c) The mountainside can be the place of redemption.

C. *The Master's plan*
(a) Here is a way which is productive.
(b) Here is a word which is inclusive.
(c) There must be a will which is submissive.

Trusting God in the dark

Isaiah 50.10: 'Who is among you that feareth the Lord, that obeyeth the voice of his servant, that walketh in darkness, and hath no light? Let him trust in the name of the Lord, and stay upon his God'

A. *The trust which is the heart of faith*
(a) The Person faith trusts.
(b) The pathway faith takes.

B. *The trials which are the test of faith*
(a) The discipline for which faith must be ready.
(b) The discoveries with which faith will be rewarded.

C. *The truths which give the rest of faith*
(a) The integrity of the Person of my Lord.
(b) The reality of the presence of my Lord.

The work of Christ

Isaiah 53.11: 'He shall see of the travail of his soul, and shall be satisfied'

A. *The solitude of the way walked by Christ*
(a) The loneliness of the path he trod.
(b) The costliness of the price he paid.

B. *The magnitude of the work wrought by Christ*
(a) The burden he bore for men.
(b) The blessing he brings to men.

C. *The gratitude of the world won by Christ*
(a) The lives which have welcomed him.
(b) The love which has worshipped him.

God's invitation to man

Isaiah 55:1–7

    A.   *The divine offer to the thirsting heart*
    (a) How the offer describes man.
    (b) How the offer directs man.

    B.   *The divine challenge to the thinking mind*
    (a) The charge of futility.
    (b) The claim to sufficiency.

    C.   *The divine warning to the trifling soul*
    (a) The warning we do well to heed.
    (b) The welcome we are wise to give.

The heart seen as a garden (1)

Isaiah 58.11: 'Thou shalt be like a watered garden'

    A.   *There is work in a garden*
    (a) Work in sowing.
    (b) Work for growing.

    B.   *There are weeds in a garden*
    (a) Think how harmful they can be.
    (b) Think how watchful we must be.

    C.   *There is wealth in a garden*
    (a) There is wealth to be seen.
    (b) There is wealth to be shared.

The heart seen as a garden (2)

Isaiah 58.11: 'Thou shalt be like a watered garden'

A. *There is work in a garden*
(a) Work by a Person.
(b) Work at a price.

B. *There are weeds in a garden*
(a) Think what they spoil.
(b) Think how they spread.

C. *There is wealth in a garden*
(a) The enjoyment for others.
(b) The enrichment of others.

Spiritual warfare

Isaiah 59.19: 'When the enemy shall come in like a flood, the Spirit of the Lord shall lift up a standard against him'

A. *There is a hostility to be met*
(a) It was experienced by our Lord.
(b) It should be expected by us.

B. *There is an intensity to be matched*
(a) Think of the attack we face.
(b) Think of the answer we give.

C. *There is a superiority to be mastered*
(a) Think of the defiance we can show.
(b) Think of the dependence we must have.

Prayer for revival

Isaiah 64.1–4: 'O that thou wouldest rend the heavens, that thou wouldest come down, that the mountains might flow down at thy presence'

 A. *The prayer to God which seeks revival*
 (a) A desire which burns steadily before God.
 (b) A dependence which bears utterly upon God.

 B. *The power of God which marks revival*
 (a) The impossible is achieved.
 (b) The unusual is accepted.

 C. *The praise to God which crowns revival*
 (a) The reproach which is removed.
 (b) The rejoicing which is released.

 D. *The presence of God which is revival*
 (a) There will be an awareness of the presence.
 (b) There will be an acceptance of the presence.

Jeremiah
The events of one hour can change the course of a life

Jeremiah 1.1–10, 17–19

 A. *The mystery of the purpose of God for his life*
 (a) The pattern which was shown.
 (b) The protest which was swift.

 B. *The adequacy of the power of God for his task*
 (a) The resources he would enjoy.
 (b) The results he could expect.

 C. *The certainty of the presence of God at his side*
 (a) The courage he would need.
 (b) The courage he would have.

A call to the backslider

Jeremiah 2.1–13: 'They have forsaken me'

   A.   *The memory love does not forget*
(a) The openness of love.
(b) The eagerness of love.
(c) The fastidiousness of love.

   B.   *The mystery love cannot resolve*
(a) There was no reason for their conduct.
(b) There was no reference to their Lord.
(c) There was no response to his grace.

   C.   *The ministry love will not discard*
(a) The condition in which they have lived.
(b) The correction through which they will learn.
(c) The compassion with which they are loved.

A Harvest message

Jeremiah 8.20: 'The harvest is past, the summer is ended, and we are not saved'

   A.   *The opportunity they had known*
(a) Within the space of a year.
(b) Within the span of a life.

   B.   *The opportunity they had lost*
(a) How stubborn was their attitude.
(b) How serious was their predicament.

   C.   *The opportunity they had still*
(a) Disaster was needless.
(b) Decision was urgent.

The relationship between God and his people: the potter and the clay

Jeremiah 18.1–6

A. *It involves a responding to the pressure of the hands of God*
(a) The pressure will be felt inwardly through conviction: Ps. 32:4.
(b) The pressure will be felt outwardly through circumstance: Ps. 31:15.

B. *It will mean a revealing of the purpose in the mind of God*
(a) The purpose of loveliness: Ps. 149:4.
(b) The purpose of usefulness: John 15:16.

C. *It will mean a relying on the patience of the love of God*
(a) The tragedy which will sometimes happen in the life of a believer.
(b) The constancy which will always be found in the love of the Father.

Finding God's blessing in an unexpected place

Jeremiah 31.2: 'The people found grace in the wilderness'

A. *A place which was desolate*
(a) The dreariness of the wilderness.
(b) The dangers in the wilderness.

B. *A path which was dreaded*
(a) The loneliness of it.
(b) The hardness of it.

C. *A plan which was discovered*
(a) The daily provision made.
(b) The divine purpose revealed.

Ambition

Jeremiah 45.5: 'Seekest thou great things for thyself? Seek them not.'

   A.   *The fact of ambition is observed*
  (a) Ambition can be desirable.
  (b) Ambition can be dangerous.

   B.   *The flaw in ambition is exposed*
  (a) The exaltation of self is rebuked.
  (b) The degradation of service is condemned.

   C.   *The flight from ambition is advised*
  (a) The humility which God demands.
  (b) The jealousy which God displays.

Lamentations

A call to compassion for a needy world

Lamentations 1.12: 'Is it nothing to you, all ye that pass by?'

   A.   *The cry we can hear*
  (a) The tragedy in which so many live.
  (b) The testimony for which so many look.

   B.   *The charge we may face*
  (a) The charge of indifference.
  (b) The charge of inaction.

   C.   *The call we must heed*
  (a) The Church is a serving church.
  (b) Our God is a saving God.

A message for a commissioning service for missionaries

Lamentations 3.23: 'Great is thy faithfulness.' The faithfulness of God will be seen in three ways.

A. *In the provision of God which we will receive for our needs*
(a) The priority we must give to his will.
(b) The sufficiency we will have for our needs.

B. *In the protection of God which we shall enjoy in our fight (The shield of faith or God's faithfulness, Eph. 6.16)*
(a) The dangers we will face.
(b) The shelter we will have.

C. *In the permission of God which we will discern in our trials (Ps. 119.75, 1 Cor. 10.13)*
(a) The limit which God sets to our trials.
(b) The defeat which God ends through our trials.

Ezekiel

Standing in the gap: intercession

Ezekiel 22.30: 'I sought for a man that should stand in the gap, but I found none'

A. *The land was defiled*
(a) It was a privileged land.
(b) It was a polluted land.

B. *A life was desired*
(a) The appearance of the gap.
(b) The importance of a man.

C. *The Lord was distraught*
(a) The reasons for the failure.
(b) The results of the failure.

New life in dead bones

Ezekiel 37.3: 'Can these bones live? . . . O Lord God, thou knowest'

A. *The work of grace we need to see*
(a) The condition of the people of God described.
(b) The intention of the purpose of God declared.

B. *The word of life we need to preach*
(a) It produced an adjustment.
(b) It conveyed an enablement.

C. *The war of faith we need to fight*
(a) The character of the people of God.
(b) The conflict of the people of God.

Daniel

The importance of saying 'No'

Daniel 1.8: 'But Daniel purposed in his heart that he would not . . . '

A. *The resolve in his heart*
(a) The pressures he faced.
(b) The purpose he formed.

B. *The request on his lips*
(a) The servant of God is seen alone.
(b) The Spirit of God is seen at work.

C. *The result in his life*
(a) The people he was able to help.
(b) The pathway he was able to walk.

Loyalty to God: Daniel's compatriots

Daniel 1:7

A. *We find them standing out from the others*
(a) Their consecration to God.
(b) Their vindication by God.

B. *We find them standing in with their leader*
(a) How instinctively he turned to them.
(b) How effectively they prayed for him.

C. *We find them standing fast for their master*
(a) The prominence which was unwelcome.
(b) The confidence which was unwavering.

True commitment to God

Daniel 10.11: 'A man greatly beloved'

A. *He was found on his face before God (verse 9)*
(a) The vision which forced him there.
(b) The verdict which faced him there.

B. *He was found on his knees before God (verse 10)*
(a) The intimacy he enjoyed.
(b) The fidelity he displayed.

C. *He was found on his feet before God (verse 11)*
(a) The authority which determined the manner of his life.
(b) The authority which determined the message on his lips.

Hosea

Idolatry

Hosea 4.17: 'Ephraim is joined to idols'

A. *A disobedience which was blatant*
(a) What God had required.
(b) How man had rebelled.

B. *A discipline which was bitter*
(a) The intention of God.
(b) The infection of sin.

C. *A discovery which was blessed*
(a) The sadness they would know.
(b) The goodness they would prove.

Fallow or Fruitful

Hosea 10.12: 'Break up your fallow ground: for it is time to seek the Lord'

A. *What is recalled of God's work*
(a) The times which were different.
(b) The traces which were evident.

B. *What was required by God's word*
(a) The change in their ways.
(b) The choice of their wills.

C. *What would result in God's will*
(a) How relevant the message.
(b) How confident the message.

Joel

Turning back to God

Joel 2.25: 'I will restore to you the years that the locust hath eaten'

A. *The target for sin's attack: 'The land is as the garden of Eden before them' (2.3)*
(a) How the garden was marked by an experience of God's presence.
(b) How the garden was marked by the evidence of God's power.

B. *The tragedy of sin's advent: 'behind them a desolate wilderness' (2.3)*
(a) How severe the devastation was.
(b) How sustained the duration proved.

C. *The triumph of sin's arrest*
(a) The prayer God was waiting to hear.
(b) The power God was willing to give.

A justification for mass evangelism

Joel 3.14: 'Multitudes, multitudes in the valley of decision'

A. *The dislike which some have of the methods used*
(a) A dislike based on the size of the crowds.
(b) A dislike based on the stress on a choice.

B. *The demand which men face in the message preached*
(a) The respect for human personality this kind of preaching shows.
(b) The response to authority this kind of preaching seeks.

C. *The delight which many have in the miracles wrought*
(a) The discovery so many have made in such crusades.
(b) The difference so many will know as a result of such crusades.

Amos

Travelling with the Lord

Amos 3.3: 'Can two walk together, except they be agreed?'

A. *The initial appointment*
(a) The place where we meet.
(b) The choice which we make.

B. *The continual agreement*
(a) The possibility of estrangement.
(b) The necessity of at-one-ment.

C. *The final achievement*
(a) The discoveries which will be made.
(b) The destination which will be reached.

The importance of preaching

Amos 8.11: 'A famine of the word'

A. *The place of preaching*
(a) It has had a distinguished place.
(b) Today it sometimes has a discredited place.

B. *The price of preaching*
(a) The separation to this task.
(b) The preparation for this task.

C. *The power of preaching*
(a) The truth it must proclaim.
(b) The faith it will produce.

Jonah
The gospel of the second chance

Jonah 3.1: 'And the word of the Lord came unto Jonah the second time'

- A. *The course which God planned for his servant*
- (a) The plan in the service of God which was definite.
- (b) The plight of the servant of God which was desperate.

- B. *The change which God saw in his servant*
- (a) The hold which God had on his servant.
- (b) The help which God gave to his servant.

- C. *The chance which God gave to his servant*
- (a) The request which God made.
- (b) The response which God got.

Haggai

The Lord's messenger and his message

Haggai 1.13

- A. *The messenger must be fashioned by the truth of his message*
- (a) There will be the closest of contacts with the message.
- (b) There will be the clearest of effects of the message.

- B. *The messenger will be fragrant from his touch with his message*
- (a) The source of that fragrance must be realised.
- (b) The scent of that fragrance will be recognised.

- C. *The messenger should be forgotten in the telling of his message*
- (a) The failure which must be avoided of people thinking of him.
- (b) The Saviour who must be exalted by people's trust in him.

Zechariah

Depending upon the Holy Spirit

Zechariah 4.6: 'Not by might, nor by power, but by my Spirit, saith the Lord'

A. *The message on the lips of the servant of God*
(a) The matter of the message.
(b) The manner of the messenger.

B. *The manner of the life of the servant of God*
(a) It must be consistent with the life of his Lord.
(b) He must be obedient to the will of his Lord.

C. *The methods in the work of the servant of God*
(a) There must be a dependence upon God.
(b) There must be a diligence by the servant.

D. *The motives in the heart of the servant of God*
(a) The love which must be expressed.
(b) The Lord who must be exalted.

Malachi

God's portrait of a preacher

Malachi 2.6

   A.   *The words of the preacher: 'the law of truth was in his mouth'*
(a) The accuracy which must mark his words.
(b) The authority which must mark his words.

   B.   *The walk of the preacher: 'he walked with me in peace and equity'*
(a) The intimacy enjoyed by him.
(b) The integrity evidenced by him.

   C.   *The work of the preacher: 'He did turn many away from iniquity'*
(a) It would be a difficult work.
(b) It would be a dependent work.

How God deals with his own

Malachi 3.3: 'He shall sit as a refiner and purifier of silver'

A. *The concern which motivates this relationship*
(a) The purpose about which his mind is resolved.
(b) The process by which his aim is achieved.

B. *The control which regulates this relationship*
(a) How watchful he is as he tends the process.
(b) How careful he is as he times the process.

C. *The content which consummates this relationship*
(a) The silver must be purified.
(b) The Saviour will be glorified.

Proving God (1)

Malachi 3.10: 'Bring ye all the tithes . . . and prove me now'

A. *The charge which God brought*
(a) The God who had been forsaken (3:7).
(b) The guilt which must be forgiven.

B. *The change which God pledged*
(a) The condition they had to meet.
(b) The provision God would make.

C. *The chance God gave*
(a) That he might be proved by his people.
(b) That he might be praised by his people.

Proving God (2)

Malachi 3.10

A. *The connection we can note*
(a) Giving indicates the reality of our concern.
(b) Giving increases the range of our service.

B. *The condition we must face*
(a) The attitude to giving which is rebuked.
(b) The action of giving which is required.

C. *The consequence man will see*
(a) The offer God makes of unlimited blessing.
(b) The order God makes to secure that blessing.

Matthew

Christmas is no time for fear

Matthew 1.20: 'Fear not'

A. *To the shepherds Christmas spoke of an involvement which was spiritual*
(a) The world which broke through that night.
(b) The word which brought peace that night.

B. *To Mary Christmas spoke of an involvement which was personal*
(a) The message which would ask submission of her.
(b) The miracle which would bring salvation through her.

C. *To Joseph Christmas spoke of an involvement which was social*
(a) Think of the comments they would face.
(b) Think of the comfort they would find.

'Thou shalt call his name Jesus: for he shall save his people from their sins'

Matthew 1.21

A. *The person he is*
(a) The element of mystery.
(b) The element of majesty.

B. *The purpose he had*
(a) The tragedy of sin in man.
(b) The remedy for sin through Christ.

C. *The people he saves*
(a) The claim he makes on us.
(b) The choice he asks of us.

'Emmanuel . . . God with us'

Matthew 1.23

A. *There is certainty in Christ on which I can rely*
(a) There is an authority in what Christ said.
(b) There is an adequacy in what Christ did.

B. *There is sympathy in Christ to which I can respond (cf. Heb. 2.18)*
(a) Why I am afraid of God.
(b) How I am assured in Christ.

C. *There is company in Christ in which I can rejoice*
(a) The delight I will find in his company.
(b) The desire I must have for his company.

Herod the King

Matthew 2.1–6

    A.   *Men have sensed a concern in him*
    (a) The truth he heard.
    (b) The threat he feared.

    B.   *Men have seen a contrast in him*
    (a) Look at the sincerity presented here in the Wise Men.
    (b) Look at the hypocrisy portrayed here in the wicked king.

    C.   *Men have shown a contempt for him*
    (a) The ruthlessness of the man.
    (b) The foolishness of the man.

Christmas – a time for questions

Matthew 2.2

    A.   *Why do we need him?*
    (a) The problem we have.
    (b) The promise God gave.

    B.   *Where do we find him?*
    (a) How far away he was for them.
    (b) How close at hand he is for us.

    C.   *What do we give him?*
    (a) The welcome he desires.
    (b) The worship he deserves.

The star

Matthew 2.2: 'We have seen his star in the east, and are come to worship him'

A. *The search they made*
(a) The request they made.
(b) The resolve they showed.

B. *The truth they heard*
(a) The mistake they made.
(b) The message they heard.

C. *The assurance they got*
(a) The guidance they needed.
(b) The gladness they showed.

D. *The Redeemer they found*
(a) This was no dream.
(b) There was no doubt.

Wise men still seek Jesus

Matthew 2.1–15: 'Where is he that is born King of the Jews?'

A. *The wisdom of the seekers*
(a) The truth they were determined to find.
(b) The path they were determined to tread.

B. *The witness of the Scriptures*
(a) The blunder they made.
(b) The answer they got.

C. *The worship of the Saviour*
(a) How they knelt at his feet.
(b) What they brought in their hands.

Jesus the King

Matthew 2.2: 'born King'

A. *The truth grasped about him*
(a) Named King at his birth.
(b) Named King at his death.

B. *The threat glimpsed in him*
(a) By the secular powers.
(b) By the spiritual powers.

C. *The throne given to him*
(a) By the Father.
(b) By the faithful.

Jesus is tempted in the wilderness

Matthew 4.1: 'Then Jesus was led up of the Spirit into the wilderness to be tempted of the devil'

A. *The significance of the moment*
(a) It had been a moment of resolve by Christ.
(b) It had been a moment of response from heaven.

B. *The importance of the man*
(a) The identity of the target.
(b) The variety of the tactics.

C. *The relevance of the message* •
(a) There is no need to despair when we are tempted.
(b) There is no need for defeat when we are tempted.

Being salt in the world

Matthew 5.13

    A.   *The purposes which salt should achieve*
    (a) The task it usually fulfils.
    (b) The taste it often improves.
    (c) The thirst it often creates.

    B.   *The possibilities which salt must avoid*
    (a) There is here a word to alarm.
    (b) There is here a life to alert.
    (c) There is here a fear to allay.

    C.   *The penalty which salt may have to accept*
    (a) There will be no place for it.
    (b) There will be no use for it.
    (c) There will be no thought for it.

Being the light of the world

Matthew 5.14–16

    A.   *The truth affirmed*
    (a) A declaration which is staggering.
    (b) An implication which is sobering.

    B.   *The task assigned*
    (a) The Christian is to be a witnessing light.
    (b) The Christian is to be a welcoming light (cf. Luke 8.16).

    C.   *The test applied*
    (a) We must avoid concealing the light.
    (b) We must achieve the glorifying of God.

A city on a hill

Matthew 5.14

A. *The community into which the Christian is born*
(a) There is a common life which all Christians share.
(b) There is a common Lord whom all Christians serve.

B. *The security with which the Christian is blessed*
(a) The intention of the enemy which must be faced.
(b) The protection from the enemy which may be found.

C. *The obscurity from which the Christian is brought*
(a) Why is the thought of such publicity so unacceptable?
(b) Why is the truth of this publicity so unavoidable?

Reconciliation

Matthew 5.23–24

A. *The loyalty affirmed by him*
(a) This man was in the right place.
(b) This man was doing the right thing.

B. *The memory aroused in him*
(a) The sin which was recalled.
(b) The source which was revealed.

C. *The priority assigned to him*
(a) Where he was to go.
(b) When he was to come.

Marks of Christian normality

Matthew 6.1–18: 'When you give ... When you pray ... When you fast'

A. *The heart of reality*
(a) The concern we have for others.
(b) The contact we have with our God.
(c) The control we show in our lives.

B. *The hurt of hypocrisy*
(a) The praise which some want to receive.
(b) The place which some want to be given.
(c) The people whom some want to impress.

C. *The hour of finality*
(a) The variety success can hold.
(b) The verdict success receives.
(c) The vindication success will have.

'Thy will be done' – by me, not to me!

Matthew 6.10

A. *The discernment I must have of the will of God*
(a) The attitude which must be adopted.
(b) The areas which will be affected.

B. *The commitment I must make to the will of God*
(a) My consent to the will of God.
(b) The constraint of the love of God.

C. *The enjoyment I will find in the will of God*
(a) The blunder which can be made.
(b) The blessings which will be found.

'Thine is the kingdom, and the power, and the glory, for ever'

Matthew 6.13

   A. *Committed to the will of God*
(a) The acceptance of Christ I must make.
(b) The allegiance to Christ I must give.

   B. *Confident in the power of God*
(a) The power which has been received.
(b) The power which must be released.

   C. *Concerned for the glory of God*
(a) Disturbed by the tragedies of life.
(b) Delivered from the tyranny of moods.

Christ's recipe for living

Matthew 6.33: 'Seek ye first the kingdom of God, and his righteousness; and all these [necessary] things shall be added unto you'

   A. *The presence of the King: we must have the right ingredients*
(a) There must be an acceptance of that presence.
(b) There should be an assurance of that presence.

   B. *The priority of the King: we must do things in the right order*
(a) The alternatives we can find to his will.
(b) The authority we must face in his will.

   C. *The promise of the King: we will then get the right results*
(a) There will be an abundance which will meet our every need.
(b) There must be a difference which will mark our daily life.

The answer to anxiety

Matthew 6.34: 'Don't worry' (J. B. Phillips)

A. *The anxieties by which our lives will be assailed*
(a) The uselessness of worry.
(b) The sinfulness of worry.

B. *The authority to which our lives must be aligned*
(a) Remembering our membership of the family.
(b) Maintaining our fellowship with the Father.

C. *The adequacy of which our lives will be assured*
(a) The evidence from which we can learn.
(b) The confidence with which we can live.

Two gates, two ways and two ends

Matthew 7.13–14: 'Enter ye in at the strait gate'

A. *The Christian life is exacting in what it demands*
(a) The conditions of my entry.
(b) The restrictions on my pathway.

B. *The Christian life is enriching in how it expands*
(a) Think of the impoverishment beyond the wide gate.
(b) Think of the enrichment beyond the strait gate.

C. *The Christian life is enduring in what it achieves*
(a) How tragic the end can be for the unbeliever.
(b) How thrilling the end will be for the Christian.

Living is building (1)

Matthew 7.24–27: 'Built upon the sand . . . built upon a rock'

A. *Life is creative*
(a) What is the reason for this?
(b) What are the results of this?

B. *Life is selective*
(a) Note the experience which both men shared.
(b) Note the difference which both men showed.

C. *Life is decisive*
(a) Note the experience of the various forces we will meet.
(b) Note the consequences of the various choices we have made.

Living is building (2)

Matthew 7.24–27

A. *The building which life will mean*
(a) We note that life is constructive.
(b) We note that life is selective.

B. *The battering which life will meet*
(a) The facts to recognise.
(b) The forces to reckon with.

C. *The blessing which life can miss*
(a) The equal opportunity.
(b) The final outcome.

The moment of decision

Matthew 9.9: 'Jesus . . . saw a man, named Matthew, sitting at the receipt of custom: and he said to him, "Follow me." And he arose, and followed him'

A. *Note the coming of Christ into his life*
(a) When did it happen?
(b) Where did it happen?

B. *Note the calling by Christ to His side*
(a) It was a call to follow.
(b) It was a call to forsake.

C. *Note the choosing of Christ as his Lord*
(a) The decision he made that day.
(b) The destiny he met that day.

The unpopularity which Jesus had to face

Matthew 10.25: 'It is enough that the disciple be as his master, and the servant as his lord. If they have called the master of the house Beelzebub, how much more shall they call them of his household?'

A. *In the circle of his home (Mark 3.21)*
(a) The way he spent his time.
(b) The way he served the world.

B. *The church of his day (cf. John 8.48)*
(a) The way he shattered their complacency.
(b) The way he threatened their security.

C. *The crowds on his path (cf. John 10.20)*
(a) The way he isolated the individual.
(b) The way he insisted on submission.

Coming to Christ (1)

Matthew 11.28–29: 'Come unto me, all ye that labour and are heavy laden, and I will give you rest. Take my yoke upon you, and learn of me . . . and ye shall find rest unto your souls'

A. *I find simplicity here: 'Come unto me'*
(a) Making a decision.
(b) Moving in a direction.

B. *I find authority here: 'Take my yoke upon you'*
(a) He will want to take control of my life.
(b) He will want to get consent from my heart.

C. *I find discovery here: 'and ye shall find'*
(a) The sinfulness he will lift from me.
(b) The usefulness he will find for me.

Coming to Christ (2)

Matthew 11.28–29

A. *There is a yoke to accept*
(a) The will of the Master that he would show to me.
(b) The work of the Master that I will share with him.

B. *There is a school to attend*
(a) There will be a process of learning.
(b) There should be a progress in learning.

C. *There is a rest to attain*
(a) The sufficiency discovered.
(b) The serenity displayed.

The Queen of the South

Matthew 12.42: 'The queen of the south shall rise up in judgment with this generation, and shall condemn it'

    A. *The commendation which shocked them*
    (a) The unexpected person chosen by him.
    (b) The unexplored pathway taken by her.

    B. *The comparison which shamed them*
    (a) The importance of Solomon compared with that of the Saviour.
    (b) The ignorance of their generation compared with the wisdom of the queen.

    C. *The condemnation which stunned them.*
    (a) What she was ready to do.
    (b) What they had refused to do.

What we should expect in Christian service

Matthew Chapter 13: the parable of the sower

    A. *We should expect Satan*
    (a) Note the intrusion of Satan.
    (b) Note the intention of Satan.

    B. *We should expect sadness*
    (a) The promise we shall see.
    (b) The pressures which may succeed.

    C. *We should expect success*
    (a) The grasp of the Scriptures.
    (b) The growth in the Spirit.

The parable of the tares

Matthew 13.24–30, 36–43

- A. *A problem solved*
- (a) Who is the Person who owns the world?
- (b) What is the purpose which rules the world?

- B. *The process sensed*
- (a) The intention of evil.
- (b) The inaction of God.

- C. *The prospect stated*
- (a) The limit set.
- (b) The lesson taught.

'The kingdom of heaven is like unto a merchant man'

Matthew 13.45

- A. *The investor who cannot be ignored*
- (a) The provision which must be made by the investor.
- (b) The conditions which must be met for the investor.

- B. *The labourer who cannot be ignored*
- (a) How differently the work may be done.
- (b) How diligently the work must be done.

- C. *The consumer who must not be ignored.*
- (a) The product must be acceptable to him.
- (b) The product must be available to him.

Christian compassion

Matthew 14.14: 'Jesus . . . saw a great multitude, and was moved with compassion toward them'

A. *The heart compassion fills (Matt. 14.14)*
(a) The tragedies of human need which must be faced.
(b) The reality of divine love which must be seen.

B. *The hands compassion needs (Matt. 20.34)*
(a) The concern aroused.
(b) The contact achieved.

C. *The hope compassion brings (Luke 7.11–15)*
(a) The loneliness compassion enters.
(b) The helplessness compassion ends.

The feeding of the five thousand

Matthew 14.13–23

A. *I find a tragedy here*
(a) The plight of the multitude.
(b) The plea of the disciples.

B. *I find a remedy here*
(a) The intention in the mind of Christ.
(b) The submission to the word of Christ.

C. *I find a victory here*
(a) The obedience which was given by the disciples.
(b) The abundance which was received by the multitude.

What Christ can do with what we bring (suitable for a Gift Day)

Matthew 14.15–22: 'five loaves, and two fishes'

 A. *The gift was brought: 'There is a lad here . . . ' (John 6.9)*
 (a) It was a willing gift.
 (b) It was a wanted gift.

 B. *The gift was blessed*
 (a) A new power touched it.
 (b) A new purpose transformed it.

 C. *The gift was broken*
 (a) It meant an ending for someone.
 (b) It meant an enriching for others.

The need to get alone with God

Matthew 14.23: 'Away . . . apart . . . alone'

 A. *The control the Master exercised: 'He sent the multitudes away'*
 (a) The demands of the multitude.
 (b) The dangers of the multitude.

 B. *The criticism the Master evoked*
 (a) The ignorance which inspired it.
 (b) The indifference which ignored it.

 C. *The communion the Master enjoyed*
 (a) The primacy given to prayer.
 (b) The privacy needed for prayer.

Faith amidst the storm

Matthew 14.24–33

A. *The vision of faith*
(a) The severity of the storm.
(b) The serenity of the Saviour.

B. *The venture of faith*
(a) The mastery faith seeks to share.
(b) The authority faith needs to have.

C. *The victory of faith*
(a) Its moments of danger.
(b) Its miracle of deliverance.

Insights into prayer

Matthew 14.30: 'Lord, save me!'

A. *How simply the prayer was phrased*
(a) The comfort we find in this.
(b) The challenge we face in this.

B. *How surely the prayer was heard*
(a) The Name which Peter spoke.
(b) The need which Peter stated.

C. *How swiftly the prayer was answered*
(a) How deliberately Jesus seemed to wait.
(b) How differently God seems to work.

The failure of faith

Matthew 14.30: 'Beginning to sink'

A. *The victory this man had known*
(a) The storm which was raging when Christ came to him.
(b) The steps which were responsive when Christ called to him.

B. *The vision this man had lost*
(a) The Person of Christ had been replaced by a problem.
(b) His faith had been replaced by his fear.

C. *The verdict this man now faced*
(a) The honesty of the man.
(b) The urgency of the moment.

Coming to Christ

Matthew 14.29: 'And he said, "Come" '

A. *Come and see: John 1.39*
(a) The Person he is.
(b) The purpose he has.

B. *Come and find: Matt. 11.28*
(a) The resources which are adequate in him.
(b) The results which are achieved with him.

C. *Come and kneel: Ps. 95.6*
(a) So that I am available to him.
(b) So that I am accountable to him.

Humble enough to be blessed

Matthew 15.21–31: 'crumbs from the table'

A. *She was burdened with her need*
(a) She was helpless.
(b) She was hopeful.

B. *She was brought to her knees*
(a) How she was led to Christ.
(b) What she must learn of Christ.

C. *She was blessed by her Lord*
(a) The place she was willing to take.
(b) The peace she was able to find.

What do we believe about Christ's Church?

Matthew 16.18: 'Upon this rock I will build my Church'

A. *The conviction in the Church: 'Thou art the Christ'*
(a) The Person who gives its meaning to the Church.
(b) The people who are the material for the Church.

B. *The construction of the Church: 'I will build my Church'*
(a) The progress to be achieved.
(b) The purpose to be revealed.

C. *The commission to the Church: 'The gates of hell shall not prevail'*
(a) The prospect of conflict.
(b) The promise of conquest.

The heights and the valleys of Christian experience

Matthew 7.1: 'Jesus taketh them up into a high mountain apart'

A. *The vision*
(a) His identity was clearly seen.
(b) His authority was clearly faced.

B. *The verdict*
(a) A sense of wonder.
(b) An act of worship.

C. *The valley*
(a) The prayer in the valley which had reached the heart of God.
(b) The power in the valley which could meet the needs of men.

Fixing our eyes upon Jesus

Matthew 17.8: 'They saw no man, save Jesus only'

A. *The obstacle to faith which man can become*
(a) By distorting the picture of Christ.
(b) By diverting a person from Christ.

B. *The object of faith which Christ must become*
(a) Faith in his word.
(b) Faith in his worth.

C. *The outcome of faith which life will demand*
(a) The thrill of the mountain.
(b) The task of the multitude.

The tragedy of spiritual impotence

Matthew 17.14–21: 'Why could not we cast him out?'

A. *The problem which was brought to the Church*
(a) The help which was sought.
(b) The hopes which were shattered.

B. *The presence which was found in the Church: 'they came to Him'*
(a) The confidence displayed by Jesus Christ.
(b) The deliverance bestowed by Jesus Christ.

C. *The prospect which was given to the Church*
(a) The reason for their failure.
(b) The remedy for their failure.

Christ, children and ourselves

Matthew 18.1–14

A. *What Christ bids us become*
(a) How receptive a child is in its helplessness.
(b) How responsive a child is in its trustfulness.

B. *How Christ bids us beware*
(a) Lest we despise the children.
(b) Lest we damage the children.

C. *When Christ bids us begin: when they are small. Mark 10.13*
(a) The blunder which people can make.
(b) The blessing which parents can seek.

Our need to be converted

Matthew 18.3: 'Except ye be converted, and become as little children, ye shall not enter into the kingdom of heaven'

A. *The authority of the word I must heed*
(a) The meaning of conversion.
(b) The moment of conversion.

B. *The simplicity of the way I must take*
(a) The helplessness of little children.
(b) The trustfulness of little children.

C. *The reality of the world I may know*
(a) My entrance into a new realm.
(b) My experience of a new reign.

Children are important people

Matthew 18.6

A. *The environment in which our children must live*
(a) The intrusion by the world into their lives.
(b) The intention of the world for its gain.

B. *The encouragement for which our children will look*
(a) The encouragement of example.
(b) The encouragement of experience.

C. *The equipment of which our children must learn*
(a) The problems which will baffle them.
(b) The presence which will bless them.

The importance of the little

A. *A little person: Matt. 18.6*
(a) It is possible to underrate the importance of a little person.
(b) It is terrible to overlook our influence upon a little person.

B. *A little leaven: 1 Cor. 5.6, Gal. 5.9*
(a) The observation which is undeniable.
(b) The obligation which is inescapable.

C. *A little member: James 3.5*
(a) How different the effect of the words we speak can be.
(b) How difficult the control of the words we speak can be.

The centrality of Jesus Christ

Matthew 18.20

A. *Jesus Christ: Central in the Church*
(a) How mixed are our motives in the Church.
(b) What matters is the Master in the Church.

B. *Jesus Christ: Central on the cross. John 19.18*
(a) In the making of an atonement.
(b) In the message of the atonement.

C. *Jesus Christ: Central in the home. John 20.19*
(a) The Presence which brought peace.
(b) The purpose which needed power.

D. *Jesus Christ: Central in the glory. Rev. 5.6*
(a) The Lord he is.
(b) The love he has.

The unforgiving servant

Matthew 18.21–35

   A.   *The immensity of the debt he incurred*
   (a) The hopelessness of his state.
   (b) The forgiveness of his sins.

   B.   *The absurdity of the line he pursued*
   (a) The pettiness of the matter.
   (b) The ruthlessness of the method.

   C.   *The intensity of the wrath he provoked*
   (a) The inconsistency which was rebuked.
   (b) The incompatibility which was revealed.

A message for the spiritually unemployed

Matthew 20.6: 'Why stand ye here all the day idle?'

   A.   *The tasks in which God wants us to share*
   (a) The immensity of the task.
   (b) The urgency of the task.

   B.   *The times at which God asks us to come*
   (a) It can never be too soon.
   (b) It can never be too late.

   C.   *The truths from which God asks us to learn*
   (a) The motives revealed in the story.
   (b) The message contained in the story.

Salome – an ambitious mother

Matthew 20.17–28

A. *The ambitions she cherished*
(a) The future with which she was concerned.
(b) The failure for which she is condemned.

B. *The positions she coveted*
(a) They would be related to Christ.
(b) They would be reflecting on her.

C. *The confusion she caused*
(a) The harmony which was disrupted.
(b) The humility which was demanded.

A Palm Sunday message (1)

Matthew 21.5: 'Behold, thy King cometh unto thee'

A. *A declaration which was unmistakable*
(a) Note how prophecy was fulfilled.
(b) Note how publicity was fostered.

B. *A revelation which was unacceptable*
(a) The peace which Christ had come to give.
(b) The price which Christ asked men to pay.

C. *A condemnation which was unavoidable*
(a) The opportunity given to them.
(b) The opportunity taken from them.

A Palm Sunday message (2)

Matthew 21.10: 'When he was come into Jerusalem, all the city was moved, saying, "Who is this?"'

A. *A presence experienced: 'When he was come'*
(a) The publicity surrounding Christ.
(b) The fidelity needed by Christ.

B. *A purpose envisaged*
(a) The chance they must have.
(b) The choice they must make.

C. *A people involved*
(a) Rejoicing for many.
(b) Resentment for others.

When a city is confronted with Christ

Matthew 21.10: 'When he was come into Jerusalem, all the city was moved, saying, "Who is this?"'

A. *What was the manner by which the confrontation was achieved?*
(a) The identity of Christ was clearly declared.
(b) The authority of Christ was clearly displayed.

B. *What were the dangers by which this confrontation was accompanied?*
(a) Dangers for the friends of Christ.
(b) Dangers for the foes of Christ.

C. *How was the confrontation assessed?*
(a) The condemnation of men.
(b) The coronation of Christ.

What does it take to move a city?

Matthew 21.10: 'All the city was moved'

A. *It took the crowds*
(a) The concern of the Christ.
(b) The content of the Church.

B. *It took the cheers*
(a) How they rejoiced.
(b) Why they rejoiced.

C. *It took the Christ*
(a) The claim he made.
(b) The choice they faced.

'And he left them, and went out of the city into Bethany; and he lodged there'

Matthew 21.17

A. *The warning Christ sounds*
(a) The success they enjoyed.
(b) The silence they experienced.

B. *The wisdom he shows*
(a) How wise to distance himself from the task in hand.
(b) How wise to discuss his task with others.

C. *The welcome he seeks*
(a) How unhurried they were as they listened.
(b) How unwearied they were as they laboured.

A Palm Sunday message (3)

Matthew 21.17: 'He left them . . . he lodged there'

A. *Think of the company he shunned that night*
(a) They were disturbed by him.
(b) They were displeased with him.
(c) They were discarded by him.

B. *Think of the company he sought that night*
(a) They wanted him.
(b) They welcomed him.
(c) They worshipped him.

A Communion meditation: what we face and find in the gospel

Matthew 22.1–14: 'All things are now ready: come . . .'

A. *The historical initiative*
(a) The preparations made.
(b) The invitations sent.

B. *The practical alternative*
(a) The decision the gospel demands.
(b) The division the gospel creates.

C. *The categorical imperative*
(a) The overruling authority.
(b) The overriding necessity.

The Christian's three relationships

Matthew 22.37–39: 'Thou shalt love the Lord thy God . . . and thy neighbour'

   A.   *With the Lord*
(a) A relationship made right by the obedience of Christ.
(b) A relationship kept right by the obedience of man.

   B.   *With the Church*
(a) How demanding this will be.
(b) How rewarding this will be.

   C.   *With the world*
(a) The contact the Christian will have with the world.
(b) The concern the Christian will show for the world.

God does not wait forever

Matthew 23.37: 'How often would I . . . and ye would not'

   A.   *The expectation with which love waits*
(a) The carefulness which marks the provision of love.
(b) The fruitfulness which is the intention of love.

   B.   *The consummation at which love weeps*
(a) His identity had been revealed unmistakably.
(b) His authority had been spurned unbelievably.

   C.   *The devastation of which love warns*
(a) Their punishment as the people of God.
(b) Their replacement in the purpose of God.

Persecution

Matthew 24.9: 'Ye shall be hated of all men for my name's sake'

A. *A hatred to be expected by the Christian*
(a) The prospect of it of which we are warned.
(b) The peril in it for which we must watch.

B. *A hatred to be exploited by the Christian*
(a) What we must reveal.
(b) Why we should rejoice.

C. *A hatred to be expressed by the Christian*
(a) A distinction which regulates the hatred of the Christian.
(b) A devotion which motivates the hatred of the Christian.

The fig tree budding: a symbol of Israel

Matthew 24.32

A. *The terms of Israel's relationship*
(a) The choice revealed: Gen. 12.1–3.
(b) The conditions imposed: Lev. 26, Deut. 28.
(c) The consequences foretold.

B. *The tragedy of Israel's rejection*
(a) Nationally, a scattered people.
(b) Socially, a persecuted people.
(c) Spiritually, an apostate people.

C. *The truth of Israel's return. Ezek. 36—37*
(a) The coming of the people.
(b) The condition of the land.
(c) The conversion of the nation.

The parable of the ten virgins
Matthew 25.1–13

A. *The coming*
(a) The delay in his coming.
(b) The darkness at his coming.

B. *The contrast*
(a) The visible appearance which was similar.
(b) The vital difference which was spiritual.

C. *The command*
(a) The importance of the truth.
(b) The ignorance of the time.

The parable of the talents
Matthew 25.14: 'His own servants'

A. *The trust he placed in his servants*
(a) The difference in what was received.
(b) A diligence was what was required.

B. *The time he gave to his servants*
(a) The progress they made in their work.
(b) The prospect they kept in their minds.

C. *The truth which he sought from his servants*
(a) There would be delight for some.
(b) There was distress for the one.

The failure of the man with one talent

Matthew 25.14–30

   A.   *The realm where the failure took place*
  (a) How searching this is.
  (b) How serious this is.

   B.   *The reasons why failure takes place*
  (a) He was afraid in his heart.
  (b) He was astray in his thinking.

   C.   *The results when failure takes place*
  (a) We see increased opportunities for some.
  (b) We see decreased opportunities for others.

Hospitals – an important sphere for Christian witness, by life rather than by lip

Matthew 25.31–40

   A.   *The opportunity which sickness gives*
  (a) We find all the world in hospital.
  (b) They have plenty of time there.

   B.   *The responsibility which sickness brings*
  (a) How closely related some Christians are to the patients.
  (b) How clearly Christ should be revealed in us all.

   C.   *The urgency which sickness holds*
  (a) It always is a limited opportunity.
  (b) It sometimes is a lost opportunity.

Judas's thirty pieces of silver

Matthew 26.14–15

A. *They were desired*
(a) How desperately he wanted to have them.
(b) How deliberately he worked to get them.

B. *They were disdained*
(a) Note the changed value of the silver.
(b) Note the contemptuous voices of the scribes.

C. *They were discarded*
(a) The forgotten factor, conscience.
(b) The final folly, suicide.

A message for ministers

Matthew 26.22: 'Lord, is it I?'

A. *Are the motives in my heart such that the Spirit will bless?*
(a) What are the motives in the heart of the preacher?
(b) What are the motives in the hearts of the people?

B. *Is the message on my lips such that the Spirit will bless?*
(a) What about the matter in my preaching?
(b) What about the manner of my preaching?

C. *Are the methods in my work such that the Spirit will bless?*
(a) The importance which is given to prayer.
(b) The difference which is seen through prayer.

D. *Is the manner of my life such that the Spirit will bless?*
(a) There will be a negative side to holiness.
(b) There will be a positive side to holiness.

Jesus in the Garden of Gethsemane

Matthew 26.39: 'And he went a little further'

A. *The distance he moved*
(a) Note the people he moved away from.
(b) Note the Person he was alone with.

B. *The destiny he met*
(a) The suffering which would be involved.
(b) The salvation which was at stake.

C. *The decision he made*
(a) There was abdication.
(b) There was dedication.

Peter in the Garden of Gethsemane

Matthew 26.40: 'What, could ye not watch with me one hour?'

A. *The immensity of the debt which was owed by Peter*
(a) The privileges he had known.
(b) The profession he had made.

B. *The modesty of the demand which was made by Jesus*
(a) The costliness of the path he faced.
(b) The contrast of the plea he made.

C. *The brevity of the duration which was involved*
(a) How quickly one hour is gone.
(b) How gladly one hour is given.

D. *The intensity of the desire which was there*
(a) The companionship Christ desired.
(b) The co-operation Christ sought.

Peter, the man who kept his distance from Jesus Christ

Matthew 26.58: 'Peter followed him afar off'

A. *How he spoke*
(a) The confidence his words revealed.
(b) The dependence his Lord required.

B. *When he slept*
(a) The strategic importance of the hour.
(b) The seeming indifference in their hearts.

C. *Where he sat*
(a) The lie on his lips.
(b) The look from his Lord.

The hands which lead Christ to us

Matthew 27.2: 'They led him . . . to Pontius Pilate'

A. *The confrontation we see involving Pontius Pilate*
(a) What the hour was.
(b) Whose the hands were.

B. *The complications we see disturbing him*
(a) The conflicting forces without.
(b) The compelling fears within.

C. *The condemnation we pass upon him*
(a) His futile attempts to be rid of Christ.
(b) His fatal assent to the death of Christ.

The most important question in the world

Matthew 27.22: 'What shall I do then with Jesus?' The dilemma of Pontius Pilate

A. *The intrusion he knew was inevitable*
(a) The reports which had continually come to him.
(b) The request which was finally made to him.

B. *The evasion he found was impossible*
(a) The pressures he knew.
(b) The failure he faced.

C. *The decision he made which was incredible*
(a) What were the reasons which swayed the heart of this man?
(b) What of the reproach which stained the name of this man?

The refusal of Christ

Matthew 27.34: 'They gave him vinegar to drink mingled with gall: and when he had tasted thereof, he would not drink'

A. *We see here the hurt of tragedy*
(a) The ruins which surrounded him.
(b) The pains which stabbed him.

B. *We see the hands of sympathy*
(a) It was kindly meant.
(b) It was firmly met.

C. *We see the hour of victory*
(a) The words he spoke.
(b) The work he did.

A Good Friday meditation

Matthew 27.36: 'And sitting down they watched him there'

A. *The eyes of the wicked watched him there*
(a) Think of the resentment aroused in their hearts.
(b) Think of the removal achieved by their hands.

B. *The eyes of the wondering watched him there*
(a) What men had said of him.
(b) What men had done to him.

C. *The eyes of the worshipping watched him there*
(a) Eyes which saw who the Person was on that cross.
(b) Eyes which saw what the purpose was of the cross.

The gospel according to Christ's enemies

Matthew 27.39–44: The taunts which were hurled against him, now treasured by the Christian

A. - *The bench at which he worked: 'Is not this the carpenter?'*
(a) Consider the rejection of Christ based upon this.
(b) Consider the attraction of Christ based upon this.

B. *The folk with whom he mixed: 'the friend of publicans and sinners'*
(a) The words which men flung at Christ.
(b) The warmth which men have felt in Christ.

C. *The throne of which he spoke: 'Hail, King of the Jews'*
(a) The insults with which men shamed the Kingship of Jesus.
(b) The insights with which men sensed the Kingship of Jesus.

D. *The cross on which he died*
(a) The demand which was made by men.
(b) The demand which was met by Christ.

The place of authority in our lives

Matthew 28.18–20: 'All power [authority] is given unto me in heaven and in earth'

A. *There is a hostility which challenges authority*
(a) How common this is.
(b) How costly this proves.

B. *There is a hypocrisy which condemns this revolt*
(a) The indignation of many Christians.
(b) The inconsistency of many Christians.

C. *There is a heredity which corrupts our respect for authority*
(a) The basic fact that man is born a sinner.
(b) The folly which is blind.

D. *There is a humility which consents to authority*
(a) The example of the Saviour.
(b) The enabling of the Spirit.

The Great Commission (1)

Matthew 28.18–20: 'All authority is given unto me . . . Go ye'

A. *The will of Christ to which we all must yield*
(a) The source of his authority.
(b) The scope of his authority.

B. *The work of Christ in which we all must share*
(a) The places to which we are sent.
(b) The purpose for which we are sent.

C. *The word of Christ in which we all can trust*
(a) The difference his presence makes.
(b) The assurance his promise gives.

The Great Commission (2)

Matthew 28.18–20

    A.   *The initiative the Christian must take*
    (a) The complaint which is heard in the churches: 'They won't come!'
    (b) The command which is here for the churches: 'Go ye.'

    B.   *The imperative the Christian must face*
    (a) The information conveyed by my lips.
    (b) The illustration portrayed by my life.

    C.   *The incentive the Christian will have*
    (a) The wonder of the Lord's presence in our lives.
    (b) The witness to the Lord's power through our lives.

The Great Commission (3)

Matthew 28.18–20

    A.   *The throne at which we all must bow*
    (a) His right which comes as a challenge to us.
    (b) His reign which brings a control over us.

    B.   *The task in which we all must share*
    (a) The immensity of the task.
    (b) The diversity of the gifts.

    C.   *The truth by which we all must live*
    (a) The protest we can make.
    (b) The Presence we will have.

The sin of inactivity

Matthew 28.18

A. *The directive which is plain*
(a) There is a contrast here.
(b) There is a challenge here.

B. *The duty which is personal*
(a) The ignorance I must expect.
(b) The instruction I must give.

C. *The dynamic which is provided*
(a) Power is resident in Christ.
(b) Power is released through us.

Mark

Preparation for serving God

Mark 1.12–13: 'And immediately the Spirit driveth him into the wilderness. And he was there in the wilderness forty days, tempted of Satan; and was with the wild beasts; and the angels ministered unto him'

A. *The compulsion which was irresistible*
(a) A life which knows the presence of the Holy Spirit.
(b) A life which knows the pressure of the Holy Spirit.

B. *The commission which was irreversible*
(a) How swiftly the attack was made.
(b) How surely the attack was met.

C. *The communion which was irreplaceable.*
(a) The Source of the help he got.
(b) The scale of the help he gives.

The calling of Simon and Andrew

Mark 1.17: 'Come ye after me, and I will make you to become fishers of men'

A. *The purpose in their lives*
(a) The expectation a fisherman has.
(b) The preparations a fisherman makes.

B. *The partners in their work*
(a) How much they would lean on one another.
(b) How much they would learn from one another.

C. *The presence of their Lord*
(a) The guidance he would give.
(b) The obedience he would ask.

How Jesus entered into the synagogue

Mark 1.21: 'And they went into Capernaum; and straightway on the sabbath day he entered into the synagogue, and taught'

A. *He comes as Master*
(a) The person I must see.
(b) The purposes I must serve.

B. *He comes as Teacher*
(a) We come as students.
(b) We wait in silence.

C. *He comes as Healer*
(a) His power will be experienced in the lives of men.
(b) His praise will be expressed by the lips of men.

Prayer – the example of Christ

Mark 1.35: 'In the morning, rising up a great while before day, he went out . . . into a solitary place and there prayed'

A. *The prayer which was unhurried*
(a) A contrast is seen here.
(b) A content is suggested here.

B. *The place which was undisturbed*
(a) How difficult this was to find.
(b) How determined he was to find it.

C. *The practice which was unbroken*
(a) How natural prayer was for Jesus.
(b) How needful prayer was for Jesus.

The cleansing of a leper

Mark 1.40–45

A. *Why did he come?*
(a) Think of the disease in his life.
(b) Think of the despair in his soul.

B. *How did he come?*
(a) He came with honesty.
(b) He came with humility.

C. *When did he come?*
(a) What he saw in Jesus.
(b) What he said to Jesus.

Crippled, challenged, cured

Mark 2.1–13

A. *The man was crippled*
(a) Think of the dependence he showed.
(b) Think of the experience he missed.

B. *The man was challenged*
(a) The way to Jesus posed a challenge.
(b) The words of Jesus posed a challenge.

C. *The man was cured*
(a) The power of Christ was experienced.
(b) The praise of Christ was evoked.

How four people contributed to the blessing of one life

Mark 2.3–12

A. *An impulse which was shared*
(a) The coming of the impulse.
(b) The acting on the impulse.

B. *An ingenuity which was successful*
(a) The way was blocked at first.
(b) They were determined to succeed.

C. *An insight which was startling*
(a) The man's need was deeper than they thought.
(b) The master's words were directed to his need.

C. *An impression which was surprising*
(a) People praised Christ when they saw his power.
(b) People praised Christ throughout the town.

A hand is healed

Mark 3.1–6: 'And there was a man there which had a withered hand'

A. *The significance of the hand which was withered*
(a) It could be the hand of fellowship.
(b) It could be the hand of prayer.
(c) It could be the hand which serves.

B. *The story of the hand which was healed*
(a) Here was a condition which could not be concealed.
(b) Here was a challenge which could not be evaded.
(c) Here was a command which could not be ignored.

How the Lord observed the Lord's day

Mark 3.2

A. *Where we find him going on the Lord's Day*
(a) He went to the services in the synagogue.
(b) He went into the homes of the people.
(c) He went where the people would be found.

B. *What we find him doing on the Lord's day*
(a) We find him listening.
(b) We find him witnessing.
(c) We find him ministering.

C. *How we find him speaking of the Lord's day*
(a) He speaks of the control the Lord must exercise.
(b) He speaks of the concern the day should express.
(c) He speaks of the conflict the Church can expect.

The Lord's day

Mark 3.1–5 and Luke 6.1–5

A. *The authority which rules over it*
(a) The ordering hands of the Saviour.
(b) The obedient heart of the servant.

B. *The opportunity which comes with it*
(a) The opportunity for worship.
(b) The opportunity for witness.

C. *The blessing which flows from it*
(a) The fulfilment of God's purpose.
(b) The fellowship with God's people.

A blueprint of discipleship

Mark 3.14–15: 'That they should be with him'

A. *Their enjoyment of a walk*
(a) The priority to be given to this.
(b) The quality to be gained from this.

B. *Their equipment for a work*
(a) Their employment in a task.
(b) Their enduement for the task.

C. *Their engagement in a war*
(a) There is hardship to be expected.
(b) There is comradeship to be enjoyed.

A message for the ordination of a pastor

Mark 3.14–15

A. *The communion with your Lord you are to maintain*
(a) The kinds of pressures which would endanger this.
(b) The sense of priority which can ensure this.

B. *The commission from your Lord you are to fulfil*
(a) He will tell you where you are to go.
(b) He will tell you what you are to say.

C. *The compassion of your Lord you are to portray*
(a) Men should see in your life an illustration of the love of God.
(b) Men should see in your life a demonstration of the power of God.

The unpardonable sin

Mark 3.22–30

A. *The confrontation of these men with Jesus Christ*
(a) It was inevitable.
(b) It was uncomfortable.

B. *The consideration by these men of Jesus Christ*
(a) The choice they must make about him.
(b) The charge they had brought against him.

C. *The condemnation of these men by Jesus Christ*
(a) This constitutes a warning against something which is possible.
(b) This constitutes a warning against something which would be terrible.

Careful hearing

Mark 4.24–25: 'Take heed what ye hear'

A. *How selective our hearing should be*
(a) The defilement which could be experienced.
(b) The discernment which must be exercised.

B. *How responsive our hearing should be*
(a) The intention I must have when I hear.
(b) The instruction I will get as I hear.

C. *How decisive our hearing should be*
(a) There is a prospect to be feared.
(b) There is a progress to be made.

Life without health

Mark 5.25–34

A. *A life from which health had gone*
(a) The crippling disease she had known.
(b) The crushing despair she had felt.

B. *A life in which hope was born*
(a) There had been a learning about Christ.
(b) There was a longing for Christ.

C. *A life for which help was found*
(a) What Christ gives must be received personally.
(b) What Christ does must be revealed publicly.

Peter, James and John

Mark 5.37, 9.2, 14.33

A. *What he said which enabled him to win them*
(a) An invitation to fellowship (John).
(b) A transformation of character (Peter).
(c) A satisfaction through winning men (James).

B. *What he saw which enabled him to love them*
(a) Peter was the talker.
(b) John was the dreamer.
(c) James was the fighter.

C. *What he shared which enabled him to bless them*
(a) He shared his victories with them.
(b) He shared his deity with them.
(c) He shared his agony with them.

The quiet where God is (1)

Mark 6.31: 'Come ye yourselves apart into a desert place, and rest awhile'

A. *Christ wanted them to get away from the pressures in their lives*
(a) How unceasing were the demands made upon them.
(b) How unaware they were of the dangers facing them.

B. *Christ wanted them to get away for the purposes of his love*
(a) He wanted them to learn to get some rest.
(b) He wanted them to give some time to themselves.

C. *Christ wanted them to be alone in the presence of their Lord*
(a) There would be so much he would have to say to them about their work.
(b) There would be so much he would want to share with them about his work.

The quiet where God is (2)

Mark 6.31

A. *The situation Jesus observed*
(a) He observed the demands of the people in their lives.
(b) He observed the dangers of the pressures in their lives.

B. *The obligation he imposed*
(a) The obligation of withdrawal.
(b) The obligation of renewal.

C. *The expectation he aroused*
(a) There would be an assessment which would be valuable.
(b) There would be an enjoyment which would be memorable.

Feed the hungry

Mark 6.36–37: 'They have nothing to eat . . . Give ye them to eat'

A. *The concern shown by the Master*
(a) This is recorded in the Scriptures.
(b) This must be revealed in the Church.

B. *The complaint which was made to the Master*
(a) The immensity of the task.
(b) The impossibility of the task.

C. *The command which is spoken by the Master*
(a) The duty is clear.
(b) The danger is real.

The mount of transfiguration (1)

Mark 9.2–29: 'Up into a mountain ... Down from the mountain'

A. *The majesty they had seen*
(a) The vision of their Lord.
(b) The voice of their Lord.

B. *The misery they must serve*
(a) The helplessness they would find there.
(b) The hopefulness they would face there.

C. *The ministry they could share*
(a) The deliverance which was brought.
(b) The dependence which was basic.

The mount of transfiguration (2)

Mark 9.2–29

A. *The unbroken solitude of the hills*
(a) The multitude from which they had escaped.
(b) The solitude into which they had entered.

B. *The unveiled splendour of the Lord*
(a) The vision of deity.
(b) The voice of authority.

C. *The unwelcome summons from the world*
(a) The pleasure which they had derived from the presence of Christ.
(b) The problem which was awaiting the power of Christ.

Lacking one thing (1)

Mark 10.17–22

    A.   *He had the opportunity of a godly home*
(a) The enriching ministry of such a home.
(b) The enduring memory of such a home.

    B.   *He had the sincerity of an honest mind*
(a) He was not ashamed to approach his Lord.
(b) He was not afraid to admit his need.

    C.   *He had the testimony of a good record*
(a) It held the achievement of social integrity.
(b) It held the admission of spiritual need.

    D.   *He faced the authority of a divine Lord*
(a) The recognition Christ gave to him.
(b) The requirement Christ asked of him.

Lacking one thing (2)

Mark 10.21; John 9.25; Philippians 3.13

    A.   *One thing we can lack (Mark 10.21)*
(a) How this young man felt.
(b) Who this young man faced.

    B.   *One thing we can know (John 9.25)*
(a) How blind this man had been.
(b) How blessed this man now was.

    C.   *One thing we can do (Phil. 3.13)*
(a) The fetters which he left behind him.
(b) The future which he saw before him.

An important question

Mark 10.17–31: 'What shall I do that I may inherit eternal life?'

A. *The lack this young man felt in his life*
(a) The answer he was wanting to find.
(b) The action he was willing to take.

B. *The Lord he faced at that hour*
(a) The identity of Christ had been realised by him.
(b) The authority of Christ which must be recognised by him.

C. *The loss of his wealth the young man feared*
(a) The revelation of the man's heart.
(b) The revolution in the man's life.

D. *The love the young man foiled by his sin*
(a) The nature of love.
(b) The failure of love.

The great refusal

Mark 10.17–31

A. *The life he lived*
(a) His integrity.
(b) His humility.

B. *The Lord he faced*
(a) The identity of Christ.
(b) The authority of Christ.

C. *The love he spurned*
(a) The shattered hopes of Christ.
(b) The saddened heart of Christ.

A question which Christ wants you to answer

Mark 10.46–52: 'What do you want me to do for you?'

A. *This man knew what he wanted*
(a) There was something he lacked in his life.
(b) There was something he learned from his Lord.

B. *This man said what he wanted*
(a) He was desperate.
(b) He was definite.

C. *This man got what he wanted*
(a) He faced a Lord who was willing.
(b) He found a life which was waiting.

What faith in Christ can do

Mark 10.52: 'Thy faith hath made thee whole'

A. *The expectation in the light of which faith will turn to Christ*
(a) The name which spelt hope.
(b) The need which sought help.

B. *The invitation on the strength of which faith can come to Christ*
(a) The word which comforted his heart.
(b) The word which covered his need.

C. *The healing for which faith gives praise to Christ*
(a) How the Source was recognised.
(b) How the song was released.

A Palm Sunday address

Mark 11.3: 'The Lord hath need of him'

A. *Here we have the hope of liberty*
(a) The cords which restrained the ass.
(b) The words which released the ass.

B. *Here we sense the hour of destiny*
(a) The suggestiveness of the place.
(b) The satisfaction of the person.

C. *Here we see the hands of mastery*
(a) The difficulties the ass met.
(b) The deity the ass bore.

The fig tree: Christ's only miracle of judgment

Mark 11.13–14, 20–21: 'Nothing but leaves'

A. *A simplicity which the miracle contains*
(a) How prominently the fig tree stood out.
(b) How expectantly the Saviour drew near.

B. *The sincerity which the Master requires*
(a) The profession which was obvious.
(b) The omission which was serious.

C. *The severity the message proclaims*
(a) How patiently God can wait.
(b) How finally God will act.

Near to the Kingdom, but not in it (1)

Mark 12.34: 'Thou art not far from the Kingdom of God'

A. *What can bring a person near to the Kingdom of God*
(a) His association with spiritual things.
(b) His appreciation of spiritual truth.

B. *What can hold a person back from the Kingdom of God*
(a) The reasons he may have had.
(b) The lessons we can all learn.

C. *What can take a person into the Kingdom of God*
(a) The submission he must be willing to give.
(b) The decision he must be willing to make.

Near to the Kingdom, but not in it (2)

Mark 12.34

A. *The distance this man had come*
(a) The appreciation the man showed.
(b) The aspiration the Master sensed.

B. *The danger this man was in*
(a) The danger of failing to take the final step.
(b) The danger of flinging away all the ground gained.

C. *The decision this man must make*
(a) The acceptance of the King.
(b) The allegiance to the King.

The Master and our giving

Mark 12.41–44

A. *Christ is concerned about the manner of our giving*
(a) We can give reluctantly.
(b) We can give rejoicingly.

B. *Christ is concerned about the measure of our giving*
(a) We are to give sensibly.
(b) We are to give sacrificially.

C. *Christ is concerned about the meaning of our giving*
(a) The love which should be expressed in our giving.
(b) The lives which will be enriched through our giving.

Doing what we can

Mark 14.3–9: 'She hath done what she could'

A. *A service was rendered*
(a) The person to whom this service was rendered.
(b) The purpose for which this service was rendered.

B. *A standard was reached*
(a) Her ability was limited.
(b) Her abandonment was limitless.

C. *A servant was rewarded*
(a) The murmurings which were hurtful.
(b) The Master who was grateful.

'The Master saith'

Mark 14.14

   A.   *The Master whose word love waits to hear*
  (a) The other voices which can be heard.
  (b) The one voice which love wants to hear.

   B.   *Whose wish love seeks to serve*
  (a) The anticipation of love in seeing a need.
  (b) The satisfaction of love in serving a need.

   C.   *Whose work love longs to share*
  (a) The dependence Christ reveals.
  (b) The devotion Christ rewards.

The tragedy of Peter's disloyalty

Mark 14.29

   A.   *Peter was sure of himself*
  (a) How impossible it must have seemed to him.
  (b) How incredible it must have sounded to him.

   B.   *Peter was scared by a girl*
  (a) The security he had enjoyed.
  (b) The hostility he then encountered.

   C.   *Peter was saved by his Lord*
  (a) The bitterness of the tears shed by him.
  (b) The blessedness of the trust shown in him.

When God has nothing to say to man

Mark 15.3: 'He answered nothing'

   A.   *The surprising reticence of the Master*
  (a) The importance of the men he faced.
  (b) The indifference of the Master we see.

   B.   *The suggested reasons for the mystery*
  (a) The mistaken conclusion man can reach.
  (b) The moral condition God does require.

   C.   *The shattering relevance of the message*
  (a) The silence which is possible still.
  (b) The sentence which is passed again.

The meaning of the death of Christ

Mark 15.38: 'And the veil of the temple was rent in twain from the top to the bottom'

   A.   *The purpose for which the veil was required*
  (a) The pride of man was rebuked by God.
  (b) The price of blood was required by God.

   B.   *The power by which the veil was removed*
  (a) The hand by which the veil was rent.
  (b) The hour at which the veil was rent.

   C.   *The Person by whom the veil was replaced*
  (a) Christ is the entrance through which man has now got to pass.
  (b) Through Christ man can now live in the presence of God.

Failure need never be final

Mark 16.1–8: 'Go, tell his disciples and Peter'

A. *The moment of tragedy Peter had known*
(a) He had said so much.
(b) He had sunk so low.

B. *The meeting with destiny he could have*
(a) The remorse in which he was sunk.
(b) The request by which he was summoned.

C. *The quality of ministry he would give*
(a) The test he must pass.
(b) The trust he would get.

The life of Mary Magdalene

Mark 16.9: 'Now when Jesus was risen . . . he appeared first to Mary Magdalene, out of whom he had cast seven devils'

A. *Mary's hope was born through Christ*
(a) The magnitude of the problems in her life.
(b) The gratitude to the Person of her Lord.

B. *Mary's heart was won to Christ*
(a) The wonder of her love.
(b) The welcome for her love.

C. *An honour was given to Mary by Christ*
(a) The meeting Christ had planned.
(b) The meaning which Christ made plain.

A message for the commissioning of missionaries

Mark 16.15, 20: 'And [Jesus] said unto them, "Go ye into all the world, and preach the gospel to every creature." . . . And they went forth, and preached everywhere, the Lord working with them, and confirming the word with signs following.'

A. *The reason for what you will be doing*
(a) The command you have heard.
(b) The consent you have given.

B. *The resources you will have where you will be going*
(a) The difference which the Lord's presence will make.
(b) The dependence for which the Lord's presence will ask.

C. *The results for which you will be looking*
(a) The assurance you can have.
(b) The assessment which God will make.

Luke

A prayer which changed a life
Luke 1.26–38

A. *The purpose of God which had been revealed to Mary*
(a) How personal was the relationship in the purpose of
    God.
(b) How fearful was the response to the purpose of God.

B. *The problem which must be resolved for Mary*
(a) The objection raised.
(b) The operation promised.

C. *Mary's prayer to God*
(a) The submission offered in it.
(b) The salvation achieved through it.

Mary's song

Luke 1.46–56

A. *God deals with us mercifully as he did with Mary*
(a) The place which Mary took.
(b) The grace which Mary trusted.

B. *God works in us powerfully, as he did in Mary*
(a) The destiny God had planned for her.
(b) The ministry God had pledged to her.

C. *God saves through us wonderfully, as he did through Mary*
(a) The salvation achieved through Mary.
(b) The submission offered by Mary.

What does the future hold for a child?

Luke 1.66

A. *This child's destiny was to bring gladness*
(a) To his home.
(b) Through his help.

B. *This child's destiny was to achieve greatness*
(a) The test of greatness.
(b) The cost of greatness.

C. *This child's destiny was to radiate goodness*
(a) The author of this.
(b) The advent of this.

The prophecy of Zacharias

Luke 1.68–79

A. *The deliverance which Christ brings to men*
(a) The blunder which man can make.
(b) The blessing which man can have.

B. *The deference which Christ asks of men*
(a) The confidence we will find in our service.
(b) The continuance we will know in our service.

C. *The difference which Christ makes in men*
(a) The decisive word in the life of a Christian.
(b) The distinctive factor in the life of a Christian.

Christmas lights

Luke 1.79: 'To give light to them that sit in darkness'
Like many of the other trimmings of Christmas, such as cards, gifts, carols and trees, Christmas lights can have Christian connotations.

A. *The lamp of truth which was lit by Christ*
(a) The initiative taken by God.
(b) The imperative faced in Christ.

B. *The lamp of love which was lit by Christ*
(a) In Christ we see the love of God for men revealed.
(b) Through Christ we see the love of God released through men.

C. *The lamp of hope which was lit by Christ*
(a) The impotence in man.
(b) The confidence in Christ.

Why Christmas?

Luke 2.7: 'Mary brought forth her firstborn son, and wrapped him in swaddling clothes, and laid him in a manger'

A. *The reasons for Christmas*
(a) The love of God revealed through the coming of Christ.
(b) The lives of men redeemed through the coming of Christ.

B. *The results from Christmas*
(a) The new relationship established with God.
(b) The new resources enjoyed by men.

C. *The response to Christmas*
(a) Our acceptance of him.
(b) Our allegiance to him.

'There was no room for them in the inn'

Luke 2.7

A. *The people there*
(a) There would be the important people.
(b) There would be the insistent people.

B. *The pressures there*
(a) The time he could not give to them.
(b) The truth he did not know of them.

C. *The picture there*
(a) A picture of the grace of God.
(b) A picture of the guilt of man.

A study of the inn-keeper

Luke 2.7

A. *The reasons he would have*
(a) The people to be considered.
(b) The trouble to be avoided.

B. *The results he would see*
(a) He would be glad of the peace he had gained.
(b) He would be glad because of the place they had found.

C. *The regrets he would know*
(a) The change which might come in his thinking.
(b) The chance which he had lost by not caring.

The birthday which everyone forgot – a talk for children

Luke 2.7

A. *Just imagine – no presents were sent!*
(a) What a strange day it was.
(b) What a sad day it was.

B. *Just imagine – no people came!*
(a) How he would wait for them at the window.
(b) How they would wave to him at the window.

C. *Just imagine – no party was held!*
(a) The plans he had made for them.
(b) The prizes he had bought for them.

Christmas is a time for singing

Luke 2.10: 'good tidings of great joy'

   A.   *The search for joy which so many have made*
(a) How confident the many were.
(b) How ignorant the many were.

   B.   *The source of joy which so many have found*
(a) The burdens which Christ has lifted from us.
(b) The blessings which Christ has lavished on us.

   C.   *The songs of joy which so many have sung*
(a) The wonder they want to express.
(b) The welcome they want to extend.

What kind of a day is Christmas?

Luke 2.10–14: 'Unto you is born this day . . . a Saviour, which is Christ the Lord'

   A.   *It is a day for giving*
(a) The desire love has to give.
(b) The demand love meets by giving.

   B.   *It is a day for praising*
(a) The wonder of the Name which the Gift bears.
(b) The answer to need which the Gift brings.

   C.   *It is a day for kneeling*
(a) The divinity perceived in Christ.
(b) The destiny proclaimed to men.

Do I need a Saviour?

Luke 2.11: 'Unto you is born this day . . . a Saviour, which is Christ the Lord'

    A.   *What am I to be saved from?*
    (a) The sinfulness of my own heart.
    (b) The seriousness of my own sins.

    B.   *What am I to be saved for?*
    (a) So that the real purpose of my life can be fulfilled.
    (b) So that the real problems in my life can be resolved.

    C.   *Who am I to be saved by?*
    (a) Am I looking in the wrong direction?
    (b) Am I thinking of the wrong decision?

Why is Christmas Day an extra special day?

Luke 2.11

    A.   *It is a time for memory*
    (a) It became a time of memory for Mary.
    (b) It becomes a time of memory for most of us.

    B.   *It is a time for mystery*
    (a) The element of wonder enters into it.
    (b) The element of worship enters into it.

    C.   *It is a time for ministry*
    (a) The place we must give to the message of Christmas.
    (b) The peace we will find through the meaning of Christmas.

The relevance of the Christmas message

Luke 2.11: 'Unto you is born this day . . . in the city of David a Saviour, which is Christ the Lord'

A. *It is historically based: 'born this day in the city of David'*
(a) Who he was.
(b) What he did.

B. *It is spiritually important: 'A Saviour which is Christ the Lord'*
(a) Think of the blight of sin.
(b) Think of the gift of salvation.

C. *It must be personally believed: 'unto you'*
(a) The respect which God shows for human personality.
(b) The response which God wants from our human personality.

The relevance of the Saviour

Luke 2.11

A. *The need of the sinner*
(a) How baffling is the problem of sin.
(b) How humbling is the plight of man.

B. *The Name of the Saviour*
(a) Who the Saviour is.
(b) How the Saviour saves.

C. *The 'now' of salvation: 'now is the day of salvation'*
(a) How urgent the matter is.
(b) How instant is the miracle wrought.

The theology of our Christmas carols

Luke 2.13, 20: 'Praising God'

A. *The gaiety expressed*
(a) The note of joy which is heard.
(b) The needs of man which are met.

B. *The deity encountered*
(a) The mystery of his Person.
(b) The majesty of his presence.

C. *The reality experienced*
(a) The grace received by us.
(b) The gifts required from us.

When the glory fades from our sky

Luke 2.15: 'And it came to pass, as the angels were gone away from them . . . '

A. *The vision which had stirred their hearts*
(a) A moment which was unforgettable.
(b) A message which was unmistakable.

B. *The venture which changed their lives*
(a) The fading of the splendour.
(b) The finding of the Saviour.

C. *The voices which now praised their God*
(a) The worship they gave to their Lord.
(b) The witness they bore to their world.

Christmas – a time to remember our childhood

Luke 2.15: 'Let us now go even unto Bethlehem'

A. *Christmas reminds us of the children we once were*
(a) Let us recall the home created by the love of our parents.
(b) Let us recall the hopes cherished in the hearts of our parents.

B. *Christmas reminds us of the choices we have since made*
(a) The pressures we had to face in growing up.
(b) The pathway we have since travelled as adults.

C. *Christmas reminds us of the chance we may still have*
(a) Has the past held failures which we now regret?
(b) Does the present speak of a future which can still be saved?

What do we find at Christmas?

Luke 2.16: 'They came with haste, and found Mary, and Joseph, and the babe lying in a manger'

A. *At the centre of Christmas we find a child*
(a) We think of the children we have.
(b) We think of the children we were.

B. *In the wonder of Christmas we find the Christ*
(a) There was a mystery about this child.
(b) There was a majesty about this child.

C. *At Christmas we find a choice*
(a) The action which has been taken by God.
(b) The answer we must be given by man.

The deep thoughts of Mary

Luke 2.19: 'Mary kept all these things, and pondered them in her heart'

A. *The wonder in her mind at the grace of God*
(a) What was said to her.
(b) What was said by her.

B. *The working in her life of the power of God*
(a) The protest which was offered by her.
(b) The prospect which was opened to her.

C. *The welcome in her heart to the will of God*
(a) The response which was without reservation.
(b) The result which was beyond calculation.

The boy Jesus at the temple: losing and finding Christ

Luke 2.41–52: 'Supposing him to have been in the company'

A. *The life which had been found*
(a) The wonderful companion he would be.
(b) The wonder of the communion they would have.

B. *The loss which should be feared*
(a) The carelessness through which she lost him.
(b) The ceaselessness with which she sought him.

C. *The Lord who must be faced*
(a) The thoughts revealed in what she said.
(b) The truth recalled in what he said.

What kind of a home did Jesus have?

Luke 2.51: 'And Jesus went down with them and was subject unto them'

A. *There would be happiness there*
(a) His consideration for others.
(b) His participation with others.

B. *There would be faithfulness there*
(a) Obedience would mark the way he lived.
(b) Diligence would mark the work he did.

C. *There would be loneliness there*
(a) The home would hold a tragedy for him.
(b) The home would produce a sympathy in him.

When God intervenes

Luke 3.1–22: A study on John the Baptist

A. *The message sent*
(a) The list of the people God failed to use.
(b) The life of the person God was to use.

B. *The movement sensed*
(a) The preparation by a preacher.
(b) The expectation in the people.

C. *The Master seen*
(a) The purpose with which he came.
(b) The people for whom he came.

The good habit of worshipping on the Lord's Day (1)

Luke 4.16: 'As his custom was, Jesus went into the synagogue on the sabbath day'
Hebrews 10.25: 'Not forsaking the assembling of ourselves together'

A. *The difficulties which hinder it*
(a) The trends and pressures of our times.
(b) The things and people in our lives.

B. *The discoveries which reward it*
(a) There are blessings which can be sought together.
(b) There are burdens which can be shared together.

C. *The disciplines which secure it*
(a) The bond we have in our hearts.
(b) The blend we have in our lives.

D. *The disobedience which neglects it*
(a) The life which has been expected of us.
(b) The loss which would be expensive to us.

The good habit of worshipping on the Lord's Day (2)

Luke 4.16

A. *No matter how busy our programmes might be*
(a) The involvement seen in the life of Christ.
(b) The appointment kept in the life of Christ.

B. *No matter how weary our bodies might be*
(a) Think how tired he would sometimes be.
(b) Think how he would always be there.

C. *No matter how empty the service might be*
(a) The worship he would bring to it.
(b) The witness he would bear through it.

Jesus – a preacher worth listening to

Luke 4.18

A. *A preacher worth listening to*
(a) His identity.
(b) His authority.

B. *A picture worth looking at*
(a) The method of the preacher.
(b) The message of the picture.

C. *A purpose worth living for*
(a) The involvement accepted by Christ.
(b) The equipment available to us.

The hands of Jesus

Luke 4.40: 'He laid his hands on every one of them'

A. *The people who were reached that way*
(a) How many they were.
(b) How busy he was.

B. *The purpose which was revealed that way*
(a) The motive in the heart of Christ.
(b) The message of the hands of Christ.

C. *The power which was released that way*
(a) The change wrought by his hands.
(b) The cost seen in his hands.

What is to be the measure of our giving?

Luke 6.38: 'Give, and it shall be given unto you; good measure, pressed down, and shaken together, and running over, shall men give into your bosom. For with the same measure that ye mete withal it shall be measured to you again.'

A. *Think of the opportunities which must be seized*
(a) We have so much to give away.
(b) There are so many to give to.

B. *Think of the overflow which should be spontaneous*
(a) There should be a lavishness in giving.
(b) There will be a happiness in giving.

C. *Think of the outcome which will be surprising*
(a) The development of character which will be ours.
(b) The enrichment of others through the gifts which will be received.

The compassion of Christ which should be reproduced in us

Luke 7.11–17

A. *Compassion sees*
(a) The tragedy which was observed by Christ.
(b) The sympathy which was aroused in Christ.

B. *Compassion speaks*
(a) The gentle intrusion it makes.
(b) The gracious intention it has.

C. *Compassion saves*
(a) The response compassion gets.
(b) The results compassion sees.

Jesus raises a dead young man to life

Luke 7.11–17: 'Young man, I say unto thee, arise'

A. *The miracle meant confrontation*
(a) What the confrontation would teach.
(b) How the confrontation was timed.

B. *The miracle meant transformation*
(a) The concern of the Master.
(b) The control by the Master.

C. *The miracle meant restoration*
(a) There was a restoration to life.
(b) There was a restoration to love.

Christian service

Luke 5.1–11

A. *A request which was challenging*
(a) Where they were told to go.
(b) What they were told to use.

B. *A response which was faltering*
(a) The reluctance which was shown initially by Peter.
(b) The obedience which was given ultimately by Peter.

C. *A result which was breathtaking*
(a) The extent of the success.
(b) The effect of their success.

Jesus, 'the friend of sinners'

Luke 7.34

A. *An amazing friendship*
(a) The Person he is.
(b) The people we are.

B. *A transforming friendship*
(a) How friendship shares.
(b) How friendship shapes.

C. *An enduring friendship*
(a) It is unchanging.
(b) It is unending.

Jesus is anointed by a sinful woman

Luke 7.47: 'She loved much'

A. *How close she came to her Lord*
(a) The report love heard.
(b) The resolve love makes.

B. *How much she gave to her Lord*
(a) The motive in her giving.
(b) The measure of her giving.

C. *How far she went for her Lord*
(a) Her critics who were resentful.
(b) Her courage which was rewarded.

The importance of 'How'

Luke 8.18

A   *The manner in which we hear*
(a) The opportunity which was shared.
(b) The diversity which was shown.

B.   *The motives behind the way in which we choose: Luke 14.7*
(a) The temptation which must be resisted.
(b) The exaltation which can be received.

C.   *The measure with which we give: Mark 12.41, Luke 21.1–4*
(a) How Christ is aware of our giving.
(b) How Christ will assess our giving.

The unwanted Christ

Luke 8.26–39

A.   *A life which was distressed*
(a) His helplessness.
(b) His harmfulness.

B.   *A land which was disturbed*
(a) Their amazement at what the Lord had done for the man.
(b) Their resentment at what he had done to their pigs.

C.   *A Lord who was dismissed*
(a) The request they presented to Christ.
(b) The respect they received from Christ.

Afraid of the truth

Luke 9.45: 'They feared to ask him'

    A. *They were afraid of what the truth might disclose*
(a) The person he might be.
(b) The purpose he might have.

    B. *They were afraid of what the truth might destroy*
(a) The picture they had formed of Christ.
(b) The pleasures they had found in Christ.

    C. *They were afraid of what the truth might demand*
(a) Acceptance of his word.
(b) Allegiance to his will.

Passing the tests of discipleship

Luke 9.57–62

    A. *The test of poverty*
(a) There is the possibility of deprivation.
(b) There is the certainty of compensation.

    B. *The test of urgency: verse 59*
(a) How casual the matter seemed to this man.
(b) How crucial the moment proved for this man.

    C. *The test of loyalty*
(a) The threat which others can be.
(b) The Throne which Jesus must have.

Failure in human relationships

Luke 10.25–37: Passing by on the other side

A. *A life which was seen to be in need*
(a) How personal was the hurt this man received.
(b) How practical was the help this man required.

B. *The eyes which were doomed to look in vain*
(a) The indifference shown.
(b) The inconvenience shirked.

C. *The hands which were quick to act in love*
(a) The trouble he was prepared to take.
(b) The time he was prepared to give.

The parable of the Good Samaritan

Luke 10.25–37: 'And thy neighbour'

A. *The misery to be seen*
(a) The dangers on the road.
(b) The despair in the soul.
(c) The damage to the life.

B. *The mentality to be shunned*
(a) These men were identified.
(b) These men were informed.
(c) These men were indifferent.

C. *The mercy to be shown*
(a) The heart which compassion fills.
(b) The hands which compassion needs.
(c) The hope which compassion brings.

A life which was going downhill

Luke 10.30–37: 'A certain man went down from Jerusalem to Jericho'

A. *The direction he took*
(a) His distance from the House of God.
(b) His descent from the heights of God.

B. *The disasters he met*
(a) The people who injured him.
(b) The people who ignored him.

C. *The deliverance he found*
(a) The compassion in the Samaritan's heart.
(b) The completion of the Samaritan's task.

The home-makers in Bethany

Luke 10.38

A. *Love's environment*
(a) We find love's delight in labouring.
(b) We find love's delight in listening.

B. *Love's bewilderment: John 11*
(a) How they were distressed.
(b) What they then discovered.

C. *Love's discernment: John 12*
(a) The wisdom love displays.
(b) The welcome love receives.

At the feet of Jesus

Luke 10.39

A. *We find Mary, in her love, sitting at the feet of her Lord*
(a) The proximity for which love longs.
(b) The intimacy in which love learns.

B. *We find Mary kneeling at the feet of her Lord: John 11*
(a) The anguish which filled Mary's heart.
(b) The answer which healed Mary's hurt.

C. *What we find Mary, in her love, doing at the feet of her Lord: John 12*
(a) She was able to share the moment of his need.
(b) She was able to show the measure of her love.

Too busy?

Luke 10.38–42: 'Martha was cumbered about with much serving'

A. *The Presence in which she was delighted*
(a) Her receiving of her Lord.
(b) Her rejoicing in her Lord.

B. *The pressures by which she was distracted*
(a) Think of her tasks which were demanding.
(b) Think of her thoughts which were disturbing.

C. *The priority to which she was directed*
(a) The busy-ness her Lord noticed.
(b) The blessedness her heart needed.

Prayer: a pattern, a parable, a promise

Luke 11.1–13

A. *The intimacy of prayer*
(a) The child I must be.
(b) The claim I will have.

B. *The urgency of prayer*
(a) The inadequacy of his resources.
(b) The importunity of his request.

C. *The certainty of prayer*
(a) The word of our Lord which we can trust.
(b) The way which we must leave to our Lord.

Some basic principles of true prayer

Luke 11.5–13

A. *The bankruptcy in which prayer is born*
(a) The demands faced by this man.
(b) The dismay felt by this man.

B. *The urgency by which prayer is marked*
(a) The priority this man was willing to give to prayer.
(b) The persistence this man was willing to show in prayer.

C. *The certainty on which prayer will rest*
(a) What has been contrasted in the teaching of Christ.
(b) What can be concluded from the teaching of Christ.

Jesus casts out a dumb spirit

Luke 11.14

A. *The restraint in his life observed*
(a) The life he had.
(b) The liberty he lacked.

B. *The release from his bonds desired*
(a) He was brought to Christ.
(b) He was blessed by Christ.

C. *The results for his Lord achieved*
(a) The witness given.
(b) The wonder created.

Sins of which Christian leaders should be wary

Luke 11.37–54

A. *Stressing the unimportant: verse 42*
(a) The importance assigned to some minor issues.
(b) The indifference assigned to some major issues.

B. *Seeking the unmerited: verse 43*
(a) The prominence they loved.
(b) The experience they lacked.

C. *Concealing the unworthy: verse 44*
(a) A deception which was deliberate.
(b) A presumption which was dangerous.

D. *Proclaiming the unfulfilled: verse 46*
(a) The obligations they laid on others.
(b) The obligations they left to others.

E. *Reverencing the unwanted: verse 47*
(a) The demand of orthodoxy which they were prepared to meet.
(b) The distance from reality which they were glad to maintain.

F. *Hindering the unenlightened: verse 52*
(a) The assumption made by Christ.
(b) The assertion made by Christ.

When does God call a man a fool?

Luke 12.13–21

    A.   *When a man mistakes himself for his God*
    (a) Look at the thoughts he had.
    (b) Think of the things he claimed.

    B.   *When he mistakes his body for his soul*
    (a) Note the goals he pursued.
    (b) Note the goods he possessed.

    C.   *When a man mistakes time for eternity*
    (a) Note the shortness of his pleasure.
    (b) Note the silence in his planning.

Gambling and covetousness

Luke 12.15: 'Take heed, and beware of covetousness'

    A.   *The meaning of gambling*
    (a) Can we find a statement in which it is defined?
    (b) Can we find a judgment to which it must submit?

    B.   *The motives we must face*
    (a) The motive of selfishness.
    (b) The motive of carelessness.

    C.   *The menace we must fear*
    (a) The harm it can do.
    (b) The hold it can get.

Job satisfaction in Christian service

Luke 12.37: 'Blessed are those servants'

A. *There must be a readiness about our Christian service: 'Let your loins be girded about'*
(a) God's servants must be ready for any task.
(b) God's servants must be ready at any time.

B. *There must be a holiness about our Christian living: 'Your lights burning'*
(a) Note the qualities of which the light speaks.
(b) Note the clarity with which the light shines.

C. *There must be a watchfulness about God's servants: 'Men that wait for their Lord'*
(a) The faithfulness of those who expect the coming of their Lord.
(b) The foolishness of those who neglect the coming of their Lord.

The barren fig tree (1)

Luke 13.1–10

A. *The environment which was privileged*
(a) The purpose he had for the tree.
(b) The provision he made for the tree.

B. *The disappointment which was prolonged*
(a) Note the patience shown.
(b) Note the poverty found.

C. *The judgment which was passed*
(a) The possible removal of the tree.
(b) The possible replacement of the tree.

D. *The postponement which was permitted*
(a) The labour which would mark it.
(b) The limit which would end it.

The barren fig tree (2)

Luke 13.1–10

A. *Where it was found*
(a) The attention it was bound to receive.
(b) The intention it was meant to fulfil.

B. *How it had failed*
(a) The passage of time.
(b) The wastage of space.

C. *What it must face*
(a) The process of correction.
(b) The prospect of rejection.

The barren fig tree (3)

Luke 13.1–10

A. *The claim which was made here*
(a) The person to whom the tree belonged.
(b) The purpose for which the tree existed.

B. *The charge which was brought here*
(a) The legitimate expectation.
(b) The ultimate condemnation.

C. *The chance which was given here*
(a) The treatment which was disturbing.
(b) The judgment which was decisive.

Christ's power to transform a life

Luke 13.10–17

A. *The plight in which she was found*
(a) She was helpless.
(b) She was hopeless.

B. *The power by which she was freed*
(a) The declaration of his purpose.
(b) The demonstration of his power.

C. *The praise with which she was filled*
(a) The resentment which some showed.
(b) The rejoicing which some shared.

The great banquet of the gospel (1)

Luke 14.15–24: 'A great supper'

A. *The preparations made for the gospel*
(a) The care shown in the preparation.
(b) The cost faced in the preparation.

B. *The invitation sent through the gospel*
(a) The clarity of it.
(b) The urgency of it.

C. *The revelation caused by the gospel*
(a) A revelation of human guilt.
(b) A revelation of divine grace.

The great banquet of the gospel (2)

Luke 14.15–24

A. *The love which was seen*
(a) The intention which love had.
(b) The invitation which love had sent.

B. *The lies which were said*
(a) The hypocrisy in their answers.
(b) The hostility of their attitude.

C. *The loss which was sad*
(a) Their pleas were accepted.
(b) Their places were filled.

A contract for Christian commitment

Luke 14.25–35: 'And there went great multitudes with him: and he turned, and said unto them . . .'

A. *The terms for which he asked*
(a) They meant loyalty to his Person.
(b) They meant identity with his purpose.

B. *The tasks to which he called them*
(a) He spoke of building.
(b) He spoke of battle.

C. *The truths of which he spoke*
(a) He spoke of what they would reject.
(b) He spoke of what they must renounce.

The parable of the lost sheep

Luke 15.1–7

    A. *The sheep was foolish*
    (a) In what it believed.
    (b) In how it behaved.

    B. *The sheep was frightened*
    (a) Because of its loneliness.
    (b) Because of its helplessness.

    C. *The sheep was found*
    (a) How determined the shepherd was.
    (b) How delighted the shepherd was.

Parables of the lost

Luke 15.1–32: Christ speaks of the lost sheep, the lost silver coin and the lost son

    A. *The purpose Christ has here*
    (a) There can be a contempt for men which Christ wanted to rebuke.
    (b) There is a concern for men here which Christ wanted to reveal.

    B. *The picture Christ draws here*
    (a) How different are the ways in which men are lost.
    (b) How desperate is the need of men who are lost.

    C. *The promise Christ gives here*
    (a) The promise of the action God has taken.
    (b) The promise of the answer which God gives.

The parable of the lost silver coin

Luke 15.8–10

   A.   *The responsibility assigned*
   (a) The blame for the loss of the coin.
   (b) The shame for the loss of the coin.

   B.   *The activity displayed*
   (a) The value of the silver.
   (b) The vigour of the search.

   C.   *The victory achieved*
   (a) The success of the task.
   (b) The sharing of the joy.

The parable of the lost son (1): the wonder of the Father's love

Luke 15.11–24

   A.   *The seeming helplessness of the love of God*
   (a) What the father's love had to permit the son to do.
   (b) How the father's love followed the son as he went away.

   B.   *The surging restlessness in the mind of God*
   (a) The suffering of love.
   (b) The wondering of love.

   C.   *The saving matchlessness of the grace of God*
   (a) The readiness with which it forgives.
   (b) The lavishness with which it provides.

The parable of the lost son (2): man's misguided search for happiness without God

Luke 15.11–24

A. *The desires which mastered the younger son*
(a) He was selfish in his desires.
(b) He was sincere in his desires.
(c) He was stubborn in his desires.

B. *The disasters which he met*
(a) He lost his wealth.
(b) He lost his freedom.
(c) He lost his self-respect.

C. *The discoveries which made him*
(a) He discovered the failure he was.
(b) He discovered the father he had.
(c) He discovered the fullness he sought.

The parable of the lost son (3): man in revolt

Luke 15.11–24

A. *The rebel he was*
(a) The active dislike of his father's control.
(b) The achieved distance from his father's control.

B. *The results he faced*
(a) The liberty he lost.
(b) The poverty he found.

C. *The return he made*
(a) The discoveries which caused his return.
(b) The destiny which crowned his return.

The parable of the lost son (4): the man who nearly made a mess of his life

Luke 15.11–24

A. *The convictions which swayed him*
(a) The authority he was determined to discard.
(b) The ability he was determined to display.

B. *The confusion which swamped his life*
(a) The unexpected failure which shattered him.
(b) The unexplored future which frightened him.

C. *The conversion which saved him*
(a) The truth he faced.
(b) The path he found.

The elder son (1): the sin of self-pity

Luke 15.25–32: 'Thou never gavest me a kid'

A. *The curse of self-pity*
(a) It destroys our happiness.
(b) It destroys our usefulness.
(c) It destroys our one-ness.

B. *The cause of self-pity*
(a) His restricted vision.
(b) His distorted values.
(c) His outraged virtue.

C. *The cure of self-pity*
(a) He would have the father's abiding presence.
(b) He would enjoy the father's abundant provision.
(c) He would fulfil the father's achieved purpose.

The elder son (2): the man who did not know he was lost

Luke 15.25–32

A. *His lostness was revealed by the return of a lost soul*
(a) Think of the wonder of that.
(b) Think of the welcome of that.

B. *His lostness was revealed by the resolve of a little mind*
(a) How restricted he was in outlook.
(b) How resentful he was towards others.

C. *His lostness was revealed in the rebuke of a loving heart*
(a) There had been a fitness in their rejoicing.
(b) There had been a failure in their relationship.

The elder son (3): the man who did not know he was lost

Luke 15.25–32

A. *His uprightness was undeniable*
(a) The familiarity he enjoyed with his father.
(b) The fidelity he displayed to his father.

B. *His attitudes which were indefensible*
(a) The tragic wrongness of his attitude to what had happened.
(b) The basic weakness of his attitude to what had happened.

C. *His solitude which was inescapable*
(a) The stranger he knew himself to be.
(b) The anger he allowed himself to feel.

The Christian's use of money

Luke 16.1–14: 'Make to yourselves friends [by means of riches, but when they fail] they may receive you into everlasting habitations'

A. *The certainty we must face: 'When they fail'*
(a) The love which is perilous.
(b) The loss which is obvious.

B. *The opportunity we must use*
(a) How useful money can be.
(b) How grateful many can be.

C. *The possibilities we can see*
(a) The form our service can take.
(b) The fruit our service will have.

Forgiving others

Luke 17.3–4

A. *It is commanded*
(a) The motivation I will have.
(b) The condemnation I may earn.

B. *It is conditioned*
(a) The right to rebuke is stated.
(b) The need to repent is stressed.

C. *It is complete*
(a) No restriction in time.
(b) No reservation in kind.

The importance of saying 'Thank you' to Jesus (1)

Luke 17.11–19

A. *How rich was the blessing which provoked his thankfulness*
(a) How desperate his need.
(b) How adequate his help.

B. *How right was the return which expressed his thankfulness*
(a) The place taken by man.
(b) The praise given to God.

C. *How rude was the failure which neglected thankfulness*
(a) There is something shameful here.
(b) There is something hurtful here.

The importance of saying 'Thank you' to Jesus (2) (a talk for children)

Luke 17.11–19

A. *What this man was told*
(a) The need which troubled him.
(b) The news which thrilled him.

B. *How he had to trust*
(a) The word they were given.
(b) The way they were healed.

C. *How he gave thanks*
(a) What he had received.
(b) How he would rejoice.

An Advent message

Luke 17.20–37: 'As it was in the days of Noah'

A. *The wickedness which had provoked the judgment of God*
(a) The guilt of man which was undeniable.
(b) The grace of God which was unacceptable.

B. *The faithfulness which had marked the people of God*
(a) The righteousness of their lives.
(b) The restlessness in their hearts.

C. *The suddenness of the action of God*
(a) The futility of trying to find out when he will come.
(b) The finality of what will happen when he does come.

Religion – counterfeit and true

Luke 18.9–14

A. *Religion is here (verse 10)*
(a) There are places associated with religion.
(b) There are practices associated with religion.

B. *Rejection is here*
(a) The assurance displayed by the Pharisee.
(b) The acceptance denied to the Pharisee.

C. *Redemption is here*
(a) The request of the publican.
(b) The return of the publican.

Grasping the opportunity of a lifetime

Luke 18.37: 'Jesus of Nazareth passeth by'

A. *The chance given to him*
(a) The reports he had heard.
(b) The request he made.

B. *The choice made by him*
(a) In spite of discouragement.
(b) In spite of entanglement.

C. *The change wrought in him*
(a) How frankly the Lord was faced.
(b) How fully his need was met.

The story of Zacchaeus (1): the need to hurry

Luke 19.5: 'Make haste, and come down; for today I must abide at thy house'

A. *The chance which was given to Zacchaeus*
(a) The curiosity which had been aroused by Christ.
(b) The opportunity which had been arranged by Christ.

B. *The choice which was asked of him*
(a) The request which Jesus made.
(b) The response which Jesus got.

C. *The change which was seen in him*
(a) The transformation of his life.
(b) The exhortation of his Lord.

The story of Zacchaeus (2): the unexpectedness of Jesus Christ

Luke 19.1–10

> A. *The unexpectedness of the man involved with Christ*
> (a) The longing this man had in his heart.
> (b) The length to which this man went in his search.
>
> B. *The unexpectedness of the message spoken by Christ*
> (a) The intimacy desired by Christ.
> (b) The urgency displayed by Christ.
>
> C. *The unexpectedness of the miracle wrought by Christ*
> (a) His acceptance of Christ.
> (b) His assurance from Christ.

The story of Zacchaeus (3): a day full of surprises

Luke 19.1–10

> A. *A surprising resolve*
> (a) The wish to see Christ.
> (b) The way he saw Christ.
>
> B. *A surprising request*
> (a) The desire in the heart of Christ.
> (b) The delight in the heart of Zacchaeus.
>
> C. *A surprising result*
> (a) What was said.
> (b) What was seen.

The story of Zacchaeus (4): the importance of today

Luke 19.5: 'Make haste, and come down; for today I must abide at thy house'

A. *Today can be an opportunity for responding to the grace of God*
(a) The request by Christ.
(b) The response to Christ.

B. *Today it may be necessary to react to the voice of God: 'Today, if you will hear his voice' (Ps. 95.7–8)*
(a) Here we have a sense of wonder.
(b) Here we have a note of danger.

C. *Today may show us our responsibility to relate to the will of God (Matt. 21.28)*
(a) The plan God has for this world.
(b) The place God has for us in his work.

D. *Today may bring us rejoicing into the presence of God: 'Today, thou shalt be with me in paradise' (Luke 23.43)*
(a) We do not know when that day will come for us.
(b) We do know what that day will hold for us.

Homes which were blessed by Christ

A. *The home of Zacchaeus, where Christ was welcomed: Luke 19.5–6*
(a) What Christ said to this man.
(b) What Christ did for this man.

B. *The home of Jairus, where Christ was wanted: Luke 8.41–56*
(a) Jairus didn't know what to do.
(b) Jairus did know whom to go to.

C. *The home at Bethany, where Christ was worshipped: Luke 10.38–42*
(a) The proximity desired by love.
(b) The activity displayed by love.

A Palm Sunday meditation (1)

Luke 19.38: 'Blessed be the King that cometh in the name of the Lord'

A. *How scriptural the affirmation was*
(a) The kingship which was attributed to him.
(b) The kingship which was accepted by him.

B. *How superficial the acclamation proved*
(a) The truth which thrilled their hearts.
(b) The threats which stilled their praise.

C. *How sensational the application is*
(a) The coronation of our Lord in our lives.
(b) The transformation of our lives by his grace.

A Palm Sunday meditation (2): a plea for enthusiasm

Luke 19.40: 'If these should hold their peace, the stones would immediately cry out'

A. *The record we have read*
(a) How spontaneous this enthusiasm was.
(b) How infectious this enthusiasm was.

B. *The reasons we can find*
(a) The truth they had grasped about him.
(b) The thanks they must give to him.

C. *The rebuke we should heed*
(a) The attempts the critics made to silence the songs.
(b) The answer they got.

God can weep

Luke 19.41: 'And when he was come near, he beheld the city, and wept over it'

A. *He came*
(a) The different reasons men had for coming to the city.
(b) The definite reasons he had for coming to the city.

B. *He saw*
(a) He saw the crowds in their need.
(b) He saw the cross which would meet that need.

C. *He wept*
(a) He knew how men would respond.
(b) He knew how men would reject him.

Jesus and the collection

Luke 21.1–4

A. *Where he sat*
(a) What the money would reveal.
(b) Why the money is required.

B. *What he saw*
(a) The least important person.
(b) The least impressive gift.

C. *What he said*
(a) His evaluation of the gifts.
(b) His commendation of the giver.

The ministry of the un-named

Luke 22.12: 'He shall show you a large upper room, furnished'

A. *How frequently this ministry was relied on*
(a) There was never any doubt in Christ's mind.
(b) There was never any delay in Christ's work.

B. *How faithfully this ministry was rendered*
(a) There was a willingness about it.
(b) There was a thoroughness about it.

C. *How kindly this ministry was rewarded*
(a) They were rewarded by the Presence they secured.
(b) They were rewarded by the purposes they served.

A Communion meditation (1)

Luke 22.15: 'With desire I have desired to eat this passover with you'

A. *The company which love craves*
(a) The preparation by the hands of men.
(b) The expectation in the heart of Christ.

B. *The fidelity to which love speaks*
(a) The wounds of love.
(b) The work of love.

C. *The memory in which love lives*
(a) The simplicity which is seen here.
(b) The perpetuity which is sought here.

A Communion meditation (2)

Luke 22.19: 'This do in remembrance of me'

A. *The wish to be remembered*
(a) That heart is dead where the wish is not present.
(b) The hurt is deep where the wish is not granted.

B. *The work to be remembered*
(a) How deeply blessed we are through his work for us.
(b) How dearly bought was his work for us.

C. *The way to be remembered*
(a) Love wants to be remembered frequently.
(b) Love wants to be remembered faithfully.

Jesus' gratitude towards the disciples

Luke 22.28: 'Ye are they which have continued with me in my temptations'

A. *How few their numbers were*
(a) How insignificant to the world.
(b) How inadequate for the work.

B. *How faithful their natures were*
(a) The pressures on their lives.
(b) The presence of their Lord.

C. *How fragrant their names were*
(a) Their recognition by the Master.
(b) Their recollection by the Church.

The trial of faith

Luke 22.31–32: 'I have prayed for thee, that thy faith fail not'

    A.   *The assailant he would meet*
    (a) His target.
    (b) His tactics.

    B.   *The assurance he would have*
    (a) The divine control.
    (b) The divine concern.

    C.   *The assessment Christ would make*
    (a) The battering of a servant.
    (b) The bettering of the service.

'And Peter followed afar off'

Luke 22.54

    A.   *The contact with his Lord he had enjoyed*
    (a) How Peter had loved it.
    (b) How Peter had lost it.

    B.   *The contempt of his friends his lies evoked*
    (a) He had said so much for so long.
    (b) He had sunk so low for so little.

    C.   *The concern for his soul the Lord expressed*
    (a) The trust revealed by that look.
    (b) The tears released by that look.

A Good Friday meditation (1)

Luke 23.33: 'And when they were come to the place, which is called Calvary, there they crucified him'

A. *The centrality of the cross*
(a) The cross was central in the thinking of Christ.
(b) The cross is central in the teaching of the Church.

B. *The finality of the cross*
(a) There was an element of necessity about his death.
(b) There was an element of sufficiency about his death.

C. *The regality of the cross*
(a) The authority which men had always sensed in him.
(b) The identity which men now clearly saw in him.

A Good Friday meditation (2): a remarkable prayer

Luke 23.42: 'Lord, remember me when thou comest into thy kingdom'

A. *The despair in which his faith was born*
(a) There was a confession of his sin.
(b) There was a concern with his God.

B. *The discernment with which his faith was blessed*
(a) The contact he had with Christ.
(b) The conviction he reached about Christ.

C. *The deliverance to which he was brought*
(a) How sure was the promise which was made.
(b) How sweet was the Presence which he would know.

The road to Emmaus

Luke 24.13–35

   A. *The problems which crushed these men*
   (a) How differently things had turned out from what they had expected.
   (b) How despondent they were in what they now believed.

   B. *The Presence which changed them*
   (a) The Person he was.
   (b) The purpose he had.

   C. *The prospect which cheered them*
   (a) The need which they must now serve.
   (b) The news which they must now spread.

An Easter meditation (1)

Luke 24.15: 'Jesus himself drew near, and went with them'

   A. *The Person of Jesus Christ*
   (a) There is an explanation we must find for the Person of Jesus Christ.
   (b) There are implications we must face concerning the Person of Jesus Christ.

   B. *The Purpose of Jesus Christ*
   (a) His purpose was to reveal the love of God.
   (b) His purpose was to redeem the lives of men.

   C. *The Presence of Jesus Christ*
   (a) The difference which his presence will make in our lives.
   (b) The permanence which his presence will have in our lives.

An Easter meditation (2): the journey from doubt to faith

Luke 24.29

A. *Their bewilderment*
(a) Their conception of the Christ.
(b) Their rejection of the cross.

B. *Their enlightenment*
(a) The divine presence enjoyed by them.
(b) The divine purpose explained to them.

C. *Their astonishment*
(a) The opportunity they seized.
(b) The discovery they shared.

An Easter prayer

Luke 24.29: 'Abide with us: for it is toward evening, and the day is far spent'

A. *Their walk with Christ*
(a) The contact he sought with them.
(b) The concern he had for them.

B. *Their wish for Christ*
(a) The illumination they had found.
(b) The termination they now feared.

C. *Their words to Christ*
(a) The request they made to him.
(b) The response they got from him.

A message of hope for the fallen

Luke 24.34: 'The Lord is risen indeed, and hath appeared to Simon'

A. *The sense of surprise that is here*
(a) The despair which life can hold.
(b) The desire which love will have.

B. *The shroud of silence*
(a) How exclusive the meeting was.
(b) How effective the meeting was.

C. *The sequel of service*
(a) The love which Peter had for his Lord.
(b) The lives which he won for his Lord.

John

The coming of Christ

John 1.11–13: 'He came unto his own, and his own received him not. But as many as received him, to them gave he power to become the sons of God'

A. *The ignorance which his coming dispelled*
(a) The initiative God takes.
(b) The intention God has.

B. *The indifference which his coming exposed*
(a) The disturbance they resented.
(b) The destruction they planned.

C. *The experience which his coming bestowed*
(a) It means receiving the Christ.
(b) It means becoming a child.

Becoming a child of God
John 1.11–13

A. *There is a warning to heed – we do not become children of God because of:*
(a) The parents we have.
(b) The efforts we make.
(c) The pressures we face.

B. *There is a welcome to give*
(a) The chance he will give to us.
(b) The choice he will ask of us.
(c) The change he will make in us.

C. *There is a wonder to know*
(a) The access to the Father in which the child can rejoice.
(b) The goodness of the Father on which the child can rely.
(c) The likeness of the Father which the child will reflect.

The Incarnation (1)
John 1.14: 'The Word was made flesh, and dwelt among us, (and we beheld his glory, the glory as of the only begotten of the Father,) full of grace and truth'

A. *The possibility of this must be admitted*
(a) In the light of the limited extent of man's knowledge.
(b) In the light of the basis of man's knowledge (initially all is revealed).

B. *The necessity of this must be asserted*
(a) Human love demands the making of such a revelation.
(b) Human life determines the manner of such a revelation.

C. *The authority of this must be accepted*
(a) There is a submission which must be given to Christ.
(b) There is a salvation which may be received through Christ.

The Incarnation (2)

John 1.14

A. *The humanity through which the glory shone*
(a) There is a mystery which can be seen.
(b) There is a ministry which must be shared (the Word becomes flesh again in the Christian).

B. *The proximity at which the glory showed*
(a) The contact which love longs to have with those it loves.
(b) The content which love longs to share with those it loves.

C. *The divinity of which the glory spoke*
(a) The wonder evoked.
(b) The worship expressed.

Jesus manifests his glory

John 1.14: '(We beheld his glory, the glory as of the only begotten of the Father), full of grace and truth.'
John 2.11: 'This beginning of miracles did Jesus in Cana of Galilee, and manifested forth his glory; and his disciples believed in him'
In many places in the Gospels Jesus took something humble and manifested his glory through it.

A. *He took the water at Cana: this speaks of the unexciting duties in life*
(a) There is a monotony in life which can be dull.
(b) There can be a miracle in life which is divine.

B. *He took a boy's forgotten lunch: this speaks of the seemingly unimportant details in life*
(a) How little that packet of lunch seemed.
(b) How many that little packet of lunch served.

C. *He took some dust and opened a blind man's eyes: this speaks of the unrelieved darkness in life*
(a) Think of the depths of this man's need.
(b) Think of the dirt on the Master's hand.

D. *He took a towel and washed the disciples' feet: this speaks of the unjustified demands in life*
(a) There was no trace of rightness in his doing that work.
(b) There was no tinge of resentment as he did it.

E. *He took a cross and died on it: this speaks of the ungranted desires in life*
(a) There was a bitter onslaught.
(b) There was a blessed outcome.

Christmas – a time for greetings

John 1.14: 'The Word was made flesh, and dwelt among us'

    A. *The Sender of the greeting*
    (a) Consider his divinity.
    (b) Consider his authority.

    B. *The Bearer of the greeting*
    (a) Consider the method employed.
    (b) Consider the message conveyed.

    C. *The reader of the greeting*
    (a) Consider the arrival of the greeting.
    (b) Consider the acceptance of the greeting.

A study of John the Baptist

John 1.23: 'I am the voice of one crying in the wilderness'

    A. *The solitude he experienced*
    (a) His communion with his God.
    (b) His rejection of his world.

    B. *The silence he ended*
    (a) The testimony which was authentic.
    (b) The toleration which was attacked.

    C. *The Saviour he exalted*
    (a) The relationship which would be restored through Christ.
    (b) The resources which would be available in Christ.

Jesus, the Lamb of God (1)

John 1.29: 'Behold the Lamb of God, which taketh away the sin of the world'

A. *The load of sin*
(a) How heavy the burden can be.
(b) How helpless the bearer can be.

B. *The Lamb of God*
(a) The meaning of the name.
(b) The meeting of a need.

C. *The look of faith*
(a) The truth we need to know about him.
(b) The trust we need to place in him.

Jesus, the Lamb of God (2)

John 1.29,36

A. *The Person seen here*
(a) His destiny seen here.
(b) His deity seen here.

B. *The purpose served here*
(a) The type to which John refers.
(b) The truth to which John relates.

C. *The problem solved here*
(a) The relationship adjusted by Christ.
(b) The resources available in Christ.

The first disciples (1)

John 1.29–42

   A.   *The message they heard with their ears*
   (a) What they were able to learn.
   (b) Where they were asked to look.

   B.   *The meeting they had with their Lord*
   (a) How Jesus saw them.
   (b) What Jesus said to them.

   C.   *The moment they held in their hearts*
   (a) The conviction which gripped their hearts.
   (b) The compulsion which constrained their wills.

The first disciples (2)

John 1.35–42

   A.   *There was proclamation*
   (a) They were attracted to John.
   (b) They were directed to Jesus.

   B.   *There was confrontation*
   (a) Note what Jesus said to them.
   (b) Note what Jesus showed to them.

   C.   *There was transformation*
   (a) They faced a mastery to which they must bow.
   (b) They found a ministry in which they would share.

'What are you looking for?' – a suitable question for a communion service

John 1.38: 'What seek ye?'

A. *We can expect to find God here*
(a) Think of the Lord who presides at the table.
(b) Think of the Lord who provides the table.

B. *We can expect to find guilt here*
(a) Think of the condemnation which is faced by the sinner.
(b) Think of the hesitation which may be felt by the sinner.

C. *We can expect to find grace here*
(a) Think of the sufficiency of the work which Christ did for us.
(b) Think of the simplicity of the way which Christ planned for us.

Bringing others to Jesus

John 1.42: 'He brought him to Jesus'

A. *The wonder of the message*
(a) The channel God used.
(b) The challenge men face.

B. *The witness to the Master*
(a) The response which some made.
(b) The resolve which some formed.

C. *The working of a miracle*
(a) The bringing was a miracle.
(b) The blessing was a miracle.

Andrew (1) – one of the first disciples

John 1.29–41

A. *Andrew the persistent man: he knew how to use his tongue*
(a) He was convinced of the wonder of his Lord.
(b) He was convincing in his witness to his Lord.

B. *Andrew the observant man: he knew how to use his eyes (John 6.5–14)*
(a) The problem which confronted them.
(b) The Person who concerned him.

C. *Andrew the listening man: he knew how to use his ears (John 12.20–22)*
(a) He was a good listener.
(b) He was a good leader.

Andrew (2) – The first evangelist

John 1.42: 'He brought him to Jesus'

A. *The man he was*
(a) The discovery he had made.
(b) The identity he could use.

B. *The work he did*
(a) He went to his brother.
(b) He walked with his brother.

C. *The goal he reached*
(a) The silence of the sinner.
(b) The statement by the Saviour.

Andrew (3): his spiritual know-how

John 1.42

A. *He knew how to use his tongue*
(a) The Person of whom Andrew was ready to speak.
(b) The person to whom Andrew was ready to speak.

B. *He knew how to use his eyes: John 6.5–14*
(a) The problem which could be sensed by anyone.
(b) The problem which could be solved by only One.

C. *He knew how to use his ears: John 12.20–23*
(a) Note the request with which they had come.
(b) Note the response with which they were met.

Jesus' first miracle (1)

John 2.1–12: 'And Jesus was called to the marriage'

A. *The invitation*
(a) The request being made to him.
(b) The response they got from him.

B. *The interruption*
(a) The worry which crept in.
(b) The wisdom which cried out.

C. *The intervention*
(a) The seeming irrelevance of his words.
(b) The swift obedience to his will.

Jesus' first miracle (2)

John 2.1–12

A. *Christ was wanted there*
(a) The presence of the Lord had been desired by them.
(b) The problem in their lives could be referred to him.

B. *Christ was working there*
(a) The control he must have.
(b) The consent we must give.

C. *Christ was worshipped there*
(a) The truth learned by them.
(b) The trust placed in him.

Jesus' first miracle (3): an insight into Christian service

John 2.9: 'But the servants which drew the water knew'

A. *The anxieties which troubled their minds*
(a) They were concerned about their resources, which seemed inadequate.
(b) They were concerned about the reproach which seemed inevitable.

B. *The activities which tested their faith*
(a) The apparent uselessness of Christ's request.
(b) The absolute thoroughness of their response.

C. *The adequacy which thrilled their souls*
(a) The mystery which was baffling.
(b) The ministry which was blessed.

The importance of the new birth (1)

John 3.7: 'Ye must be born again'

A. *A problem which is baffling*
(a) The nature of man.
(b) The failure of man.

B. *A process which is humbling*
(a) To admit my need.
(b) To accept God's gift.

C. *A prospect which is thrilling*
(a) To experience an abundance which will meet my every need.
(b) To enjoy an assurance which will still my every fear.

The importance of the new birth (2)

John 3.7

A. *The pathway by which Nicodemus had come*
(a) The inadequacy of his conception of Christ.
(b) The timidity of his confession to Christ.
(c) The sincerity of his coming to Christ.

B. *The precepts to which Nicodemus must yield*
(a) The authority of the Speaker.
(b) The necessity of the experience.
(c) The severity of the language.

C. *The process through which Nicodemus could live*
(a) The wish he must have.
(b) The way he must come.
(c) The world he could know.

The importance of the new birth (3)

John 3.7

A. *The authority which proclaimed it*
(a) The authority was royal.
(b) The audience was respectable.

B. *The absurdity which seemed to preclude it*
(a) How desirable it was.
(b) How impossible it seemed.

C. *The agency which procures it*
(a) The commencement of the new life.
(b) The development of the new life.

The importance of the new birth (4)

John 3.7

A. *The way Nicodemus came*
(a) He came personally.
(b) He came purposefully.

B. *The words Nicodemus heard*
(a) The authority with which Christ spoke.
(b) The necessity of which Christ spoke.

C. *The world Nicodemus found*
(a) He heard of a new realm which he could enter.
(b) He heard of a new rule to which he must submit.

The importance of the new birth (5): Nicodemus – the man who should have known better

John 3.10: 'Art thou a master of Israel, and knowest not these things?'

    A.   *Where Nicodemus was found*
    (a) He was instructed in the word of God.
    (b) He was involved in the work of God.

    B.   *How Nicodemus had failed*
    (a) He must have been aware of his need.
    (b) He may have been afraid of the way.

    C.   *What Nicodemus had to face*
    (a) There had to be a willingness to respond on his part.
    (b) There was a readiness to reveal on Christ's part.

The Holy Spirit: a talk for children

    A.   *The Bible speaks of the Holy Spirit as a wind which blows: John 3.8*
    (a) We can't see the wind.
    (b) We can feel the wind.

    B.   *The Bible speaks of the Holy Spirit as a fire which blazes: Matt. 3.11*
    (a) What the fire burns out.
    (b) What the fire burns in.

    C.   *The Bible speaks of the Holy Spirit as a gift which blesses: Acts 2.38*
    (a) The Holy Spirit is a living gift.
    (b) The Holy Spirit is a loving gift.

The cross seen through the eyes of Christ

John 3.14–15: 'As Moses lifted up the serpent in the wilderness, even so must the Son of man be lifted up: that whosoever believeth in him should not perish, but have eternal life'

A.   *Sovereignty is here*
(a) The plan of salvation was designed by God.
(b) The plan of salvation was declared by man.

B.   *Simplicity is here*
(a) The message was so simple that everyone could understand it.
(b) The way was so simple that anyone could undertake it.

C.   *Sufficiency is here*
(a) The message was inclusive of all men.
(b) The message was effective for all sin.

The greatest text in the Bible (1)

John 3.16: 'For God so loved the world, that he gave his only begotten Son, that whosoever believeth in him should not perish, but have everlasting life'

A.   *The greatest love we can ever know*
(a) The importance which love gives to a life.
(b) The difference which love makes to a life.

B.   *The greatest gift we can ever have*
(a) The desire love has to give.
(b) The demand love meets in giving.

C.   *The greatest choice we can ever make*
(a) The respect for us which God shows.
(b) The response from us which God seeks.

The greatest text in the Bible (2)

John 3.16

    A.   *The attitude revealed in the cross*
    (a) The world embraced by that love.
    (b) The wonder evoked by that love.

    B.   *The action recorded here*
    (a) Christ was given to die on the cross.
    (b) Christ is given to dwell in our lives.

    C.   *The answer required here*
    (a) The simplicity of God's way.
    (b) The security through God's word.

The greatest text in the Bible (3)

John 3.16

    A.   *The grounds on which my faith can rest*
    (a) What most people believe.
    (b) What most people forget.

    B.   *The gifts by which my needs are met*
    (a) The problems which have baffled the minds of men.
    (b) The Person who can transform the lives of men.

    C.   *The goal to which my life will lead*
    (a) The final enemy who has to be faced.
    (b) The total victory which Christ has won.

The greatest text in the Bible (4): the giving of love

John 3.16

    A.   *The desire which constrains the giving of love*
    (a) The happiness the gift will bring.
    (b) The usefulness the gift will have.

    B.   *The demand which confronts the giving of love*
    (a) How costly the gift may prove.
    (b) How gladly the price is paid.

    C.   *The delight which completes the giving of love*
    (a) How glad love is when the gift is received.
    (b) How sad love is when the gift is refused.

Jesus and the Samaritan woman

John 4.4–42

    A.   *The setting for what happened that day*
    (a) The people the woman passed on the way.
    (b) The Person she found at the well.

    B.   *The secret of what happened that day*
    (a) The offer he made to her.
    (b) The answer she gave to him.

    C.   *The sequel to what happened that day*
    (a) The love which must speak of Christ.
    (b) The lives which were brought to Christ.

Revival at Sychar

John 4.4–42

   A.   *A note of warning*
   (a) Were the disciples prejudiced?
   (b) Were the disciples preoccupied?

   B.   *A sense of wonder*
   (a) Think of the grace revealed.
   (b) Think of the gift received.

   C.   *A place of witness*
   (a) The Person who had borne her witness.
   (b) The people who were blessed through her witness.

When Jesus was tired

John 4.6: 'Jesus therefore, being wearied with his journey, sat . . . on the well'

   A.   *A Christ who was tired*
   (a) The compulsion which drove him.
   (b) The exertion which drained him.

   B.   *A Christ who was talking*
   (a) His need of her.
   (b) Her need of him.

   C.   *A Christ who was thrilled*
   (a) He was thrilled with the response in one life.
   (b) He was thrilled with the results in other lives.

The progress of faith

John 4.46–54

A. *Faith hears*
(a) The need he had.
(b) The news he heard.

B. *Faith seeks*
(a) The duration of the search.
(b) The desperation in his heart.

C. *Faith pleads*
(a) The reality of his faith had been proved.
(b) The quality of his faith was being probed.

D. *Faith rests*
(a) Note the prayer which ceased.
(b) Note the peace which came.

'Wilt thou be made whole?'

John 5.6

A. *This man had become accustomed to his lot*
(a) The expectancy with which he used to come.
(b) The lethargy in which he was now sunk.

B. *This man was accosted by his Lord*
(a) Note the tragedy Jesus saw in him.
(b) Note the honesty Jesus sought from him.

C. *What was accomplished in his life*
(a) New resources were brought to bear on his life.
(b) New requirements were being asked by his Lord.

'I am the bread of life'

John 6.35

   A.   *The claim which must arrest me*
   (a) The Name he claims to bear.
   (b) The needs he claims to meet.

   B.   *The Christ who would indwell me*
   (a) He is a living Person.
   (b) He brings a lasting presence.

   C.   *The choice which now confronts me*
   (a) The constraint which love applies.
   (b) The consent which love awaits.

The message of the fragments which remained

John 6.12–13: '"Gather up the fragments that remain, that nothing be lost." Therefore they gathered them together, and filled twelve baskets with the fragments.'

   A.   *There is no shortage when Christ is at work*
   (a) The needless anxiety of the disciples.
   (b) The boundless adequacy of the Lord.

   B.   *There is no wastage when Christ is at work*
   (a) How careful the Master was.
   (b) How useful the fragments were.

   C.   *There is no garbage when Christ is at work*
   (a) How thoughtful Christ was of others.
   (b) How grateful others were to Christ.

Rivers of living water

John 7.37–39: 'If any man thirst, let him come unto me, and drink. He that believeth on me . . . out of his [innermost being] shall flow rivers of living water (this spake he of the Spirit)'

A. *How arresting the offer was*
(a) How inclusive the offer was: 'If any man'.
(b) How exclusive the offer was: 'If any man thirst'.

B. *How abounding the supply was*
(a) Note its dimension: 'the rivers'.
(b) Note its direction: 'out of'.

C. *How abiding the results were*
(a) The difference which water makes.
(b) The distance which water travels.

A woman caught in adultery

John 8.2–11: 'Neither do I condemn thee: go, and sin no more'

A. *The fairness of Jesus*
(a) He did not deny the charge.
(b) He would not limit the charge.

B. *The kindness of Jesus*
(a) We see this in the privacy he sought for her.
(b) We see this in the courtesy he showed to her.

C. *The forgiveness of Jesus*
(a) He could see a change in her heart.
(b) He could see a cross on a hill.

D. *The holiness of Jesus*
(a) Something had to stop in her life.
(b) Something could then start in her life.

The light of the world

John 8.12: 'I am the light of the world: he that followeth me shall not walk in darkness, but shall have the light of life'

A. *The supremacy which Christ claims*
(a) In Christ there is a splendour which will excel.
(b) In Christ there is a splendour which will expose.

B. *The proximity which Christ seeks*
(a) The intimacy he wants us to enjoy.
(b) The authority he asks us to obey.

C. *The security which Christ gives*
(a) Avoidance of the perils which can destroy our lives.
(b) Assurance of a Presence which can direct our lives.

Freedom in Christ

John 8.36: 'If the Son . . . shall make you free, ye shall be free indeed'

A. *Freedom in Christ from the blunders which can blight a man's life*
(a) The decisions my life will hold.
(b) The direction my life can have.

B. *Freedom in Christ from the burdens which can break a man's heart*
(a) There are burdens man cannot bear.
(b) There are burdens man need not bear.

C. *Freedom in Christ from the bondage which can bind a man's soul*
(a) The tyranny imposed by sin.
(b) The liberty enjoyed through Christ.

What Jesus has to say about himself

John 8.42: 'I came from God'

A. *The Person he was*
(a) His conviction about his deity.
(b) His conviction about his destiny.

B. *The purpose he had*
(a) The plight of the world.
(b) The price of the way.

C. *The problem he is*
(a) The destruction resented by men.
(b) The decision required of men.

They asked, 'How?' and he answered, 'Jesus!'

John 9.10–11

A. *This miracle records the activity of Christ*
(a) The real presence of Christ.
(b) The redemptive purpose of Christ.

B. *This miracle presumes the authority of Christ*
(a) The control of the master.
(b) The consent of the man.

C. *This miracle portrays the adequacy of Christ*
(a) The curiosity he evoked.
(b) The loyalty he portrayed.

The doorway to salvation

John 10.9: 'I am the door: by me if any man enter in, he shall be saved, and shall go in and out, and find pasture'

A. *The sovereignty which is claimed by Christ*
(a) The imperative which men must accept.
(b) The alternatives which men will attempt.

B. *The security which is pledged by Christ*
(a) The direction which my life must take.
(b) The protection which my life will have.

C. *The serenity which is gained through Christ*
(a) The anxiety from which my mind is released.
(b) The activity for which my strength is renewed.

Good shepherding

John 10.1–31

A. *The good shepherd speaks of 'my sheep'*
(a) The shepherd's responsibility must be assessed.
(b) The shepherd's relationship must be achieved.

B. *The good shepherd speaks of 'my voice'*
(a) There must be a hearing of the voice of the shepherd.
(b) There must be a heeding of the voice of the shepherd.

C. *The good shepherd speaks of 'my hand'*
(a) The dangers of which the shepherd is aware.
(b) The demands for which the shepherd is prepared.

D. *The good shepherd speaks of 'my life'*
(a) The life of service from which there is no release.
(b) The life of sacrifice to which there is no limit.

E. *The good shepherd speaks of 'my Father'*
(a) The shepherd is thinking of the trust which has been placed in him.
(b) The shepherd is thinking of the task which will be completed by him.

When love is tried and tested

John Chapter 11: the story of Lazarus being raised from death

    A.   *The trials through which love must pass*
    (a) The debt which Christ owed to that home.
    (b) The doubts which Christ created in those hearts.

    B.   *The tarrying from which love would shrink*
    (a) The deliberate delay we see here.
    (b) The ultimate desire which is shown here.

    C.   *The triumph in which love will share*
    (a) The anger of Christ.
    (b) The action of Christ.

Martha, Mary and Lazarus

John 11.5: 'Jesus loved Martha, and her sister, and Lazarus'

    A.   *The swiftness of the love which was found in Martha*
    (a) The demands she would gladly meet in serving him.
    (b) The delight she would surely find in serving him.

    B.   *The nearness of love which was found in Mary*
    (a) The insight love would gain.
    (b) The contact love must have.

    C.   *The quietness of love which was found in Lazarus*
    (a) The silence our Lord would need at times.
    (b) The service our Lord would receive at times.

Facing bewilderment

John 11.7–8: 'Jesus said unto his disciples, "Let us go into Judaea again." His disciples say unto him, "Master, the Jews of late sought to stone thee; and goest thou thither again?"'

A. *The amazement his actions provoked in the minds of some*
(a) The path was seen clearly.
(b) The price might prove costly.

B. *The alignment his action proclaimed with the will of God*
(a) There were the other ways open to Christ.
(b) There was the only way taken by Christ.

C. *The achievement his action procured for the good of men*
(a) There is an intimate connection we see here between what we do and what God does.
(b) There is the ultimate conclusion we reach here that we have no choice but to do his will.

What the Bible has to say about our tears

John 11.35: 'Jesus wept'

A. *The Bible notes when tears can be shed in vain*
(a) Think when tears are worthless (cf. Heb. 12.16–17).
(b) Think when tears are wasted.

B. *The Bible also shows that tears can express love*
(a) We read of the giving of love: Luke 7.38–44.
(b) We read of the grieving of love: Luke 19.41.

C. *The Bible speaks of a place and time where tears will cease forever: 'And God shall wipe away all tears'. Rev. 7.17*
(a) The cause for tears will be removed.
(b) The Christ will be revealed.

The ministry of grateful love

John 12.1–11

A. *The quality which marks the ministry of grateful love*
(a) The extravagance of it.
(b) The fragrance of it.

B. *The sympathy which guides the ministry of grateful love*
(a) The wisdom it reveals.
(b) The welcome it receives.

C. *The memory which crowns the ministry of grateful love*
(a) It will have an enduring memory.
(b) It will have an enriching memory.

'Sir, we would see Jesus'

John 12.21

A. *The purpose which brought them there*
(a) What they did.
(b) What they said.

B. *The people who helped them there*
(a) How they were attracted to Philip.
(b) How they were assisted by Philip.

C. *The Person who faced them there*
(a) What did Christ say to them?
(b) What did Christ seek from them?

The prayer Jesus didn't pray

John 12.27–28: 'Now is my soul troubled; and what shall I
say? "Father, save me from this hour?" But for this cause
came I unto this hour. "Father, glorify thy Name." Then
came there a voice from heaven, saying, "I have both glorified
it, and will glorify it again."'

A. *A soul which was troubled*
(a) The suffering envisaged.
(b) The solitude entailed.

B. *A heart which was tempted*
(a) The helplessness which seeks the help of God.
(b) The selfishness which would shrink from the will of
God.

C. *A love which was trusted*
(a) The confidence which lay behind the prayer.
(b) The consequence which lay beyond the prayer.

The appeal of the cross

John 12.32–33: '"And I, if I be lifted up from the earth, will
draw all men unto me." This he said, signifying what death
he should die.'

A. *The appeal which the story of the cross conveys*
(a) The people to whom the cross appeals.
(b) The Person to whom the cross attracts.

B. *The action which the story of the cross contains*
(a) We see the necessity of the cross.
(b) We see the finality of the cross.

C. *The answer which the story of the cross requires*
(a) Our acceptance of the cross as the way to God.
(b) Our allegiance to the Christ and the will of God.

A study of Simon Peter

John 13.8: 'If I wash thee not, thou hast no part with me'

A. *He was a man with defiled feet*
(a) The nature of the man.
(b) The need of the man.

B. *He was a man with a defiant heart*
(a) The refusal Peter made.
(b) The risk Peter ran.

C. *He was a man with a desperate cry*
(a) A truth which was unbearable.
(b) A trust which was unreserved.

Washed by Jesus

John 13.8

A. *The wonder of his grace*
(a) The Person he was.
(b) The purpose he had.

B. *The warning of his love*
(a) The word which could have been final.
(b) The way which would have been fatal.

C. *The welcome for his hands*
(a) The resistance which was broken.
(b) The assurance which was given.

Love – the hallmark of the Christian

John 13.35: 'By this shall all men know that ye are my disciples, if ye have love one to another.'
1 John 3.14: 'We know that we have passed from death unto life, because we love.'

A. *When does this love come into my life? (cf. Rom. 5.5)*
(a) Where does this love reside?
(b) When is this love received?

B. *What will this love do in my life?*
(a) It will change my values.
(b) It will clear my vision.

C. *How can this love grow in my life?*
(a) The intimacy in which this love will grow.
(b) The intensity with which this love will control.

Jesus – the way, the truth and the life

John 14.6: 'I am the way, the truth and the life: no man cometh unto the Father, but by me'

A. *In Christ there is the way I must find*
(a) Christ is the only way.
(b) Christ is the open way.

B. *In Christ there is the truth I must learn*
(a) The authority we must accept.
(b) The futility we must admit.

C. *In Christ there is the life I can have*
(a) The pattern he is for life.
(b) The power he brings to life.

Three claims – one choice

John 14.6

A. *'I am the way'*
(a) There must be a making of the way.
(b) There must be a taking of the way.

B. *'I am the truth'*
(a) The blunders I can make which can spell loss in my life.
(b) The answer Christ gives which can shed light on my path.

C. *'I am the life'*
(a) The reason for the offer Christ makes.
(b) The response to the offer which we make.

The meaning of the love of God

John 14.18–24

A. *The proximity for which love longs*
(a) The wonder of this love.
(b) The welcome of this love.

B. *The intimacy to which love leads*
(a) The privilege of love.
(b) The proving of love.

C. *The eternity through which love lasts*
(a) The challenge I face in this.
(b) The comfort I find in this.

What makes our hearts afraid of death?

John 14.27: 'Let not your heart be troubled, neither let it be afraid'

A. *Our sinfulness makes us afraid*
(a) What we face in ourselves.
(b) What we find in our Saviour.

B. *Our loneliness makes us afraid*
(a) Loneliness that life holds.
(b) A loneliness which Christ ends forever.

C. *Our helplessness makes us afraid*
(a) The impotence we feel in the face of death.
(b) The assurance he gives in the face of death.

A message for Harvest Thanksgiving

John 15.5: 'I am the vine, ye are the branches'

A. *A life communicated*
(a) The absurdity we must see.
(b) The activity we must share.

B. *A life cultivated*
(a) The unsatisfied heart.
(b) The unsparing hand.

C. *A life consummated*
(a) The goal we must reach.
(b) The glory we may bring.

'Ye are the branches'

John 15.5

    A.   *Christ speaks of a sharing in the life of the vine*
    (a) There must be an acceptance in our lives of Christ.
    (b) There must also be a dependence in our lives upon Christ.

    B.   *Christ speaks of a bearing of fruit by the vine*
    (a) We must consider the meaning of the fruit.
    (b) We must consider the measure of the fruit.

    C.   *Christ speaks of a caring for the health of the vine*
    (a) Think of the pain endured.
    (b) Think of the praise evoked.

Depending upon Christ

John 15.5: 'Without me ye can do nothing'

    A.   *Christ is speaking of our involvement in his service*
    (a) We see there is so much to be done.
    (b) Christ needs so many to do it.

    B.   *Christ speaks of a detachment from his Spirit*
    (a) The rejection of his presence.
    (b) The rebellion against his purpose.

    C.   *Christ speaks of an assessment by his standards*
    (a) The amazement by which he would startle us.
    (b) The achievement to which he would summon us.

Friends of Christ (1)

John 15.14: 'Ye are my friends if ye do whatsoever I command you'

    A. *The gift of this friendship with Christ*
    (a) The welcome to his friendship I must give.
    (b) The wonder of his friendship I will know.

    B. *The growth of this friendship with Christ*
    (a) There will be a constant talking together.
    (b) There will be a constant walking together.

    C. *The goal of this friendship with Christ*
    (a) The enrichment of the other.
    (b) The enjoyment of the other.

Friends of Christ (2)

John 15.14

    A. *The place we shall be asked to make for this friendship*
    (a) The welcome in my life.
    (b) The wonder of his love.

    B. *The proof we shall be asked to give of this friendship*
    (a) The requests friendship can make.
    (b) The response friendship should get.

    C. *The price we shall be asked to pay for this friendship*
    (a) The environment he asks us to shun.
    (b) The resentment he asks us to share.

Chosen by Christ

John 15.16: 'Ye have not chosen me, but I have chosen you'

A. *The orders I must take*
(a) The tasks he will give to me.
(b) The trust he must get from me.

B. *The others I will meet*
(a) How much we lean on others.
(b) How much we learn from others.

C. *The outcome I will seek*
(a) The battle I will have.
(b) The blessing I will know.

Living in enemy-occupied territory

John 15.19: 'I have chosen you out of the world'

A. *The authority which the world apparently prefers to the will of God*
(a) The person who is ruler of this world.
(b) The people who are ruled in this world.

B. *The affinity with the mind of God which the world obviously lacks*
(a) The blindness which exists in the world.
(b) The bitterness which is felt by the world.

C. *The activity which the world urgently demands from the Church of God*
(a) A contact to be maintained with the world.
(b) A concern to be manifested towards the world.

The Christian's answer to loneliness

John 16.32: 'Alone . . . yet . . . not alone'

A. *The reality of loneliness*
(a) The fact of loneliness.
(b) The forms of loneliness.

B. *The tragedy of loneliness*
(a) There are burdens we cannot bear alone.
(b) There are blessings we cannot share with others.

C. *The remedy for loneliness*
(a) The presence of God we can have in our lives.
(b) The people whom God will bring into our lives.

The Lord's Prayer

John Chapter 17

A. *He is concerned about the mission on which they must embark*
(a) The ignorance to be dispelled by Christ.
(b) The obedience which had been displayed by Christ.

B. *He is concerned about the menace for which they must watch*
(a) He speaks of the hostility they will provoke.
(b) He speaks of the integrity they must preserve.

C. *He is concerned about the manner in which they must live*
(a) He stresses the wonder of their unity in him.
(b) He speaks of the witness of this unity to the world.

The Christian and the world

John 17.15,18: Not taken out of the world but sent into the world

A. *The throne of which the Scriptures speak*
(a) The power which controls the minds of people.
(b) The people who are controlled by this power.

B. *The threat of which the Scriptures warn*
(a) The Scriptures speak of the world's opposition to the Christian way.
(b) The Scriptures speak of the attraction of the Christian to the world.

C. *The thrust to which the Scriptures call us*
(a) The world is to be the sphere of the witness of the Christian.
(b) The world will see the strength of the witness of the Christian.

A five-word prayer: 'For thee ... for them ... Amen'

John 17.19: 'For their sakes I sanctify myself'

A. *Love's concern: 'for thee'*
(a) The reproach love feels.
(b) The resolve love makes.

B. *Love's contact: 'for them'*
(a) The desire love has.
(b) The delight love finds.

C. *Love's consent: 'Amen'*
(a) The task love undertakes.
(b) The trust love fulfills.

(The idea of the five-word prayer originally comes from Bishop J. Taylor Smith.)

Christian unity

John 17.21: 'That they all may be one: as thou, Father, art in me, and I in thee, that they also may be one in us: that the world may believe that thou hast sent me'

A. *The prayer of the Lord*
(a) The witness through unity which is stated.
(b) The way to unity which is stated.

B. *The problems in the way*
(a) We have to take into account the problems of taste.
(b) We have to take into account the problem of truth.

C. *The prospects in our day*
(a) We need to know the dangers in the present situation.
(b) We need to know the duty we have in the present situation.

'Art thou also one of this man's disciples?'

John 18.17

A. *The conception of the man which the words contained*
(a) The Master they had in mind.
(b) The meaning behind the question.

B. *The content in the mind which the words conveyed*
(a) Their bitter resentment against Christ.
(b) Their utter rejection of Christ.

C. *The confession of the Master which the words compelled*
(a) The suddenness of the thrust.
(b) The solitariness of the test.

The kingship of Jesus (1)

John 19.5,14: 'Then came Jesus forth, wearing the crown of thorns, and the purple robe. And Pilate said unto them . . . "Behold your King!"'

A. *His presentation as King*
(a) The sovereignty which men faced in him.
(b) The authority which men found in him.

B. *His humiliation as King*
(a) The ignorance of the soldiers who named him King.
(b) The impenitence of the scribes who named him King.

C. *His exaltation as King*
(a) We see here the start of this exaltation.
(b) We see now the scope of his exaltation.

The kingship of Jesus (2)

John 19.14: 'Behold your King!'

A. *The search in which men sought Jesus as King*
(a) Their sincerity.
(b) Their humility.

B. *The scorn with which men mocked Jesus as King*
(a) The mockery made of him at his trial.
(b) The majesty men met in him at his trial.

C. *The scene at which men crowned Jesus as King*
(a) The discernment in the minds of men.
(b) The enthronement in the hearts of men.

The cross (1)

John 19.18: 'They crucified him, and two [thieves] with him, on either side one, and Jesus in the midst'

A. *What the cross declares*
(a) It declares the love of God.
(b) It reveals the sin of man.

B. *What the cross demands*
(a) The first demand is repentance.
(b) The next demand is acceptance.

C. *How the cross divides*
(a) There were those who were blind.
(b) There were those who were blessed.

The cross (2)

John 19.30: 'It is finished'

A. *The work he came to do*
(a) He had come that the sinner should be saved.
(b) He had come that the Father should be seen.

B. *The way he cried aloud*
(a) The achievement in which he triumphed.
(b) An amazement with which men trembled.

C. *The word he chose to use*
(a) Listen again to the taunts I can hear.
(b) Think again of the trust I must have.

The cross (3)

John 19.30: 'It is finished'

A. *The will of God was completely finished*
(a) How clearly the will of God was seen by Christ.
(b) How costly the will of God would prove for Christ.

B. *The work of grace was completely finished*
(a) The necessity of the cross.
(b) The sufficiency of the cross.

C. *The way to glory was completely finished*
(a) The assurance we can now have.
(b) The acceptance we must now make.

Sentences which sustain faith

John 19.30: 'It is finished'
Matthew 4.4: 'It is written'
Matthew 14.27: 'It is I'

A. *'It is finished': this speaks of the sufficiency to which faith must look*
(a) The foolish way in which we can think.
(b) The finished work in which we must trust.

B. *'It is written': this speaks of the security on which faith can rest*
(a) There is a faithfulness to trust.
(b) There is a fearfulness to doubt.

C. *'It is I': this speaks of the serenity with which faith may walk*
(a) The storm which meant conflict.
(b) The sight which brought comfort.

The garden of the Resurrection

John 19.38–42a: 'In the place where he was crucified there was a garden; and in the garden a new sepulchre, wherein was never a man yet laid. There they laid Jesus.'

A. *A garden speaks of life*
(a) The weakness from which the life will spring.
(b) The quietness with which the life will come.

B. *A garden speaks of love*
(a) The design of love seen in a garden.
(b) The desire of love sought from a garden.

C. *A garden speaks of light*
(a) I see in this garden the darkness of a broken heart.
(b) I see in this garden the dawning of a blessed hope.

The first Easter as Mary Magdalene would have remembered it

John 20.11: 'Mary stood without at the sepulchre weeping'

A. *She would have remembered that the nights had been sleepless*
(a) The tragedy she had seen.
(b) The agony she had suffered.

B. *She would have remembered that her eyes had been sightless*
(a) How she could not delay in getting to the tomb.
(b) What she could not believe when she got there.

C. *She would have remembered that her joy had been speechless*
(a) She would recall the moment in which all was changed.
(b) She would recall the message with which she was charged.

Jesus the Gardener

John 20.15: 'Supposing him to be the gardener'

A. *The gardener's is the hand which plants*
(a) The preparing of the soil.
(b) The planting of the seed.

B. *The gardener's is the hand which prunes*
(a) The reason for pruning.
(b) The results of pruning.

C. *The gardener's is the hand which plucks*
(a) The right which belongs to him.
(b) The reasons which vary with him.

'Woman, why weepest thou?'

John 20.15

A. *The tragedy she felt so deeply*
(a) The tragedy of her bereavement.
(b) The tragedy of her bewilderment.

B. *The reality she faced so blindly*
(a) How gently Christ reproached her.
(b) How firmly Christ restrained her.

C. *The testimony she bore so gladly*
(a) It was a radiant testimony.
(b) It was a relevant testimony.

What the risen Christ gives to his Church

John 20.19–29

A. *The gift of a divine pardon*
(a) The past they had known.
(b) The price he had paid.

B. *The gift of a divine purpose*
(a) The responsibility he purposed for them.
(b) The resources he promised to them.

C. *The gift of a divine presence*
(a) How Thomas had been hurt.
(b) How Thomas could be helped.

Sent by Jesus

John 20.21: 'As my Father hath sent me, even so send I you'

A. *The Person we are sent by*
(a) The divine imperative by which our lives are ruled.
(b) The human initiative to which my life is called.

B. *The people we are sent to*
(a) The name by which they have been called.
(b) The need in which they will be found.

C. *The purpose we are sent for*
(a) The purpose of revelation.
(b) The purpose of restoration.

Spiritual absenteeism

John 20.19,24: 'Then came Jesus . . . But Thomas was not
with them'

    A.   *The Lord who had come*
    (a) He brought the word of peace.
    (b) He spoke the word of power.

    B.   *The lives which were changed*
    (a) The worship of their Lord.
    (b) The witness on their lips.

    C.   *The loss which was caused*
    (a) What was the reason?
    (b) What was the result?

When faith confronts doubt

John 20.25: 'Except I shall see in his hands the print of the
nails, and put my finger into the print of the nail, and thrust
my hand into his side, I will not believe'

    A.   *The experience shared by the disciples*
    (a) The coming of their Lord.
    (b) The changing of their lives.

    B.   *The eloquence shown by the disciples*
    (a) The conviction with which they would speak.
    (b) The rejection by which they were shocked.

    C.   *The evidence sought from the disciples*
    (a) Evidence which must be visible.
    (b) Evidence which would be credible.

A study of the character of Doubting Thomas (1)

John 20.24–29

A. *We find him following*
(a) The call he was willing to heed.
(b) The cost he was willing to pay.

B. *We find him faltering*
(a) His absence from the fellowship.
(b) His presence in the fellowship.

C. *We find him finishing*
(a) How faithful he proved in the end.
(b) How fruitful he became in his life.

A study of the character of Doubting Thomas (2)

John 20.29: 'Blessed are they that have not seen, and yet have believed'

A. *The blunder he made*
(a) The responsibility he shirked.
(b) The opportunity he lost.

B. *The danger he ran*
(a) The exclusion resented by him.
(b) The evidence requested by him.

C. *The wonder he faced*
(a) The reality of the Presence he had not seen.
(b) The divinity of the Person he could not doubt.

Backsliding

John 21.3: 'I go a fishing'

   A.   *They went back*
   (a) The tug of the old life.
   (b) The talk of their old friends.

   B.   *They woke up*
   (a) The weary hearts of these men.
   (b) The waiting Lord on the shore.

   C.   *They worked on*
   (a) The test applied by Christ.
   (b) The task accepted by them.

The Gospel of the Dawn

John 21.4: 'When the morning was now come, Jesus stood on the shore.'
Another translation: 'Just as the dawn began to break . . . '
Another translation: 'Morning came and there stood Jesus.'

   A.   *We find Jesus standing in the dawn light historically*
   (a) The glimpses of the truth which men had had.
   (b) The glory of the truth which Christ now brought.

   B.   *We find Jesus standing in the dawn light personally*
   (a) The Presence I must heed.
   (b) The prospect I will have.

   C.   *We find Jesus standing in the dawn light prophetically*
   (a) The failure which will be complete.
   (b) The future that will be certain.

Darkness, dawn, day

John 21.4

A. *We have darkness here*
(a) Peter had felt the pull of the old life.
(b) Peter had found the poverty of the old life.

B. *We have dawn here*
(a) For Peter it was a moment of memory.
(b) For Peter it was a moment of privacy.

C. *We have day here*
(a) It would bring a new humility to his love.
(b) It would bring a new responsibility to his life.

An interview which put a man on his feet again

John 21.15–22

A. *The tragedy which Christ had sensed in Peter*
(a) The disgrace of Simon Peter which was well known.
(b) The despair of Simon Peter which was unknown.

B. *The honesty which Christ sought from Peter*
(a) There was something Christ wanted to face alone with him.
(b) There was something Christ wanted to find alive in him.

C. *The destiny which Christ shared with Peter*
(a) The responsibility which Christ was willing to entrust to him.
(b) The reliability which Christ was waiting to receive from him.

The birth of a leader

John 21.15–25

A. *The tests which leadership must pass*
(a) The test of devotion.
(b) The test of degree.

B. *The truths which leadership must learn*
(a) The need for openness towards his Lord.
(b) The need for obedience in his life.

C. *The tasks which leadership will face*
(a) The compassion which the words of Christ portrayed.
(b) The commission which the words of Christ bestowed.

Acts

The Resurrection in the New Testament

Acts 1.3

   A.   *The Resurrection was predicted in the ministry of Jesus*
   (a) It was recorded in the sayings of Jesus.
   (b) It was recalled by the enemies of Jesus.

   B.   *The Resurrection was presented as a miracle of God*
   (a) Note the details in its description.
   (b) Note the difficulties in its denial.

   C.   *The Resurrection was proclaimed in the message of the Church*
   (a) As the seal and vindication of Christ's work.
   (b) As the secret and victory of the Christian's life.

The challenge of the Spirit
Acts 1.1–12

A. *The challenge of a programme*
(a) What they were to be.
(b) What they were to do.
(c) Where they were to go.

B. *The challenge of a Presence*
(a) There is a life which the Spirit wants to live in me.
(b) There is a gift which the Spirit wants to give to me.
(c) There are things which the Spirit wants to do in me.

C. *The challenge of a prospect: 'This same Jesus shall come again . . . '*
(a) The certainty of judgment.
(b) The urgency in service.
(c) A sanctity in living.

The problem of powerlessness in the light of the promise of Pentecost

Acts 1. 4–14

A. *How the Spirit has been received by every believer*
(a) When does the believer receive the Holy Spirit?
(b) Why does the believer require the Holy Spirit?

B. *How the Spirit can be restrained in any believer*
(a) The objections which some may raise to this truth about the Spirit.
(b) The obstructions which some Christians would put in the way of the Spirit.

C. *How the Spirit must be released in every believer*
(a) There are some distinctions we must make in our thinking about the Spirit.
(b) There are some disciplines we must maintain in our relationship to the Spirit.

Witnesses for Jesus

Acts 1.8: 'Ye shall be witnesses unto me'

A. *A witness is someone who has seen*
(a) The ignorance which the witness confronts.
(b) The importance which the witness assumes.

B. *A witness is someone who can speak*
(a) Because of the ministry of the Holy Spirit.
(b) Because of the liberty of the Holy Spirit.

C. *A witness is someone who will stand*
(a) The position which the witness will take.
(b) The conviction which the witness will have.

The promise of Christ's Second Coming

Acts 1.11: 'This same Jesus shall so come in like manner as ye have seen him go'

A. *The voice of the Church*
(a) In her creeds.
(b) In her praise.
(c) In her prayers.

B. *The verdict of the Book*
(a) The unfulfilled prophecies of the Old Testament.
(b) The unmistakable testimony of Jesus Christ.
(c) The unwavering expectancy of the Early Church.

C. *The vision of faith*
(a) The comfort faith derives from this truth.
(b) The climax faith discerns in this truth.
(c) The coming faith desires in this truth.

What we should expect a sermon to do

Acts 2.14–47

A. *The preaching of the word will disturb*: *'They were pricked in their hearts' (2.37)*
(a) The reason for this disturbance.
(b) The response to this disturbance.

B. *The preaching of the word should direct*
(a) The clarity in what was said.
(b) The certainty in what was said.

C. *The preaching of the word will divide*
(a) The positive attitude of reception.
(b) The negative attitude of rejection.

The birth of faith

Acts 2.37: 'What shall we do?'

A. *The person about whom faith must learn*
(a) The blunder which folk can make.
(b) The blessing which faith can find.

B. *The pathway along which faith must move*
(a) They must repent.
(b) They would receive.

C. *The people among whom faith would live*
(a) The answer to loneliness.
(b) The answer to uselessness.

Christian fellowship

Acts 2.44: 'All that believed were together'

A. *The demands of fellowship*
(a) There must be time.
(b) There must be truth.
(c) There must be trust.

B. *The dangers of fellowship*
(a) It can be a selfish fellowship.
(b) It can be a shallow fellowship.
(c) It can be a substitute for fellowship with God.

C. *The discoveries of fellowship*
(a) There can be enrichment.
(b) There can be encouragement.
(c) There can be enjoyment.

D. *The dynamic of fellowship*
(a) The inspiration of it.
(b) The attraction of it.
(c) The invitation to it.

What the Bible says about being converted

Acts 3.19

A. *How it humbles*
(a) What we like to think.
(b) What we need to learn.

B. *What it holds*
(a) Something required of me.
(b) Something received by me.

C. *When it happens*
(a) When man's pride is broken.
(b) When God's path is taken.

The ministry of encouragement: the character of Barnabas

Acts 4.36

A. *What he was able to give*
(a) His material substance.
(b) His personal presence.

B. *What he was able to do*
(a) How watchful were his eyes.
(b) How fruitful was his work.

C. *What he was able to say*
(a) The problems which were arising.
(b) The presence which was asked for.

Stephen

Acts 6.5: 'a man full of faith and of the Holy Ghost'

A. *How fullness serves*
(a) The lowliness of the service asked of him.
(b) The faithfulness in the service showed by him.

B. *How fullness speaks*
(a) The insights he had into the truth of God.
(b) The impact he made in his witness to Christ.

C. *How fullness shines*
(a) The proximity at which the glory showed.
(b) The divinity of which the glory spoke.

The man whom God uses

Acts 8. 1–10

A. *The obedience which God asks from the man whom he uses*
(a) How actively he was involved in the service of God.
(b) How flexibly he was in touch with the Spirit of God.

B. *The opportunity which God gives to the man whom he uses*
(a) How hungry the hearts of men can be.
(b) How ready the man of God must be.

C. *The outcome which God conceals from the man whom he uses*
(a) The wonder of what God can do through the life which he uses.
(b) The wisdom in what God can conceal from the man whom he uses.

The conversion of Saul of Tarsus (1)

Acts 9.1–22

A. *The hostility of Saul*
(a) It was constantly displayed.
(b) It was secretly disturbed.

B. *The honesty of Saul*
(a) The vision he received.
(b) The verdict he reached.

C. *The humility of Saul*
(a) Ready to admit the blunder he had made.
(b) Ready to accept the blessing which God would give.

The conversion of Saul of Tarsus (2)

Acts 9.6: 'Lord, what wilt thou have me to do?'

A. *A confrontation with a Person*
(a) The light that shone around him.
(b) The Lord who stood above him.

B. *A consummation of a process*
(a) His resistance to the truth of the gospel.
(b) His acceptance of the truth of the gospel.

C. *A consecration to a purpose*
(a) The will of God which was unfolded to him.
(b) The work for God which was undertaken by him.

The conversion of Saul of Tarsus (3)

Acts 9.27: 'But Barnabas took him . . . '

A. *A conversion which was undeniable*
(a) How impossible it must have seemed.
(b) How incredible it must have sounded.

B. *A reception which was unforgiveable*
(a) The expectations which would have sustained Saul on his way.
(b) The confrontation which must have shattered him on the day.

C. *An exception which proved invaluable*
(a) How deceptive the appearance of Saul could have been.
(b) How decisive the influence on Saul was to prove.

The fact of conversion: Three conversions in Acts, Chapters 9 and 16

Matthew 18.3: 'Except ye be converted, and become as little children, ye shall not enter into the kingdom of heaven'

A. *The experience of conversion which may be different*
(a) The clearness with which Saul's conversion was marked.
(b) The quietness with which Lydia's conversion was marked.
(c) The suddenness with which the jailer's conversion was marked.

B. *The essence of conversion which must be divine*
(a) The light of God's truth is revealed.
(b) The life of God's Son is received.
(c) The love of God's Spirit is released.

C. *The evidence of conversion which must be revealed*
(a) The changed purpose we can see in Saul.
(b) The changed pocket we can see in Lydia.
(c) The changed person we can see in the jailer.

Three places where the disciples are called Christians

Acts 11.26

A. *Christians are people who stand out from the crowd: Acts 11.25–26*
(a) They are distinct from other people.
(b) They are discussed by other people.

B. *Christians are people who speak out for their Lord: Acts 26.28*
(a) We see one man mastered by the truth – Paul.
(b) We see another man menaced by the truth – Agrippa.

C. *Christians are people who sing out in their joy: 1 Peter 4.16*
(a) The shame of rejection endured by them.
(b) The sounds of rejoicing expressed by them.

A glimpse of the life of a New Testament Christian home

Acts 12.12: 'And when he had considered the thing, he came to the house of Mary the Mother of John, whose surname was Mark; where many were gathered together praying'

A. *It was a home to which people turned in need*
(a) Because of the warmth of Christian love which would be shown there.
(b) Because of the wealth of Christian grace which would be shared there.

B. *It was a home in which people knelt in prayer*
(a) There was a place reserved for prayer.
(b) There was a power released through prayer.

C. *It was a home from which people went in service*
(a) Think of the spiritual activity centred in Mary's house.
(b) Think of the personal ambition (for Mark) cherished in Mary's heart.

A plea for united prayer and for attendance at prayer meetings

Acts 12.12

    A. *The encouragements to united prayer which are recorded*
    (a) The promise which suggests it: Matthew 18.19.
    (b) The practice which supports it: Acts 12.12.
    (c) The purpose which secures it.

    B. *The arrangements required for united prayer*
    (a) The information for prayer which will be supplied.
    (b) The limitations in prayer which will be applied.
    (c) The inspiration for prayer which will be found.

    C. *The enrichment received through united prayer*
    (a) The burden of responsibility will be shared.
    (b) The bonds of fellowship will be strengthened.
    (c) The blessing of God will be secured.

Mark, the Christian who made a wonderful come-back

Acts 12.12

A. *The testimony we would hear from him*
(a) Concerning the mother he had had.
(b) Concerning the preachers he had heard.

B. *The timidity we can sense in him*
(a) His selection for service.
(b) His defection from service.

C. *The tenacity we can see in him*
(a) The encouragement he got (cf. Acts 15.39).
(b) The enrichment he gave – not as a preacher but as a writer.

The conversion of the jailer

Acts 16.30: 'Sirs, what must I do to be saved?'

A. *The people to whom he was able to turn*
(a) Who they were said to be.
(b) What they were said to know.

B. *The problem about which he was anxious and troubled*
(a) The words with which he came.
(b) The way in which he came.

C. *The Person in whom he was asked to trust*
(a) There is simplicity here.
(b) There is security here.

The birth of a church

Acts 17.10–14

A. *They received the word*
(a) The message declared to them.
(b) The manner displayed by them.

B. *They searched the Scriptures*
(a) The time they were willing to give.
(b) The truth they were wanting to know.

C. *They trusted the Saviour*
(a) The response of faith.
(b) The results of faith.

The command to repent

Acts 17.30: 'God commandeth all men everywhere to repent'

A. *'Repent' is an inclusive word: 'all men everywhere'*
(a) There is no escape from it.
(b) There is no excuse for man.

B. *'Repent' is a decisive word*
(a) It will involve recollection.
(b) It will demand resolution.

C. *'Repent' is a productive word*
(a) What must be forsaken.
(b) What will be forgiven.

The importance of what happens at the end of a sermon

Acts 17.32–34

A. *The reaction of resentment*
(a) The majesty of God proclaimed by Paul.
(b) The mockery by men provoked by Paul.

B. *The reaction of postponement*
(a) How attractive postponement can seem.
(b) How deceptive postponement can prove.

C. *The reaction of commitment*
(a) The response which God desires.
(b) The reserve which God displays.

A partnership of love: Aquila and Priscilla

Acts Chapter 18

A. *The way they came into the fellowship together: Acts 18.1–3*
(a) The move they were forced to make.
(b) The man they were meant to meet.

B. *The help they were in the fellowship together: Romans 16.3*
(a) The help they were to the preacher.
(b) The help they were to the people.

C. *The love they showed to the fellowship together*
(a) A love which was costly: Romans 16.4.
(b) A love which was constant: 2 Tim. 4.19.

Receiving the Holy Spirit

Acts 19.2: 'Have ye received the Holy Ghost since ye believed?' (AV); 'Did ye receive the Holy Ghost when ye believed?' (RSV)

A. *The belief which Paul challenged*
(a) Their faith was an incipient faith.
(b) Their faith was an inadequate faith.

B. *The burden which Paul carried*
(a) The instrument which was required by God.
(b) The ignorance which was revealed by Paul.

C. *The blessing which Paul coveted*
(a) The Spirit transcends the physical limits experienced by Christ.
(b) The Spirit transforms the spiritual lives receptive to him.

What does serving the Lord entail?

Acts 20.19

A. *The need for humility*
(a) The acceptance of injury without resentment.
(b) The obedience to authority without reservation.

B. *The call for fidelity*
(a) What the servant says.
(b) How the servant serves.

C. *The fact of hostility*
(a) The enemy we must expect.
(b) The victory we can enjoy.

Paul's ministry

Acts 20.24: 'The ministry which I have received'

A. *His work as a servant*
(a) His accountability to God.
(b) His availability to men.

B. *His words as a speaker*
(a) The range he covered in his preaching.
(b) The results he coveted in his preaching.

C. *His wounds as a soldier*
(a) Wounds had been received.
(b) Wounds had been rewarded.

The gladness of giving

Acts 20.35: 'It is more blessed to give than to receive'

A. *The delight which love finds in giving*
(a) The pleasure given.
(b) The pleasure gained.

B. *The demand which love faces in giving*
(a) How costly the gift must be.
(b) How worthy the gift must be.

C. *The delay in giving which love hates*
(a) How inevitable delays can sometimes be.
(b) How unbearable delays will always be.

The inconvenience of becoming a Christian

Acts 24.25: 'When I have a convenient season, I will call for thee'

A. *A message which was disturbing*
(a) His contentment was broken.
(b) His resentment was spoken.

B. *A Master who was demanding*
(a) An acceptance of his way was demanded.
(b) An acceptance of his will was demanded.

C. *A moment which was decisive*
(a) The note of urgency which is here.
(B) The note of tragedy which is here.

Paul witnesses to Agrippa (1)

Acts 26.19: 'I was not disobedient to the heavenly vision'

A. *The vision granted*
(a) Of the Person of his Lord.
(b) Of the purpose for his life.

B. *The voices silenced*
(a) The persistence of his foes.
(b) The indulgence of the flesh.

C. *The verdict passed*
(a) The endurance demanded.
(b) The relevance discerned.

Paul witnesses to Agrippa (2)

Acts 26.28: 'Almost thou persuadest me to be a Christian'

A. *The start of it*
(a) A display which was lavish.
(b) A desire which was latent.

B. *The thrust of it*
(a) The personal reality of Paul's witness.
(b) The scriptural authority of Paul's witness.

C. *The hurt of it*
(a) Agrippa's recognition of the issue before him.
(b) His rejection of the issue before him.

When the voyage of life is nearing its end

Acts 27.27: 'About midnight the shipmen deemed that they drew near to some country'

A. *The presentiment they had*
(a) They sensed the approach of the land.
(b) They sounded the depth of the sea.

B. *The preparations they made*
(a) The strengthening of their bodies.
(b) The lightening of their load.

C. *The prospect they faced*
(a) The destruction of their ship.
(b) The deliverance of themselves.

Romans

The Christian – a slave of Jesus Christ

Romans 1.1

A. *The employment of the slave*
(a) The authority to which the slave is obedient.
(b) The activity in which the slave is occupied.

B. *The environment of the slave*
(a) He lives in the presence of his Lord.
(b) He lives for the service of his Lord.

C. *The enjoyment of the slave*
(a) The paradox we find here in God's service.
(b) The pleasure we find here in God's service.

Paul, a servant of Jesus Christ

Romans 1.1

A. *The accountability of the servant*
(a) The foolishness which the servant must avoid.
(b) The faithfulness which the servant must display.

B. *The availability of the servant*
(a) That means a readiness which needs no preparation.
(b) That means a willingness which makes no reservation.

C. *The adaptability of the servant*
(a) The changing factors in the service of Jesus Christ.
(b) The changeless function of the servant of Jesus Christ.

The importance of attitudes to people

Romans 1.8–16

A. *Paul's appreciation of others: 'First, I thank my God for you all' (verse 8)*
(a) He appreciated their faithfulness.
(b) He appreciated their fellowship.

B. *Paul's supplication for others*
(a) His prayers for them were sustained.
(b) His purpose for them was sincere.

C. *Paul's obligation to others*
(a) There was a trust of which he would be worthy.
(b) There was a task for which he must be ready.

The importance of being prepared

Romans 1.15: 'I am ready'

   A.   *The Christian must be ready to speak*
   (a) The evidence he had seen.
   (b) The confidence he would show.

   B.   *The Christian must be ready to serve*
   (a) His concern for people.
   (b) His contempt for trouble.

   C.   *The Christian must be ready to stand*
   (a) There was no retreat from the will of God.
   (b) There would be no regrets before the Throne of God.

Proclaiming the gospel (1)

Romans 1.16: 'I am not ashamed of the gospel of Christ: for it is the power of God unto salvation to every one that believeth'

   A.   *The gospel speaks of the existence of a danger*
   (a) The sinfulness of man.
   (b) The seriousness of sin.

   B.   *The gospel speaks of the experience of a dynamic*
   (a) It speaks of God working in the history of humanity.
   (b) It speaks of God working in the hearts of humanity.

   C.   *The gospel speaks of the emergence of a decision*
   (a) Think what faith demands.
   (b) Think of what faith will do.

Proclaiming the gospel (2): The temptation to be ashamed of Christ

Romans 1.16

    A.   *The sense of shame which was felt*
    (a) The humility which the gospel imposes.
    (b) The authority which the gospel reveals.

    B.   *The sense of shame which had stayed*
    (a) There was a temptation to conceal.
    (b) There might be a reaction of resentment.

    C.   *The sense of shame which was spurned*
    (a) Because of the sufficiency of the gospel.
    (b) Because of the simplicity of the gospel.

Proclaiming the gospel (3)

Romans 1.16

    A.   *The danger which has been revealed by the Gospel*
    (a) The sinfulness of man.
    (b) The seriousness of sin.

    B.   *The power which can be found in the Gospel*
    (a) What God has done for man in Christ.
    (b) What God can do in man with Christ.

    C.   *The response which must be made to the Gospel*
    (a) The options which are opened to us.
    (b) The actions to be taken by us.

Proclaiming the gospel (4)

Romans 1.16

A. *The Person who is revealed in the Gospel*
(a) The wonder felt by Paul.
(b) The blunder made by man.

B. *The power which is released in the Gospel*
(a) The help which can meet the needs of men.
(b) The hope which can fill the hearts of men.

C. *The people who are renewed by the Gospel*
(a) How inclusive the gospel is in its offer.
(b) How divisive the gospel is through man's answer.

Living by faith

Romans 1.17: 'The just shall live by faith'

A. *The response which faith is*
(a) What faith must know (cf. Rom. 10.14,17).
(b) What faith will do.

B. *The resources which faith taps*
(a) The wealth of grace which will meet my needs.
(b) The wisdom of God which will guide my steps.

C. *The results which faith sees*
(a) It should mean a different life.
(b) It should mean a triumphant life.

Godless humanity

Romans 1.21: 'Neither were [they] thankful'

   A.   *The revelation which man had received*
   (a) It had been a revelation of the truth of God.
   (b) It had been a revelation of the wrath of God.

   B.   *The recognition which man has withheld*
   (a) The conceit of man.
   (b) The contempt for God.

   C.   *The retribution which man has provoked*
   (a) What God has done.
   (b) Where man has gone.

The reality of sin

Romans 3.23: 'For all have sinned, and come short of the glory of God'

   A.   *What sin is*
   (a) Sin has to do with the nature which I have.
   (b) Sin has to do with the failure which I am.
   (c) Sin has to do with the bondage which I hate.

   B.   *What sin does*
   (a) Sin mars a life.
   (b) Sin masters a life.
   (c) Sin mocks a life.

   C.   *What sin needs*
   (a) The person who the Saviour is.
   (b) The purpose which the Saviour has.
   (c) The process which the Saviour starts.

The blessedness of forgiveness

Romans 4.7–8: 'Blessed are they whose iniquities are forgiven, and whose sins are covered. Blessed is the man to whom the Lord will not impute sin.'

   A. *Forgiveness means the lifting of a load: Isaiah 53.4–6*
  (a) How wearying the burden of sin is.
  (b) How wonderful the blessing of rest is.

   B. *Forgiveness means the ending of a war: Romans 5.10*
  (a) The suffering which marks warfare.
  (b) The surrender which ends warfare.

   C. *Forgiveness means the finding of a way: John 14.6*
  (a) The blunders we can make.
  (b) The Leader we can have.

The love of God

Romans 5.5: 'The Love of God is shed abroad in our hearts'

   A. *Love comes as a gift from God*
  (a) There will have been an acceptance of a new life.
  (b) There will be an emergence of a new love.

   B. *Love grows in communion with God: Philippians 1.9*
  (a) The time which will be spent with him.
  (b) The truths which will be learned of him.

   C. *Love constrains us in our serving God: 2 Corinthians 5.14*
  (a) The involvement which love demands.
  (b) The discernment which love displays.

   D. *Love yields in our obedience to God: Romans 12.1*
  (a) The gladness with which love will yield.
  (b) The completeness with which love will yield.

New life through Christ

Romans Chapter 6

A. *Here we read of an accomplished fact*
(a) The problem of our lives.
(b) The provision of God's love.

B. *Here we have an appropriating faith*
(a) The continuing of the presence of sin.
(b) The counting on the power of the cross.

C. *Here we have an abiding fruit: Romans 6.22*
(a) There will be a growing likeness.
(b) There will be a glorious liberty.

The surrendered life

Romans 6.13: 'Yield yourselves unto God, as those that are alive from the dead, and your members as instruments of righteousness unto God'

A. *There must be a surrender to a Person*
(a) The measure of the surrender.
(b) The moment of the surrender.

B. *There must be a surrender for a purpose*
(a) The intentions in the mind of God.
(b) The instruments in the hands of God.

C. *There must be a surrender at a price*
(a) There is a loss to be faced.
(b) There is a life to be found.

Man's surrender to God's sovereignty

Romans 6.13

    A.   *Why should I yield to God?*
    (a) Because of the Lord he is.
    (b) Because of the love he has.

    B.   *What should I yield to God?*
    (a) The personality I am.
    (b) The potentiality I have.

    C.   *How should I yield to God?*
    (a) I should yield decisively.
    (b) I should yield continually.

Eternal life – the gift of God (1)

Romans 6.23

    A.   *The choosing of the gift*
    (a) How important the person may be.
    (b) How different the purpose may prove.

    B.   *The paying for the gift*
    (a) Whom the price is paid by.
    (b) What the price amounts to.

    C.   *The getting of the gift*
    (a) The excitement which the receiving of it will cause.
    (b) The enjoyment which the receiving of the gift will bring.

Eternal life – the gift of God (2)

Romans 6.23

    A.   *The life he gives: Romans 6.23*
    (a) The blunder which many have made.
    (b) The blessing which any can have.

    B.   *The word he gives: John 17.14*
    (a) The decisions I must make in life.
    (b) The directions I can have in life.

    C.   *The peace he gives: John 14.27*
    (a) The failing of my resources.
    (b) The finding of his resources.

True Liberty in Christ

Romans 8.21: 'the glorious liberty of the children of God'

    A.   *A claim which is dishonest: 2 Peter 2.19*
    (a) So many are held by habit: John 8.34.
    (b) So many are fettered by fear: Proverbs 29.25.
    (c) So many are caught by consequences: Galatians 6.7.

    B.   *A condition which is dishonouring: Luke 13.11–17*
    (a) Dishonouring in its ugliness.
    (b) Dishonouring in its sinfulness.
    (c) Dishonouring in its hopelessness.

    C.   *A challenge which is divine: John 8.36*
    (a) The past he forgives.
    (b) The power he bestows.
    (c) The prospect he creates.

'We know that all things work together for good to them that love God'

Romans 8.28

A. *The purpose which God has for my life*
(a) Concerning the person I am.
(b) Concerning the people I touch.

B. *The process which God suits to my need*
(a) No exceptions must be made.
(b) No contradictions will be found.

C. *The patience which God asks of my love*
(a) What trust will reject.
(b) What time will reveal.

Where the gospel begins

Romans 8.29–30: 'For whom he did foreknow, he also did predestinate to be conformed to the image of his Son, that he might be the firstborn among many brethren. Moreover whom he did predestinate, them he also called: and whom he called, them he also justified: and whom he justified, them he also glorified.'

A. *Where the gospel begins: in the grace of God*
(a) There is mystery here in the foreknowledge of God.
(b) There is sovereignty here in the way in which men are to be saved through Christ.

B. *What the gospel bestows*
(a) The responsibility which is personal: to respond to the call.
(b) The relationship which is possible: being justified with God.

C. *What the gospel becomes*
(a) A transforming power in life: being glorified now.
(b) A transcendent power in death: being glorified hereafter.

Spiritual warfare

Romans 8.31–39

A. *The target which has been selected*
(a) The people who are selected for this attack.
(b) The purpose which can be sensed in this attack.

B. *The tactics which can be detected*
(a) An insistence on guilt.
(b) An instilling of doubt.

C. *The triumph which should be reflected*
(a) The sphere of our triumph.
(b) The scale of our triumph.

God's unsparing love

Romans 8.32: 'He that spared not his own Son, but delivered him up for us all, how shall he not with him also freely give us all things?'

A. *The measure of God's love is shown here*
(a) The possibility which love discards.
(b) The activity which love displays.

B. *The meaning of God's love is seen here*
(a) Our involvement is declared.
(b) Our enslavement is destroyed.

C. *The moment sought by love*
(a) The acceptance we must make.
(b) The assurance we can have.

Scaling the heights

Romans 8.37: 'Nay, in all these things we are more than conquerors through him that loved us'

A. *The sphere of our victory*
(a) Victory where no escape is provided.
(b) Victory where no exception is permitted.

B. *The scale of our victory*
(a) There is to be no delay.
(b) There is to be no doubt.

C. *The source of our victory*
(a) A life which is triumphant.
(b) A love which is trustworthy.

The task for which the Church exists

Romans 10.13–17

A. *The wonder which thrilled Paul*
(a) He was thrilled by the simplicity of the gospel.
(b) He was thrilled with the sufficiency of the gospel.

B. *The worry which troubled him*
(a) He was worried by the ignorance of so many.
(b) He was worried by the indifference of so many.

C. *The welcome which touched him*
(a) How fruitful his preaching had been.
(b) How grateful his people had been.

A pattern for progress in the Christian life

Romans 12.1–2

A. *The exhortation we must heed*
(a) The lover whom God is.
(b) The logic which Paul sees.

B. *The presentation we must make*
(a) Paul speaks of the moment of surrender.
(b) Paul speaks of the measure of surrender.

C. *The separation we must face*
(a) Paul notes the existence of the world.
(b) Paul notes the resistance to the world.

D. *The transformation we will know*
(a) Where the process begins.
(b) What the people become.

E. *The confirmation we will find*
(a) Note the order Paul stresses.
(b) Note the outcome Paul seeks.

Living sacrifices

Romans 12.1–2

A. *The presentation to make*
(a) A presentation which will be inclusive.
(b) A presentation which will be decisive.

B. *The transformation to know*
(a) There will be the inward experience.
(b) There will be the outward difference.

C. *The confirmation to have*
(a) Note the order we must follow.
(b) Note the outcome we will find.

Renewal of the mind

Romans 12.2

A. *The influence of the mind is recognised in the Scriptures*
(a) The Scriptures speak of the creative effect of thought.
(b) The Scriptures recognise the constant exercise of thought.

B. *The importance of the mind is faced by the Saviour*
(a) This is seen in the assessment he made of sin.
(b) This is seen in the discernment we must have about sin.

C. *The improvement of the mind is included in our salvation*
(a) The practical action we can take about this.
(b) The positive attitude we must adopt about this.

Time to wake up

Romans 13.11: 'It is high time to awake out of sleep'

A. *It is time to come alive with the life of Jesus Christ*
(a) The life of Christ must be received by men.
(b) The love of Christ will be revealed in men.

B. *It is time to get aligned with the mind of Jesus Christ*
(a) Think of the ignorance which Christ will dispel.
(b) Think of the obedience which Christ will demand.

C. *It is high time to speak aloud in the name of Jesus Christ*
(a) Think of the Person of whom we are to speak.
(b) Think of the people to whom we are to speak.

Some things which belong to the Lord

Romans 14.8: 'We are the Lord's'

A. *There is the Lord's day: Revelation 1.10*
(a) What God wanted to ensure through the Lord's day.
(b) How God wanted to enrich through the Lord's day.

B. *There is the Lord's house: Haggai 1.2*
(a) The Presence we expect to find there.
(b) The people we expect to meet there.

C. *There is the Lord's table: 1 Corinthians 10.21*
(a) It is his decision as to who will sit at the table.
(b) It is his decision as to what is set on the table.

The God of hope

Romans 15.13: 'Now the God of hope fill you with all joy and peace in believing, that you may abound in hope, through the power of the Holy Ghost'

A. *Hope in the light of the failure in his life which man cannot erase*
(a) The guilt I feel.
(b) The grace I find.

B. *Hope in the light of those factors in his life which man cannot resolve*
(a) The person I am.
(b) The Presence I can have.

C. *Hope in the light of the future for his life which man cannot foresee*
(a) The confusion which man cannot resolve.
(b) The intrusion which man cannot resist.

Phebe – a lesser saint

Romans 16.1–2

   A. *The sister she was*
   (a) The miracle Paul sees in her.
   (b) The ministry Paul seeks for her.

   B. *The service she gave*
   (a) The tasks done by her.
   (b) The trust shown in her.

   C. *The succour she brought*
   (a) The difficulties so many had met.
   (b) The difference so many had found.

Paul's lasting regret

Romans 16:7: 'Who were in Christ before me'

   A. *The reproach he faced which these words contain*
   (a) How stubborn he had been.
   (b) How stupid he had been.

   B. *The regeret he felt which these words suggest*
   (a) The time he had thrown away.
   (b) The tasks he must leave undone.

   C. *The resolve he formed which these words reveal*
   (a) There would be an urgency in his spirit.
   (b) There would be a quality in his service.

1 Corinthians and 2 Corinthians

1 Corinthians

Chosen

1 Corinthians 1.27

  A. *The people found in the church*
  (a) The voice which had summoned them.
  (b) The choice which had surprised them.

  B. *The power felt in the church*
  (a) The creative power in their lives.
  (b) The corrective power in their lives.

  C. *The purpose fulfilled through the church*
  (a) The pride which must be broken in man.
  (b) The praise which must be given to God.

The reflections of a pastor at the end of a year

1 Corinthians 2.1–12

A. *The truths he will have wanted his people to hear*
(a) Truths centred on the Person of Jesus Christ.
(b) Truths concerned with the passion of Jesus Christ.

B. *The trust he will have wanted his people to have*
(a) The fears he shares with them.
(b) The faith he seeks for them.

C. *The things he will have wanted his people to learn*
(a) The things which have been prepared for them.
(b) The things which must be explored by them.

Jesus Christ crucified

1 Corinthians 2.2: 'I determined not to know anything among you, save Jesus Christ, and him crucified'

A. *How Jesus Christ died voluntarily*
(a) The purpose of the coming of Christ.
(b) The pressure of the conflict for Christ.

B. *How Jesus Christ died vicariously*
(a) The necessity for his death.
(b) The sufficiency of his death.

C. *How Jesus Christ died victoriously*
(a) The shout of victory.
(b) The signs of victory.

Three Levels of Living

1 Corinthians 2.6—3.9

A. *Paul speaks of the blindness of the natural man*
(a) What are the reasons for this?
(b) What are the results of this?

B. *Paul speaks of the weakness of the carnal man*
(a) His identity is established.
(b) His inability is exposed.

C. *Paul speaks of the fullness of the spiritual man*
(a) His apprehension of the truth of God.
(b) His abandonment to the Spirit of God.

Spiritual babies

1 Corinthians 3.1: 'babes in Christ'

A. *How utterly dependent babies are*
(a) They have to be fed by others.
(b) Food they have to be fed with.

B. *How constantly divided the Corinthians were*
(a) The independence from others which little children want.
(b) The interference with others which little children show.

C. *How easily diverted they were*
(a) How worthless were the objects of their love.
(b) How useless was the pattern of their lives.

Thoughts on the quality of a year's work in a church

1 Corinthians 3.9: 'Ye are God's building'

A. *The work in which we have shared*
(a) How different are the contributions which we have made.
(b) How dependent the contributions have been.

B. *The way in which we have built*
(a) The essential foundation of our work.
(b) The material we have used in our work.

C. *The worth of what we have done*
(a) The test our work will meet.
(b) The truth the day will reveal.

Living under the constant judgment of divine love

1 Corinthians 4.4: 'He that judgeth me is the Lord'

A. *The vision we need to share with Paul*
(a) His total availability to Christ.
(b) His personal accountability to Christ.

B. *The voices we need to scorn with Paul*
(a) There will be the other voices.
(b) There will be the inner voice.

C. *The verdict we will need to seek with Paul*
(a) How complete Christ's judgment is in its knowledge.
(b) How constant Christ's judgment is in its exercise.

Fences around our freedom

1 Corinthians 6:12; 10.24

A. *The expediency of my behaviour which must be considered*
(a) The need for discernment.
(b) The need for discipline.

B. *The exposure to danger which must be avoided*
(a) The existence of this kind of danger.
(b) The avoidance of this kind of danger.

C. *The example to others which must be constructive*
(a) The hurt we can bring to other lives.
(b) The help we can be to other lives.

D. *The excellence of character which must be achieved*
(a) The waste which is possible of our lives.
(b) The work which will be permanent in our lives.

We belong to God

1 Corinthians 6.19–20: 'Ye are not your own . . . ye are bought with a price'

A. *The claim here which men have to forgo*
(a) The liberty on which men's hearts are resolved.
(b) The slavery to which men's lives are reduced.

B. *The Christ here whom men have to confront*
(a) The Person he is.
(b) The purpose he has.

C. *The choice here which men want to evade*
(a) Some choices we are willing to accept.
(b) This choice we want to avoid.

The problem of alcohol

1 Corinthians 8.9: 'take heed lest by any means this liberty of yours becomes a stumbling block to them that are weak'

A. *The choices we must face about alcohol*
(a) What are the reasons for the pressure brought upon us by society?
(b) What are the results of the pressure brought upon us by society?

B. *The charges we can bring*
(a) How inconsistent are people who consume alcohol.
(b) How indifferent they are to the consequences of consuming alcohol.

C. *The chances we must take*
(a) The opportunity there is to stand out from the crowd.
(b) The opportunity there is to speak up for Jesus Christ.

The summons to excellence

1 Corinthians 9.24–27

A. *The desire for excellence*
(a) Where we should look for it.
(b) Why we should long for it.

B. *The demands of excellence*
(a) There will be things which we must be willing to forgo.
(b) There are those whom we are not allowed to forget.

C. *The dangers of excellence*
(a) The fears in our hearts.
(b) The fight on our hands.

The Lord's table

1 Corinthians 10.21

   A. *What is displayed here*
   (a) The simplicity of what is displayed here.
   (b) The significance of what is displayed here.

   B. *What is desired here*
   (a) The hands which must be willing to receive by faith.
   (b) The hearts which are willing to respond in love.

   C. *What is declared here*
   (a) The action taken by God.
   (b) The answer given by man.

All for the glory of God

1 Corinthians 10.31: 'Whatsoever ye do, do all to the glory of God'

   A. *What I must learn*
   (a) The communion I must have with God.
   (b) The comparisons I will make with others.

   B. *What I must leave*
   (a) The displeasure I may arouse.
   (b) The discipline I must accept.

   C. *How I must live*
   (a) The conception of life which the Christian has.
   (b) The compulsion of love which the Christian will know.

Women in the Church

1 Corinthians 11.2–16, 14.34–40; 1 Timothy 2.8–15; Ephesians 5.25–33; Colossians 3.18–19

A. *The ministry which Paul sees as valuable*
(a) It was a vocal ministry.
(b) It was a vital ministry.

B. *The modesty which Paul sees as desirable*
(a) The total disregard which some actions can show for the customs of the community.
(b) The social disrepute which some actions can bring within the community.

C. *The mastery which Paul sees as acceptable*
(a) In the homes of their husbands.
(b) In the hearts of their husbands.

Holy Communion (1) – A service of thanksgiving

1 Corinthians 11.24: 'And when he had given thanks'

A. *There will be thanksgiving because of what I recall in this service*
(a) When I think of what the love of God has done for me in Christ.
(b) When I think of what the love of God has said to me in Christ.

B. *There will be thanksgiving because of what I receive in this service*
(a) There will be my acceptance of God's gift.
(b) There will be the assurance I can have of God's grace.

C. *There will be thanksgiving because of what I renew in this service*
(a) When I think of the reminder it will bring to me.
(b) When I think of the surrender it will ask of me.

Holy Communion (2) – The obligation which Christ lays on his Church

1 Corinthians 11.24–25: 'This do'

A. *What we are asked to do*
(a) We are asked to recall the Saviour in his dying love.
(b) We are asked to receive the symbols of his dying love.

B. *How we are asked to do it*
(a) We are asked to do it with simplicity.
(b) We are asked to do it with sincerity.

C. *Why we are asked to do this*
(a) Think of the evidence which God's love wants us to hold in our hands.
(b) Think of the assurance which God's love wants us to have in our hearts.

Holy Communion (3) – A service of witness

1 Corinthians 11.26: 'Ye do shew [or proclaim] the Lord's death till he come'

A. *Our witness to the fact of the Cross*
(a) There is a reminder here of the historical reality of the death of Christ.
(b) There is a reminder here of the sufficiency of the death of Christ.

B. *Our witness to the faith we have in the Christ*
(a) We recall the necessity of faith.
(b) We recall the simplicity of faith.

C. *Our witness to the fellowship of the Church*
(a) The diversity which is found within the Church.
(b) The testimony which is given by the Church.

Holy Communion (4) – the need for preparation

1 Corinthians 11.28: 'Let a man examine himself'

A. *The suggestion of the task we need to perform*
(a) The subject of this examination.
(b) The standard of this examination.

B. *The selection of a time for this preparation*
(a) The profession which must be examined.
(b) The presumption which must be avoided.

C. *The submission to a truth in this examination*
(a) How humbling it can be.
(b) How helpful it will be.

The Church of Jesus Christ

1 Corinthians 12.12–27

A. *The Church as the Body of Christ*
(a) This involves the possession of the life of Christ.
(b) This involves a submission to the will of Christ.
(c) This involves the expression of the mind of Christ.

B. *The Church as the Bride of Christ*
(a) The relationship which the Bride enjoys.
(b) The resources which she receives.
(c) The radiance which she reflects.

C. *The Church as the Building of Christ*
(a) There will be a design for the Building.
(b) There will be a development of the Building.
(c) There will be a destiny for the Building.

Love – the greatest thing in the world

1 Corinthians Chapter 13

   A. *The pre-eminence of love*
   (a) The deceptive values which can be found in Christian experience.
   (b) The decisive verdict which is passed on Christian experience.

   B. *The portrayal of love*
   (a) The distinctive facets of love
   (b) The attractive facets of love

   C. *The permanence of love*
   (a) The passing elements in Christian experience.
   (b) The permanent facts which endure in Christian experience.

The love of God

1 Corinthians 13.13: 'The greatest of these is love'

   A. *The love of God is an embracing love*
   (a) The wonder we face in this love.
   (b) The answer we find in this love.

   B. *The love of God is an enriching love*
   (a) The happiness which is the intention of love in its giving.
   (b) The costliness which will mark the provision of love in its giving.

   C. *The love of God is an enduring love*
   (a) How fickle our human love can be.
   (b) How stable our Saviour's love will prove.

The Christian home

1 Corinthians 16.19: 'The church that is in their house'

A. *The people who are found in a Christian home*
(a) The new life which permeates that home.
(b) The new Lord who dominates that home.

B. *The purposes which are fulfilled in a Christian home*
(a) The Lord who will be loved there.
(b) The lives which will be touched there.

C. *The pattern which will be filled out in a Christian home*
(a) The sacrifice which will be seen in such a home.
(b) The salvation which will be traced to such a home.

2 Corinthians

The God of all comfort

2 Corinthians 1.3–4

A. *The need of the comfortless*
(a) Our need for a Presence.
(b) Our need for a prospect.

B. *The Name of the Comforter*
(a) The assurance we can have.
(b) The abundance we can tap.

C. *The news of the comforted*
(a) The others we will meet.
(b) The offer we can make.

The promises of God

2 Corinthians 1.20

A. *The making of the promises of God*
(a) The need God sees.
(b) The Name God has.

B. *The guarding of the promises of God*
(a) Am I in the position to claim the promises of God for myself?
(b) Have I met the conditions which enable the promises of God to be kept?

C. *The keeping of the promises of God*
(a) There should be an expectancy which will fill our hearts.
(b) There should be an experience which will praise our God.

The fragrance or perfume of Christ

2 Corinthians 2.14–15: 'Thanks be to God who leads us wherever we are on Christ's triumphant way and makes our knowledge of him spread throughout the world like a lovely perfume. We Christians have the unmistakable fragrance of Christ.'

A. *How pervasive a perfume can be*
(a) A perfume travels.
(b) A perfume lingers.

B. *How expensive a perfume can be*
(a) There is a costliness which the giving of love demands.
(b) There is a carelessness which the giving of love displays.

C. *How attractive a perfume can be*
(a) The appreciation which will be shown.
(b) The motivation which will be sensed.

D. *How distinctive a perfume can be*
(a) How different perfumes are.
(b) How permanent perfume is.

Being a letter from Christ

2 Corinthians 3.2–3: 'As for you, it is plain that you are a letter that has come from Christ, given to us to deliver. A letter written, not with ink, but with the Spirit of the Living God. Written, not on stone tablets, but on the pages of the human heart.'

A. *The Writer from whom the letter has come*
(a) The person by whom the letter has been written.
(b) The purpose for which the letter has been written.

B. *The paper on which the letter is written*
(a) How different paper can be.
(b) How important people are.

C. *The reader for whom the letter is meant*
(a) The letter must be close enough for them to read it.
(b) The letter must be clear enough for them to understand it.

A message to ministers

2 Corinthians 4.2: 'Handling the word of God'

A. *We must handle the word of God accurately*
(a) This will affect the matter of our preaching.
(b) This will affect the manner of our preaching.

B. *We must handle the word of God attractively*
(a) There is a perfection we must seek to achieve.
(b) There is a presumption we must seek to avoid.

C. *We must handle the word of God acceptably*
(a) In a way which is acceptable to man.
(b) In a way which is acceptable to God.

The face of Jesus Christ

2 Corinthians 4.6: 'The glory of God in the face of Jesus Christ'

A. *The transfiguration which was seen in the face of Jesus Christ (Matthew 17.2)*
(a) This established a fact.
(b) This encouraged a faith.

B. *The determination which was seen in the face of Jesus Christ (Luke 9.51)*
(a) How costly the task was for him.
(b) How costly the terms are for us.

C. *The renunciation which was seen in the face of Jesus Christ (Matthew 26.39)*
(a) How desperate was his desire to avoid the cross.
(b) How deliberate was his decision to accept the cross.

D. *The humiliation which was seen in the face of Jesus Christ (Matthew 26.67)*
(a) How shameful this was.
(b) How hopeful this proves.

The wonder of the gospel

2 Corinthians 5.17: 'If any man be in Christ, he is a new creature'

A. *A message which is inclusive*
(a) How universal it is in its appeal.
(b) How individual it is in its application.

B. *A miracle which is creative*
(a) The difference it will make in my life.
(b) The relevance it will have in my life.

C. *A moment which is decisive*
(a) The new relationship entered into.
(b) The new resources enjoyed.

Ambassadors for Christ

2 Corinthians 5.20

A. *The dignity of the Ambassador's person*
(a) The rank of the ambassador.
(b) The residence of the ambassador.

B. *The directness of his access to his sovereign*
(a) The existence of his privilege is recognised.
(b) The importance of his privilege is realised.

C. *The delivery of his message from his sovereign*
(a) How watchfully he will live.
(b) How faithfully he will speak.

D. *The end of his term of office*
(a) The recall he will hear.
(b) The reward he will receive.

The grace of generosity

2 Corinthians 8.7: 'See that ye abound in this grace also'

A. *The manner of their giving*
(a) The motive behind it.
(b) The music within it.

B. *The measure of their giving*
(a) The principle by which it was evaluated.
(b) The example by which others were stimulated.

C. *The meaning of their giving*
(a) The revelation of love which it was.
(b) The repercussion on lives which it had.

The spiritual conflict of the believer

2 Corinthians 10.4: 'The weapons of our warfare are not carnal, but mighty through God to the pulling down of strongholds'

A. *Paul speaks of warfare*
(a) The opposition we must face.
(b) The objective we must gain.

B. *Paul speaks of weapons*
(a) There are the weapons which we must discard.
(b) There are the weapons which God will provide.

C. *Paul speaks of winning*
(a) The success we should see.
(b) The soldiers God will need.

Christ, the Lord of our thoughts

2 Corinthians 10.5: 'Bringing into captivity every thought to the obedience of Christ'

A. *The conflict with our thoughts*
(a) The importance of our thoughts.
(b) The influence of our thoughts.

B. *The capture of our thoughts*
(a) We must be alive to the peril.
(b) We must be active in our purpose.

C. *The control over our thoughts*
(a) The authority which will frame our thoughts.
(b) The activity which will fill our thoughts.

The simple gospel

2 Corinthians 11.3: 'The simplicity that is in Christ'

A. *Christ's dealings with men*
(a) The initiative taken by the love of God.
(b) The imperative spoken by the word of God.

B. *Christ's dying for men*
(a) The necessity of the cross.
(b) The simplicity of the choice.

C. *Christ's dwelling in man*
(a) The transformation which the presence of Christ will achieve.
(b) The obligations which the presence of Christ will create.

Paul's escape

2 Corinthians 11.33

A. *The need to escape*
(a) The peril which lurked within the walls.
(b) The purpose which lay beyond the walls.

B. *The road of escape*
(a) The window we will need.
(b) The basket we can use.

C. *The aids in escape*
(a) The hands which were faithful.
(b) The heart which was grateful.

From difficulty through discovery to doxology

2 Corinthians 12.1–10

A. *There is difficulty here*
(a) There was a pressure which seemed unhelpful.
(b) There was a prayer which seemed unheard.

B. *There is discovery here*
(a) The unrecognised purpose of God.
(b) The unrestricted plenitude of grace.

C. *There is doxology here*
(a) Paul's attitude is changed.
(b) Paul's acceptance is complete.

The discipline of disappointment

2 Corinthians 12.7–10

    A. *The frustration we find here*
    (a) The pressure of a sore trial.
    (b) The persistence of a sore trial.

    B. *The revelation we find here*
    (a) There was an unexpected purpose.
    (b) There was an unlimited provision.

    C. *The transformation we find here*
    (a) The transformation of weakness into strength.
    (b) The transformation of sadness into joy.

A short prayer which says everything

2 Corinthians 13.14: 'The grace of our Lord Jesus Christ, and the love of God, and the communion of the Holy Ghost, be with you all. Amen.'

    A. *The grace of the Lord Jesus Christ speaks of adequacy*
    (a) The acceptable relationship which we can enjoy with our God.
    (b) The inexhaustible resources which we have in our Lord.

    B. *The love of God the Father speaks of security*
    (a) The sense of importance given to the child of God.
    (b) The sense of assurance enjoyed by the child of God.

    C. *The fellowship of the Holy Spirit speaks of intimacy*
    (a) There will be a sharing with us.
    (b) There will be a sharing by us.

Galatians to 1 Thessalonians

Galatians

Christian unity

Galatians 3.28: 'All one in Christ Jesus'
John 17.21: 'That they . . . may be one in us: that the world may believe that thou has sent me'

A. *The warning which we should heed*
(a) The condemnation by the world which is not valid.
(b) The motivation of those within the Church which is not worthy.

B. *The wonder which we can know*
(a) There is a unity which is spiritual.
(b) There is a diversity which is functional.

C. *The witness which we should bear*
(a) The separation which is the mark of sin.
(b) The transformation which is the work of Christ.

The Christian's vanished joy

Galatians 4.15: 'Where is then the blessedness ye spake of?'

A. *The quality which had marked their Christian experience*
(a) The joy of that experience.
(b) The joy of their enthusiasm.

B. *The tragedy which now marred their Christian experience*
(a) The reasons sought.
(b) The results seen.

C. *The remedy which could solve the problem*
(a) The confession required.
(b) The communion restored.

The Church – the mother of us all

Galatians 4.26: 'Jerusalem which is above . . . is the mother of us all'
Hebrews 12.22: 'ye are come unto mount Zion, and unto the city of the living God, the heavenly Jerusalem'

A. *The cost to a mother of the birth of her child*
(a) The magnitude of the cost.
(b) The attitude to the cost.

B. *The care of the mother for the health of her child*
(a) How varied are the needs of the children.
(b) How vital is the role of a mother.

C. *The claims of a mother on the strength of her child*
(a) How great the debt of the children will be.
(b) How glad the heart of the mother should be.

When things go wrong in the life of a Christian (1)

Galatians 5.7: 'Ye did run well, who did hinder you?'

  A. *The progress which these Christians had made*
  (a) There had been a decision taken by them.
  (b) There was this description given of them.

  B. *The problem which these Christians had to solve*
  (a) The scale of the tragedy they had to face.
  (b) The source of the tragedy which could be traced.

  C. *The prospect which these Christians had to face*
  (a) What the danger was.
  (b) Where the answer lay.

When things go wrong in the life of a Christian (2)

Galatians 5.7

  A. *The progress which their faith had made*
  (a) They had started well.
  (b) They had stopped dead.

  B. *The problem which their failure had raised*
  (a) How persuasive sin is.
  (b) How corrosive sin is.

  C. *The prospect which the future would hold*
  (a) The confidence which Paul found in Christ.
  (b) The certainty of judgment which they faced.

The true nature of Christian love

Galatians 5.22: 'The fruit of the Spirit is love'

A. *When does Christian love begin?*
(a) The Bible speaks of this as something which has been given to us: Romans 5.5.
(b) The Bible speaks of this as something which should be growing in us: Philippians 1.9.

B. *What does Christian love become?*
(a) It provides the motive for my service: 2 Corinthians 5.14.
(b) It decides the measure of my surrender: Romans 6.13; Exodus 21.1–6.

C. *How does Christian love behave?*
(a) There is a perception which Christian love will display: Philippians 1.9–11.
(b) There is a perfection which Christian love will demand: Philippians 1.10; 1 Corinthians chapter 13.

How reliable are you?

Galatians 5.22: 'The fruit of the Spirit is faithfulness'
Matthew 25.14–30

A. *The divine Spirit creates faithfulness*
(a) In lives in which the ministries of the Holy Spirit are being exercised.
(b) In lives in which the identity of the servant of God can be recognised.

B. *The divine service demands faithfulness*
(a) The involvement in Christian service which we must expect to find.
(b) The requirement in Christian service which we should expect to face.

C. *The Divine Saviour rewards faithfulness*
(a) What the service of God reveals in us.
(b) How the Saviour of men rewards us.

Sowing and reaping (1)

Galatians 6.7–8: 'Be not deceived; God is not mocked: for whatsoever a man soweth, that shall he also reap. For he that soweth to his flesh shall of the flesh reap corruption; but he that soweth to the Spirit shall of the Spirit reap life everlasting'

A. *Living is sowing*
(a) Actions may seem isolated.
(b) Results will be implicated.

B. *Living is choosing*
(a) There is a restricted choice.
(b) There is a responsible choice.

C. *Living is growing*
(a) The nature of living leads to development.
(b) The numbers in living which warns us of involvement.

D. *Living is reaping*
(a) The contrast we see here.
(b) The caution we face here.

Sowing and reaping (2)

Galatians 6.7–10: 'Whatsoever a man soweth, that shall he also reap'

A. *The Lord whom men think they can mock*
(a) The form of their mocking.
(b) The folly of their mocking.

B. *The laws which men find they must face*
(a) The sowing of the seed.
(b) The growing of the seed.

C. *The lives which men make for themselves*
(a) What can be lost.
(b) What will last.

Never give up

Galatians 6.9: 'Let us not be weary in well doing: for in due season we shall reap, if we faint not'
'Never grow tired of doing what is right' (Moffatt's translation)

A. *The discernment which a Christian must have*
(a) There must be an understanding of what is right.
(b) There must be an undertaking of what is right.

B. *The discouragement which a Christian will meet*
(a) The reasons a Christian may have.
(b) The resources a Christian must use.

C. *The development which a Christian will see*
(a) How costly responsibility is.
(b) How surely results will come.

Suffering – one of the marks of a valid Christian experience

Galatians 6.17: 'From henceforth let no man trouble me: for I bear in my body the marks of the Lord Jesus'

A. *The identity which suffering portrays*
(a) The forms which suffering may take.
(b) The marks which suffering may leave.

B. *The authority which suffering bestows*
(a) The critics which Paul had.
(b) The challenge which Paul makes here.

C. *The entreaty which suffering provokes*
(a) The waste which Paul wants to avoid.
(b) The work which Paul wants to achieve.

Ephesians
Three kinds of forgiveness of sins

Ephesians 1.7: 'In whom we have redemption through his blood, the forgiveness of sins, according to the riches of his grace'

A. *The forgiveness of sins which involves God*
(a) God has made forgiveness possible.
(b) We must make forgiveness personal.

B. *The forgiveness of sins which involves others*
(a) The forgiveness which I may have to show to others: Matthew 6.14–15.
(b) The forgiveness which I may have to seek from others: Matthew 5.23–24.

C. *The forgiveness of sins which involves myself (sometimes Christians say 'I cannot forgive myself')*
(a) The pride which must be broken.
(b) The peace which can then be gained.

What does it mean to be 'sealed with the Spirit'?

Ephesians 1.13: 'Sealed with that Holy Spirit of promise'

A. *A seal implies contact*
(a) The meaning of his indwelling.
(b) The moment of his incoming.

B. *A seal indicates ownership*
(a) That means a new authority is brought into my life.
(b) That means a new security is given to my life.

C. *A seal imparts likeness*
(a) That means a new love will have come into my life.
(b) That means a new light will be seen in my life.

441

'Your faith in the Lord Jesus Christ'

Ephesians 1.15

    A.   *Failing always, I turn to him*
    (a) There will have been a discovery of my weakness.
    (b) There will have been a discovery of his worth.

    B.   *Forsaking all, I take him*
    (a) The claim he makes.
    (b) The choice I make.

    C.   *Feeling afraid, I trust him*
    (a) The difficulties I can see.
    (b) The adequacy I will prove.

    D.   *Finding another, I tell him*
    (a) What faith sees in the world.
    (b) What faith shares with the world.

The salvation of the Christian

Ephesians 2.8–9: 'By grace are ye saved through faith; and that not of yourselves: it is the gift of God: not of works, lest any man shold boast'

    A.   *Where my salvation begins*
    (a) The condition of man.
    (b) The compassion of God.

    B.   *What my salvation demands*
    (a) The simplicity of faith.
    (b) The necessity of faith.

    C.   *What my salvation secures*
    (a) What I am saved from.
    (b) What I am saved for.

Christless living

Ephesians 2.12: 'Without Christ'

A. *Christless living is lightless living*
(a) It involves man's separation from God.
(b) It involves man's condemnation by God.

B. *Christless living is powerless living – Romans 5.6: 'When we were yet without strength'*
(a) How powerless man is to secure the pardon from sin he needs.
(b) How powerless man is to find the power over sin he needs.

C. *Christless living is hopeless living – Ephesians 2.12: 'Having no hope'*
(a) Man has no word of excuse.
(b) Man finds no way of escape.

The nature of the Church (1)

Ephesians 2.22: 'Builded together for an habitation of God through the Spirit'

A. *The presence of God will be sensed here*
(a) The voice which men will hear.
(b) The vision which men should have.

B. *The purposes of God will be served here*
(a) The activity which will centre in the home.
(b) The authority which will be obeyed in the home.

C. *The praises of God will be sung here*
(a) When the goodness of God is considered.
(b) How gladness of man will be expressed.

The nature of the Church (2)

Ephesians 2.22

> A. *Its foundations*
> (a) The person of Christ.
> (b) The people of God.
>
> B. *Its furnishings*
> (a) The attitude of love found there.
> (b) The atmosphere of light felt there.
>
> C. *Its fellowship*
> (a) How attractive that fellowship should be.
> (b) How decisive that fellowship can prove.

Paul's conception of his task as a minister of the gospel

Ephesians 3.7–13

> A. *An abiding sense of wonder (verse 8)*
> (a) Paul's thoughts about himself.
> (b) Paul's task in the service of his Saviour.
>
> B. *An appointed sphere of work*
> (a) The people with whom he was concerned.
> (b) The purpose to which he was committed.
>
> C. *An abundant store of wealth*
> (a) The message proclaimed with his lips.
> (b) The manner portrayed in his life.

The Church – the Christian family (1)

Ephesians 3.14–15

A. *The way in which the family is entered*
(a) The manner of our entrance.
(b) The meaning of our entrance.

B. *The work in which the family is involved*
(a) The tasks within the family.
(b) The tasks outside the family.

C. *The wealth by which the family is enriched*
(a) The wealth of the affection shown to each member.
(b) The wealth of the achievement shared by each member.

The Church – the Christian family (2)

Ephesians 3.14–15

A. *The relationships in the family*
(a) The life which the family shares.
(b) The love which the family shows.

B. *The responsibilities of the family*
(a) There must be provision for the needs of its members.
(b) There must be a participation by its members in its life.

C. *The reproduction of the family*
(a) The sacrifices demanded by this.
(b) The survival dependent upon this.

A matter of depth

Ephesians 3.18

A. *Loving in depth*
(a) The world which love will share with the one loved.
(b) The wounds which love will bear for the one loved.

B. *Learning in depth: Romans 11.33*
(a) The capacity which has been received by the Christian.
(b) The infinity which can be explored by the Christian.

C. *Living in depth*
(a) The obedience we must give.
(b) The confidence we must have.

The fullness of God

Ephesians 3.19: 'That ye might be filled with all the fullness of God'

A. *The necessity for God's fullness*
(a) There will be a consciousness of sin.
(b) There must be a confession of sin.

B. *The sufficiency of God's fullness*
(a) The promise of fullness.
(b) The possession of fullness.

C. *The possibility of God's fullness*
(a) This is surely the purpose of God.
(b) This will surely mean the power of God.

Meekness

Ephesians 4.2

A. *How receptive meekness is*
(a) It is receptive of God's grace.
(b) It is receptive of God's guidance.

B. *How effective meekness is*
(a) Because of its gentleness with others.
(b) Because of its forgiveness of others.

C. *How attractive meekness is*
(a) There will be a loveliness associated with it.
(b) There will be a happiness resulting from it.

Christian unity

Ephesians 4.3: 'Keep the unity of the Spirit'

A. *The wonder of Christian unity – Acts 2.4: 'all that believed were together'*
(a) The preface which conditions it.
(b) The Presence which creates it.

B. *The witness of Christian unity – John 17.21: 'That the world may believe'*
(a) There will be a witness to the reality of the grace of God.
(b) There will be a witness to the relevance of the grace of God.

C. *The worship of Christian unity*
(a) There is a confidence here which can be misplaced.
(b) There is a dependence here which can be disregarded.

The ungrieved spirit

Ephesians 4.30: 'Grieve not the Holy Spirit'

A. *We have to consent to his life being lived in us*
(a) Think of his presence being a fact in our lives.
(b) Think of his presence bearing fruit in our lives.

B. *We have to consent to his gifts being used by us*
(a) The sovereignty of the Giver.
(b) The diversity of the gifts.

C. *We have to consent to his work being done in us*
(a) The ministries which he will want to exercise.
(b) The liberty which he will want to enjoy.

The nature of the Church (3)

Ephesians 5.15–33

A. *The love on which the church is built*
(a) The Person of Christ is central in her life.
(b) The passion of Christ is revealed in her life.

B. *The law by which the Church is ruled*
(a) The position given to Christ by the Father.
(b) The submission given to Christ by the fellowship.

C. *The life to which the Church is called*
(a) The perfection which Christ seeks in the Church.
(b) The provision which Christ makes for the Church.

Time – one of the most precious things we possess

Ephesians 5.15–16: 'Redeeming the time'

A. *The passage of time which we do well to heed*
(a) How swiftly it will pass.
(b) How surely it must end.

B. *The pathway through time which we have got to take*
(a) There is progress which we should make.
(b) There are people whom we will meet.

C. *The purchase of time which we are wise to make*
(a) What we must discern.
(b) What we must discard.

'Be filled with the Spirit'

Ephesians 5.18

A. *The command to be obeyed*
(a) The obligation which these words lay upon us.
(b) The implication which these words lay before us.

B. *The condition to be maintained*
(a) Discoveries which must be made.
(b) Disciplines which must be maintained.

C. *The Christ who is to be revealed*
(a) The perfection of this revelation.
(b) The attraction of this revelation.

The armour of God

Ephesians 6.10–18: 'Put on the whole armour of God'

A. *Our involvement with the enemy of God*
(a) The person he is.
(b) The purposes he has.

B. *Our equipment from the armoury of God*
(a) The identity of the armour.
(b) The totality of the armour.

C. *Our enjoyment of the victory of God*
(a) The unending conflict which we are prepared to accept.
(b) The unbroken contact which we must always maintain.

The weapon of prayer

Ephesians 6.19: 'Praying always with all prayer and supplication in the Spirit, and watching thereunto with all perseverance and supplication for all the saints and for me'

A. *The variety of the forms which prayer will adopt*
(a) There will be an adaptability about prayer.
(b) There will be an availability for prayer.

B. *The intensity of the fight which prayer will provoke*
(a) There will be an endurance which must be displayed.
(b) There will be an assistance which can be had.

C. *The reponsibility for the field which prayer will accept*
(a) How extensive the battle is.
(b) How carefully selected the targets will be.

Philippians

Paul's prayer for the church at Philippi

Philippians 1.9–11

A. *That profusion which is the mark of true love*
(a) The gift of love which has been received by every believer.
(b) The growth of love which should be revealed in every believer.

B. *That perception which guides the ministry of true love*
(a) The communion in which love will learn.
(b) The confusion through which love will lead.

C. *That perfection which is the must of true love*
(a) The pains which love will take for the Lord's sake.
(b) The praise which love will bring to the Lord's Name.

Handling the happenings of life with praise

Philippians 1.12–21: 'The things which happened unto me'

A. *The pattern of his life had been smashed*
(a) The work he had loved had come to an end.
(b) The way he had lived had come to an end.

B. *The pressures upon his faith can be sensed*
(a) He is tempted to think that his life is useless.
(b) He is tempted to think that his Lord is faithless.

C. *The praises of his Lord were being sung*
(a) He was thinking of the other people whom he could now reach.
(b) He was thinking of the better person he could now be.

451

What it meant to Paul to be a Christian

Philippians 1.21: 'To me to live is Christ'

A. *It meant something personal: 'To me'*
(a) Personal in his acceptance of Christ.
(b) Personal in his allegiance to Christ.

B. *It meant something practical: 'to live'*
(a) Every moment of his life would be spent with him.
(b) Every matter in his life would be shared with him.

C. *It meant something possible: 'is Christ'*
(a) This life is available to all who are in Christ.
(b) This life is attainable by all through Christ.

The fellowship of the Spirit

Philippians 2.1

A. *The conditions to be fulfilled*
(a) The indwelling of the life of the Spirit of God.
(b) The initiative of the love of the Spirit of God.

B. *The character to be displayed*
(a) The depth of the fellowship.
(b) The delights in the fellowship.

C. *The correctives to be applied*
(a) The tragedies which can spoil.
(b) The remedies which can save.

Growing up into spiritual fulfilment

Philippians 2.12–13: 'Work our your own salvation [experience of God's saving grace] with fear and trembling [to its completeness]. For it is God which worketh in you both to will and to do of his good pleasure.'

   A. *Variations in the purposes of God for our lives: 'your own'*
   (a) There is encouragement here for our hearts.
   (b) There is enrichment here for the Church.

   B. *Operation of the Spirit of God in our lives: 'God worketh in you'*
   (a) The Spirit of God can be restrained.
   (b) The Spirit of God must be released.

   C. *Motivation of the fear of God in our lives: 'with fear and trembling'*
   (a) The failure which love dreads to be.
   (b) The pleasure which love longs to give.

Paul's ambition as a Christian

Philippians 3.10: 'That I may know him, and the power of his [risen life], and the fellowship of his sufferings'

   A. *The Person of the risen Christ he wanted to know*
   (a) The conditions of knowing him.
   (b) The consequences of knowing him.

   B. *The power of the risen Christ he wanted to have*
   (a) The weakness in his life which he had discovered.
   (b) The witness to his Lord demanded by Christ.

   C. *The purpose of the risen Christ he wanted to share*
   (a) The burdens he must bear.
   (b) The blessings he would bring.

Paul's story

Philippians 3.10

    A.   *Captivated by a Person*
    (a) The memory of that hour.
    (b) The ministry with his Lord.

    B.   *Liberated by a power*
    (a) The wonder of that power in his life.
    (b) The witness of that power to his Lord.

    C.   *Dominated by a purpose*
    (a) How clearly that purpose had been revealed.
    (b) How costly that purpose had then proved.

The secret of Paul's influence

Philippians 3.12–13: 'I follow after, if that I may apprehend that for which also I am apprehended of Christ Jesus. Brethren, I count not myself to have apprehended: but this one thing I do . . . '

    A.   *The vision given to him*
    (a) The pattern which was seen clearly.
    (b) The pathway which would prove costly.

    B.   *The verdict passed by him*
    (a) The achievements of this man which were astounding.
    (b) The assessment by this man which was amazing.

    C.   *The vigour shown by him*
    (a) The concentration shown by him.
    (b) The consummation sought by him.

Behind, before, beyond

Philippians 3.12–14

A. *What lay behind*
(a) Paul's gratitude for it.
(b) Paul's attitude to it.

B. *What lay before*
(a) The purpose to be revealed.
(b) The people to be reached.

C. *What lay beyond*
(a) The voice he must obey.
(b) The verdict he would receive.

The importance of forgetting

Philippians 3.13: 'Forgetting those things which are behind'

A. *The past behind*
(a) The record which the past held.
(b) The resolve which Paul made.

B. *The path before*
(a) His dedication as he faced the future.
(b) His expectation as he faced the future.

C. *The prize beyond*
(a) The summons he was determined to obey.
(b) The success he was determined to achieve.

Living in the presence of the Lord

Philippians 4.5: 'The Lord is at hand'

A. *The presence of the Lord of which we are sure*
(a) The acceptance there must be of that presence.
(b) The assurance we can have of that presence.

B. *The presence of the Lord with whom we can share*
(a) Every moment of our lives will be spent with him.
(b) Every matter in our lives will be shared with him.

C. *The presence of the Lord by which we are saved*
(a) The anxiety in our hearts which is understandable.
(b) The adequacy of our Lord which is inexhaustible.

Contentment

Philippians 4:11: 'I have learned, in whatsoever state I am, therewith to be content'

A. *A commandment which the Christian must heed: Hebrews 13.5: 'Be content'*
(a) The concern which lies behind that commandment.
(b) The consent which lies before the Christian.

B. *An attainment which the Christian must learn: Philippians 4.11: 'I have learned'*
(a) The changes which life had brought to him.
(b) The chances which change had held for him.

C. *An enrichment which the Christian will find: 1 Timothy 6.6: 'Godliness with contentment is great gain'*
(a) The needs in the world which can then be met.
(b) The Name of the Lord which will then be glorified.

God will provide

Philippians 4.13

A. *An assurance upon which faith can rest: 'My God'*
(a) All the years in which Paul had served him.
(b) All the times when Paul had proved him.

B. *An assistance upon which faith can count: 'Your need'*
(a) The supplying of the need.
(b) The safeguarding of the Name.

C. *An abundance upon which faith can draw: 'His riches'*
(a) The wealth which is stored in Christ.
(b) The wealth which he will share with us.

Colossians

Essential principles for living the Christian life

Colossians 1.3: 'Always'

A. *The Christian will be always in touch with the Throne of God*
(a) The immediacy of the contact.
(b) The intensity of the concern.

B. *The Christian will be always in tune with the will of God: Philippians 2.12*
(a) How many there are who must be reached.
(b) How many there are who will be required.

C. *The Christian will be always in triumph by the grace of God: 2 Corinthians 2.14*
(a) The source of our victory.
(b) The strength of our testimony.

Lessons from the life of Epaphras

Colossians 1.7, 4.12–13; Philippians 2.25

A. *A partner in the work*
(a) The affliction which this man endured.
(b) The affection which this man evoked.

B. *A wrestler at the Throne*
(a) His praying was continuous.
(b) His praying was strenuous.

C. *A seeker of the best*
(a) The contrast which this man affords.
(b) The concern which this man displays.

A spiritual check-up

Colossians 1.9–11

    A.   *How decisive is the will of God in my thinking?*
    (a) What was the pattern of my thinking before I became a Christian?
    (b) What is the pattern now that I am a Christian?

    B.   *How attractive is my walk with God?*
    (a) The intention which God has.
    (b) The impression which I give.

    C.   *How effective is my work for God?*
    (a) The resources which have been provided.
    (b) The results which should be expected.

Three different kinds of Christians

Colossians 1.18: 'That in all things he might have the pre-eminence'

    A.   *The Christian in whose life Christ is present*
    (a) In receiving Christ he is right.
    (b) In restricting Christ he is wrong.

    B.   *The Christian in whose life Christ is prominent*
    (a) He is not ashamed of the Lord in his life.
    (b) Christ is not allowed to be Lord of his life.

    C.   *The Christian in whose life Christ is pre-eminent*
    (a) He will have been tested by God.
    (b) He will be trusted by God.

'Christ in you'

Colossians 1.27

A. *The life he wants to begin in you*
(a) There is an enslavement which he wants to break.
(b) There is an enrichment which he wants to bring.

B. *The love he wants to beget in you*
(a) The correction which love brings to our thinking.
(b) The compulsion which love brings to our living.

C. *The Lord he wants to become in you*
(a) The control which he would assume.
(b) The consent which he must await.

Knowing the will of God

Colossians 4.12: 'That ye may stand perfect and complete in all the will of God'

A. *The conviction will persist*
(a) There will be the experience of a pressure.
(b) There will be the emergence of a picture.

B. *The Church will perceive*
(a) The Christian will be active in the fellowship.
(b) The Christian will be approved by the fellowship.

C. *The circumstances will permit*
(a) The authority which will control the course of my life.
(b) The ability which will confirm the call of my Lord.
(*Main headings from H. W. Cragg.*)

1 Thessalonians

The hallmarks of a Christian

1 Thessalonians 1.3, 9–10

A. *What Christian faith does*
(a) It will turn from.
(b) It will trust in.

B. *How Christian love toils*
(a) The new motive which the Christian has.
(b) The new Master whom the Christian serves.

C. *Why Christian hope waits*
(a) The problems which assail the Christian.
(b) The promise which assures the Christian.

Paul's relationship with the gospel

1 Thessalonians 2.1–13

A. *The proclamation of the gospel I must make with my lips*
(a) How courageous our words must sometimes be.
(b) How contentious our words will sometimes prove.

B. *The obligation I must face of living out the gospel in my life*
(a) The trust which has been placed in me.
(b) The tests which must be passed by me.

C. *The motivation of God's love which I must have*
(a) The grace of love seen here.
(b) The goal of love sought here.

The way God wants us to live

1 Thessalonians 5.16–18

    A. *The Christian should live joyfully*
    (a) Where our joy is centred.
    (b) Why our joy is constant.

    B. *The Christian should live prayerfully*
    (a) The pressures by which the Christian is tried.
    (b) The Presence to which the Christian can turn.

    C. *The Christian should live thankfully*
    (a) How varied are the circumstances of life.
    (b) How valued are the discoveries of life.

The Holy Spirit and the Church

1 Thessalonians 5.19–22

    A. *The promptings which the Spirit will give*
    (a) The functions of the Spirit.
    (b) The failures of the Christian.

    B. *The preachers whom he will use*
    (a) The authority which we must accept.
    (b) The attitude which we must avoid.

    C. *The practice which he will seek*
    (a) The discernment he will give.
    (b) The discipline he will want.

1 Timothy to Philemon

1 Timothy

Age and youth

1 Timothy 1.1–2: 'Paul . . . unto Timothy'

  A. *The ministry which age has to youth*
  (a) The conviction which chose the path for Paul.
  (b) The conversion which crowned the preaching of Paul.

  B. *The intimacy which age shares with youth*
  (a) Their enlightenment through the Spirit of Christ.
  (b) Their enjoyment in the service of Christ.

  C. *The destiny which age seeks for youth*
  (a) The prayer he offered.
  (b) The progress he followed.

The ultimate aim of the Christian ministry

1 Timothy 1.5

A. *The openness of love*
(a) There is no concealment in love.
(b) There is no contentment like love.

B. *The sensitiveness of love*
(a) The perception which is distinctive about love.
(b) The perfection which is demanded by love.

C. *The trustfulness of love*
(a) How eagerly love responds.
(b) How utterly love relies.

Why Christ came into the world

1 Timothy 1.15: 'This is a faithful saying'

A. *The Person of whom the gospel speaks*
(a) The imperative which we face in Christ.
(b) The initiative which we find in Christ.

B. *The purpose of which the gospel speaks*
(a) What are we to be saved from?
(b) Who are we to be saved by?

C. *The people of whom the gospel speaks*
(a) We must admit what we are.
(b) We must accept what we need.

A plea for self-examination

1 Timothy 4.16: 'Take heed unto thyself'

A. *Am I diligent?*
(a) The menace of sloth.
(b) The motive of service.

B. *Am I disciplined?*
(a) The spheres of danger.
(b) The denials it demands.

C. *Am I discerning?*
(a) The perception I must exercise.
(b) The perfection I must attain.

The love of money

1 Timothy 6.10

A. *How powerful is the appeal of money*
(a) How attractive money can seem to be.
(b) How deceptive money can prove to be.

B. *How perilous is the pursuit of money*
(a) How prolific the damage can be socially.
(b) How specific the damage can be spiritually.

C. *How productive is the right use of money*
(a) The limited opportunities we may have.
(b) The limitless possibilities we must grasp.

465

2 Timothy

The contents of the past: a New Year message

2 Timothy 1.3, 1.12, 4.7

- A. *His enlistment in the faith*
- (a) The discovery of the saviourhood of Jesus Christ.
- (b) The discovery of the sovereignty of Jesus Christ.

- B. *His enjoyment of the fellowship*
- (a) The blessing we are meant to be to one another.
- (b) The burdens we are meant to bear for one another.

- C. *His engagement in the fight*
- (a) How numerous the enemies had been.
- (b) How glorious the victories had been.

'Stir into flame the gift of God which is in thee'

2 Timothy 1.6

- A. *The quality of the Spirit which is stressed here*
- (a) There is a destructive quality about fire.
- (b) There is an attractive quality about fire.

- B. *The tragedy in the life of the servant of God which is sensed here*
- (a) The decline which is sensed here.
- (b) The demand which is made here.

- C. *The urgency of the Saviour which is seen here*
- (a) A concern has been revealed.
- (b) A command must be obeyed.

'God hath not given us the spirit of fear'

2 Timothy 1.7

A. *The timidity which men sometimes feel*
(a) What is the reason for this timidity?
(b) What is the reply to this timidity?

B. *The hostility which men sometimes face*
(a) The tyranny of fear.
(b) The liberty of love.

C. *The uncertainty which men sometimes find*
(a) Caused by the darkness in which fear dwells.
(b) Cured by the brightness in which faith lives.

Paul's counsel to Timothy

2 Timothy 1.8

A. *He must not be ashamed of the Lord*
(a) He must speak up for the Saviour.
(b) He must stand up for his servants.

B. *He need not be afraid of the wounds*
(a) The suffering which must be faced.
(b) The satisfaction which would be found.

C. *He would not be alone in the fight*
(a) The company which would go with him.
(b) The victory which would come to him.

The vindication of Paul's faith

2 Timothy 1.12: 'I know whom I have believed'

    A.   *The confrontation which the past had held for Paul*
    (a) A confrontation with the Person of Christ.
    (b) A confrontation with the purpose of Christ.

    B.   *The confirmation which the years had brought to Paul*
    (a) What the price had been.
    (b) What the past had held.

    C.   *The consummation which the day would hold for Paul*
    (a) It would bring the verdict of his Lord.
    (b) It would bring the vision of his Lord.

On active service in Christ's army (1)

2 Timothy 2.3: 'Endure hardness, as a good soldier of Jesus Christ'

    A.   *A soldier must be willing to go to any place*
    (a) We expect the presence of this quality of obedience from some.
    (b) We excuse the absence of this quality of obedience in ourselves.

    B.   *A soldier must be willing to move at any time*
    (a) How inconvenient the soldier's instructions can prove to be.
    (b) How unimportant the soldier's intentions are shown to be.

    C.   *A soldier must be willing to fight with any foe*
    (a) The equipment he is expected to wear.
    (b) The engagement he is expected to win.

On active service in Christ's army (2)

2 Timothy 2.3

    A.   *The conflict in which he is involved*
    (a) Due to the environment he must accept.
    (b) Due to the engagement he cannot escape.

    B.   *The comrades by whom he is sustained*
    (a) The depth at which this fellowship is enjoyed.
    (b) The length for which this fellowship is enjoyed.

    C.   *The Captain to whom he must respond*
    (a) The allegiance he will offer.
    (b) The achievement he will record.

The faithfulness of God

2 Timothy 2.13: 'He abideth faithful'

    A.   *The faithfulness in his person*
    (a) The truth declared.
    (b) The trust deserved.

    B.   *His faithfulness to his purpose*
    (a) The pressures restricted by him.
    (b) The power resident in him.

    C.   *His faithfulness to his people*
    (a) The faithfulness which will be required of us.
    (b) The faithfulness which will be rewarded by God.

Pleasing God

2 Timothy 2.15: 'Study to show thyself approved unto God'

A. *The truths which God will want us to know*
(a) What is the message of God?
(b) What are the methods of God?

B. *The tests which God will want us to pass*
(a) There will be the test of obedience.
(b) There will be the test of dependence.

C. *The tasks which God will give us to do*
(a) There will be the light which we are to shed.
(b) There will be the loads which we are to share.

Religion – a force or a farce?

2 Timothy 3.5: 'though they keep up a form of religion, they will have nothing to do with it as a force'

A. *The place which they give to their religion*
(a) The profession which they make.
(b) The practices which they maintain.

B. *The purposes which they serve by their religion*
(a) They use it as a sop to their conscience.
(b) They use it as a policy of insurance.

C. *The parody which they make of their religion*
(a) What of the character of true Christianity?
(b) What of the consequences of true Christianity?

From a child thou has known the holy Scriptures

2 Timothy 3.15

A. *The Scriptures in which he was instructed*
(a) The sensitive years of a child.
(b) The retentive mind of a child.

B. *The salvation of which he had learned*
(a) He had learned of the infection of sin.
(b) He had gained from his instruction in truth.

C. *The Saviour in whom he now trusted*
(a) He had learned of the Person of Jesus Christ.
(b) He had learned of the power of Jesus Christ.

The place of preaching in the church today

2 Timothy 4.1–5: 'Preach the word'

A. *It deals with a relationship adjusted by God*
(a) Made right through Christ's death for men.
(b) Kept right through Christ dwelling in men.

B. *It deals with a fellowship which can be enjoyed in Christ*
(a) The new life which brings us together.
(b) The new love which binds us together.

C. *It deals with a stewardship which must be discharged by us*
(a) It speaks of the immensity of the task.
(b) It speaks of the diversity of the gifts.

The task of the preacher and the sources of his message

2 Timothy 4.1–5

A. *The words of Holy Writ*
(a) The study which the Scriptures demand.
(b) The secrets which the Scriptures reveal.
(c) The standard which the Scriptures become.

B. *The works of godly men*
(a) Biography, in which their lives are revealed.
(b) Doctrine, in which the truths of God's word are explained.
(c) Sermons, through which the teaching of the godly men can be enjoyed.

C. *The world of human need*
(a) The needs in the pastor's heart and life.
(b) The needs in his people's hearts and lives.
(c) The needs in the public's hearts and lives.

The structure of the preacher's message

2 Timothy 4.1–5

A. *He must analyse the text*
(a) He must break it into pieces.
(b) He must bring together the pieces which are related.

B. *He must crystallise the truths*
(a) He must find out what each group of thoughts is saying.
(b) He must express each group in a phrase or word which will stick.

C. *He must humanise the telling*
(a) He should use illustrations as Christ did.
(b) He should apply the text to life in a way people can understand.

The minister's responsibility to God

2 Timothy 4.1–8: 'I charge thee before God . . . '

A.   *The presence in which the minister is found*
(a) So that the will of God might be perceived by him.
(b) So that the word of God might be proclaimed by him.

B.   *The pressures with which the minister must cope*
(a) There will be pressures from within.
(b) There will be pressures from without.

C.   *The prospect with which the minister is faced*
(a) The vision given by his Lord.
(b) The verdict passed on his life.

Paul's assessment of his own ministry (1)

2 Timothy 4.1–8: 'I have finished my course'

A.   *We see Paul lasting out the course*
(a) The necessity of faithfulness.
(b) The possibility of faithlessness.

B.   *We see Paul looking for the crown*
(a) The expectation of love which will be realised.
(b) The evaluation of life which will be effected.

C.   *We see Paul laying down the charge*
(a) He speaks of the time of his departure.
(b) He speaks of the task of his successor.

Paul's assessment of his own ministry (2)

2 Timothy 4.7

A. *The destiny to which his life had been called*
(a) His acceptance of the will of the Father.
(b) His endurance in the work of the Father.

B. *The tragedy from which his name had had to be cleared*
(a) The terms he had accepted.
(b) The taunts he had avoided.

C. *The victory with which his work had been crowned*
(a) The unending battle.
(b) The unceasing blessing.

Words which every Christian would want to be able to say

2 Timothy 4.7: 'I have finished my course'

A. *A fight has been fought*
(a) With our fears.
(b) With our foes.

B. *A race has been run*
(a) The grace we have known.
(b) The goal we have reached.

C. *A faith has been kept*
(a) We have been tempted to forsake it.
(b) We have been trusted to proclaim it.

Demas – a spiritual dropout?

2 Timothy 4.10; Colossians 4.14; Philemon 24

    A.   *A love which was compelled to labour*
    (a) The privileges which Demas enjoyed.
    (b) The progress which Demas experienced.

    B.   *A love which was content to listen*
    (a) The restraint in the statement.
    (b) The results in the spirit.

    C.   *A love which was seen to languish*
    (a) Note the tragic choice of the man.
    (b) Note the empty place of the man.

The importance in our lives of books other than the Bible

2 Timothy 4.13: 'Bring the books'

    A.   *Books of biography, in which the intimacies of the Christian life are exposed*
    (a) Here we may find the stimulus of vision.
    (b) Here we may learn the secrets of victory.

    B.   *Books of doctrine, in which the truths of the Christian faith are explained*
    (a) The reticence of ignorance.
    (b) The importance of knowledge.

    C.   *Books of sermons, in which the ministries of the Christian Church are enjoyed*
    (a) Some great ministries are silenced by death.
    (b) Some great ministries are separated by distance.

A request from Paul

2 Timothy 4.13

A. *The unexpected request*
(a) The meaning of such a request.
(b) The meeting of such a request.

B. *The undoubted reason*
(a) The provision would not be difficult.
(b) The programme would not be disturbed.

C. *The unavailing regret*
(a) The urgency which marks some of the opportunities we may have.
(b) The tragedy which marks some of the opportunities we may lose.

Titus

The Second Coming of Christ

Titus 2.13: 'That blessed hope'
Acts 1.11: 'This same Jesus . . . . shall so come in like manner as ye have seen him go'

A. *The watch which the Christian has to keep*
(a) The despondency which is spreading.
(b) The expectancy which is sustaining.

B. *The work which the Christian has to do*
(a) The responsibilities of the Christian.
(b) The opportunities of the Christian.

C. *The way in which the Christian has to live*
(a) The discipline which is required of the Christian.
(b) The delight which will be experienced by the Christian.

The kindness of God as seen in Jesus Christ

Titus 3.4

A. *The time he spent with those who were thought to be unimportant: Mark 10.13*
(a) Note the attitude which Christ rebuked.
(b) Note the gratitude which Christ evoked.

B. *The trust he placed in those who had proved to be unsuccessful: Luke 22.61*
(a) There was a look which thanked Peter.
(b) There was a love which trusted Peter.

C. *The touch he had for those who were seen as unattractive: Mark 1.40*
(a) The tragedy of the unattractive.
(b) The destiny for the unattractive.

D. *The task he gave to those who were known to be unacceptable: John 4.7*
(a) She felt she was rejected.
(b) She found she was required.

Preach the Word

What does the Gospel say?

Titus 3.4–8

A. *It speaks of God's revealing grace*
(a) The motivation behind the revealing grace of God.
(b) The implications within the revealing grace of God.

B. *It speaks of God's restoring grace*
(a) The condemnation in which men share.
(b) The crucifixion through which Christ saves.

C. *It speaks of God's renewing grace*
(a) The transformation which men can know.
(b) The expectation which men should have.

Philemon

Paul, a prisoner of Jesus Christ

Philemon 1

A. *The unexplained providence in his life*
(a) The seeming tragedy of it.
(b) The sensed opportunity in it.

B. *The undismayed endurance of his love*
(a) The real hardship.
(b) The rejoicing fellowship.

C. *The unshaken confidence of his faith*
(a) Confidence in the wisdom of God's permissive will.
(b) Confidence in the wealth of God's providing grace.

'The church in thy house'

Philemon 2

A. *The closeness of the bond between the Christians*
(a) The intimacy of their fellowship.
(b) The insignificance of their numbers.

B. *The costliness of the Christians' faith*
(a) The personal inconvenience.
(b) The social implications.

C. *The consecration of the Christians' homes*
(a) The sanctity of the everyday would be emphasised.
(b) The responsibility to the world would be realised.

An insight into Paul's life

Philemon

A. *Paul and his circumstances*
(a) There were difficulties.
(b) There were opportunities.

B. *Paul and his converts*
(a) The gratitude he assumes.
(b) The rectitude he shows.

C. *Paul and his colleagues*
(a) His thanks for them.
(b) His trust in them.

A personal letter from Paul

Philemon

A. *What the letter reveals*
(a) Paul's grateful appreciation of others.
(b) Paul's gracious attitude to others.

B. *What the letter requests*
(a) The relationship which Paul describes to Philemon.
(b) The fellowship which Paul desires with Philemon.

C. *What the letter recalls*
(a) The debt of which Paul reminds Philemon.
(b) The debt which Philemon had to repay.

Hebrews

The reign of Christ

Hebrews 1.8–9: 'Thy throne, O God, is for ever and ever: a sceptre of righteousness is the sceptre of thy kingdom. Thou hast loved righteousness, and hated iniquity; therefore God, even thy God, hath anointed thee with the oil of gladness above thy fellows.'

A. *The permanence which the rule of Christ demands: 'Thy throne, O God, is for ever and ever'*
(a) How intermittent is the allegiance which we offer.
(b) How inconsistent is the attitude which we adopt.

B. *The purity which the role of Christ requires: 'A sceptre of righteousness is the sceptre of thy kingdom'*
(a) There must be a recognition of sin.
(b) There will be a rejection of sin.

C. *The passion which the rule of Christ imparts: 'Thou hast loved righteousness, and hated iniquity'*
(a) There is a passion we will share.
(b) There is a passion we must show.

D. *The praise which the rule of Christ inspires: 'The oil of gladness'*
(a) The essential adjustment in our lives.
(b) The final enjoyment in our hearts.

The possibility and peril of drifting

Hebrews 2.1: 'We must pay a closer attention to what we have heard, lest we drift away from it'

A. *The picture sketched here*
(a) A movement which is almost unnoticed.
(b) A movement which is almost incredible.

B. *The peril sensed here*
(a) How perilous the drifting life becomes.
(b) How presumptuous the drifting life has been.

C. *The problem solved here*
(a) The answer revealed.
(b) The action required.

Neglect – one of the unsuspected dangers of life

Hebrews 2.3: 'How shall we escape, if we neglect so great a salvation?'

A. *The possibility of neglect*
(a) It is common.
(b) It has causes.

B. *The peril of neglect: 'How shall we escape?'*
(a) The results can be extensive.
(b) The realm can be decisive.

C. *The presumption of neglect: 'great salvation'*
(a) The greatness of our salvation.
(b) The greatness of our sin.

'Through suffering'

Hebrews 2.10

A. *The loyalty which can only be proved through suffering: Hebrews 5.8: 'Though he were a Son, yet learned he obedience by the things which he suffered'*

(a) This is illustrated by the revelation of the will of God received by Abraham.

(b) Consider the response which Abraham rendered to the will of God.

B. *The maturity which can only be gained through suffering: 2.10: 'Made perfect through suffering'*

(a) The tragedy which had touched the home of Hosea.

(b) The tenderness which transformed the ministry of Hosea.

C. *The sympathy which can only be born through suffering: 2.18: 'In that he himself hath suffered being tempted, he is able to succour them that are tempted'*

(a) The agony which Christ's sufferings meant to him.

(b) The asset which Christ's sufferings become for us.

D. *The ministry which can be shared only through suffering: 13.12: 'Wherefore Jesus also . . . suffered without the gate. Let us go forth therefore unto him without the camp'*

(a) The reproach of which the cross speaks.

(b) The result to which the cross leads.

The power of the word of God

Hebrews 4.12: 'The word of God is quick and powerful'

    A.   *The quickening into life through the word: 1 Peter 1.23*
    (a) It is a living word.
    (b) It is a lasting word.

    B.   *The strengthening of our faith through the word: Romans 10.14–17*
    (a) What faith must first know.
    (b) How faith will then act.

    C.   *The deepening of our love through the word: Philippians 1.9*
    (a) The time which must be spent together.
    (b) The things which will be shared together.

    D.   *The lighting of our path through the word: Psalm 119.105*
    (a) The darkness into which we have to travel.
    (b) The deliverance by which we can be saved.

Growing up into spiritual maturity

Hebrews 6.1: 'Let us go on to perfection' or 'Let us advance steadily towards spiritual maturity'

    A.   *The importance which this should have in our lives*
    (a) The exhortation in the Scriptures.
    (b) The example of the saints.

    B.   *The difference which it will make in our lives*
    (a) The instruction we can then take.
    (b) The interest we shall then have.

    C.   *The evidence which will show in our lives*
    (a) There will be a mastery of our lips: James 3.2.
    (b) There will be a serenity in our lives: 1 John 4.17–19.

'He is able'

Hebrews 7.25

A. *Christ is able to save*
(a) The relationship transformed by what he has done for me.
(b) The resources transformed by what he can do in me.

B. *Christ is able to keep: Jude 24*
(a) The fearfulness which can hold me back from the will of God.
(b) The faithfulness which will hold me fast in the love of God.

C. *Christ is able to do: Ephesians 3.20*
(a) Christ's ability will exceed our thoughts.
(b) Christ's ability should excite our hearts.

An end to sin

Hebrews 8.12: 'No more'

A. *Faith says 'no more' to the guilt of man's sin*
(a) Faith knows that sin can be forgiven.
(b) Faith knows that sin can be forgotten.

B. *Faith says 'no more' to the grind of sin's servitude: Galatians 4.7*
(a) The bitterness of servitude.
(b) The blessedness of sonship.

C. *Faith says 'no more' to the grief of life's sorrows: Revelation 21.4*
(a) How hurtful human sorrow can be.
(b) How hopeful the Christian's salvation will prove.

The inevitability of death

Hebrews 9.27: 'It is appointed unto men once to die, and after this the judgment'

A. *When death will come*
(a) It will come inevitably.
(b) It will come irresistibly.

B. *Where death will lead*
(a) The expectation of an after-life.
(b) The preparation for an after-life.

C. *What death will hold*
(a) A judgment which will differ.
(b) A judgment which will divide.

What should be the atmosphere in a church? Expectancy!

Hebrews 10.13: 'From henceforth expecting'

A. *What do the members have the right to expect of their minister?*
(a) As a preacher.
(b) As a pastor.

B. *What does the minister have the right to expect of his members?*
(a) The presence of his people.
(b) The prayers of his people.

C. *What does the Master have the right to expect from both minister and members?*
(a) A worship which enthrones him.
(b) A witness which exalts him.

The blood of Christ

Hebrews 10.19

   A.   *The fountain in which we can be cleansed: 1 John 1.7*
(a) The Person whose blood was shed.
(b) The people whose sins are cleansed.

   B.   *The fetters from which we can be freed: Ephesians 1.7*
(a) The transaction which has been carried out.
(b) The translation into a new world which can be enjoyed.

   C.   *The fellowship in which we can now live*
(a) The peace with God which is now possible: Romans 5.9.
(b) The peace with men which is now possible: Ephesians 2.13.

A threefold invitation to faith

Hebrews 10.19–25: 'Let us draw near ... Let us hold fast ... Let us stir up' (RSV)

   A.   *The communion with his God which the Christian is meant to enjoy*
(a) How dearly bought this communion is.
(b) How deeply blessed this communion will prove.

   B.   *The confession of his faith which the Christian is meant to express*
(a) The hope we have found in Christ.
(b) The help we will find in Christ.

   C.   *The companions on the road whom the Christian is meant to inspire*
(a) How thoughtful of one another Christians should be.
(b) How helpful to one another Christians should prove.

The obedience of faith

Hebrews 11.8: 'By faith Abraham when he was called to go out . . . obeyed; and he went out, not knowing whither he went'

A. *The response which faith is*
(a) There had been a revealing by God of his Person and of his purpose.
(b) There had been a response of trust and obedience from man.

B. *The resources which faith taps*
(a) What an abundance there will be to meet my need.
(b) What a difference that will make in my life.

C. *The result which faith sees*
(a) The people whom God will bless through me.
(b) The presence which God will give to me.

Faith in the life of Moses

Hebrews 11.23–31

A. *The faith which surrounded him as a child*
(a) His parents' intercession for him.
(b) His parents' instruction of him.

B. *The faith which separated him from the crowd*
(a) The attractions in the world which he resisted.
(b) The afflictions of his people which he resented.

C. *The faith which sustained him on his way*
(a) The vision he had.
(b) The action he took.

The biggest choice which any man has to make

Hebrews 11.25: 'Choosing . . . God'

A. *The discovery which arrested Moses*
(a) The influences this man had known.
(b) The inferences this man had drawn.

B. *The decision which alarmed him*
(a) The love he would seem to spurn.
(b) The lot he would have to share.

C. *The destiny which awaited him*
(a) The obscurity into which he must first retreat.
(b) The opportunity for which he was then recalled.

'Looking unto Jesus'

Hebrews 12.1–4

A. *What we must leave: 'Let us lay aside every weight, and the sin which does so easily beset us'*
(a) This calls for an ability to discern what hinders.
(b) This calls for an ability to discard what hinders.

B. *Where we must look*
(a) We can look around at the spectators.
(b) We must look ahead at the Saviour.

C. *How we must last: 'Run with patience (or endurance)'*
(a) How sad it would be if we failed.
(b) How glad we will be if we finish.

Where faith will look

Hebrews 12.1–3

A. *Faith can look gratefully backward*
(a) The examples which will encourage.
(b) The exceptions which could discourage.

B. *Faith will look joyfully forward*
(a) There will be an acceptance of the cost of victory.
(b) There will be an endurance in the race to victory.

C. *Faith will look trustingly upward*
(a) The authority to which faith must yield.
(b) The adequacy on which faith can count.

A time to look forward

Hebrews 12.1–2

A. *The great past*
(a) The writer speaks of the conquests behind them.
(b) The writer speaks of the contest before them.

B. *The new race*
(a) The hindrances the runner will remove.
(b) The endurance the runner will require.

C. *The same Lord*
(a) The direction of their gaze.
(b) Their dependence on his grace.

The race of faith (1)

Hebrews 12.1–2: 'Let us run with patience the race that is set before us'

A. *The progress to which faith is called*
(a) The importance of how we prepare for the race.
(b) The endurance with which we will persist in the race.

B. *The witness by which faith is cheered*
(a) The enablement which the witnesses receive.
(b) The encouragement which the witnesses become.

C. *The success with which faith is crowned*
(a) The commencement of the race.
(b) The completion of the race.

The race of faith (2)

Hebrews 12.1–2

A. *Stripping for the race: 'Let us lay aside'*
(a) There are things we must put off.
(b) There are things we must put on.

B. *Starting the race: 'Let us run'*
(a) The decision we must make.
(b) The direction we must take.

C. *Staying in the race: 'Let us run with patience'*
(a) There are those who give up.
(b) There are those who go on.

Disciplined by God (1)

Hebrews 12.3–13: 'The chastening of the Lord'

A. *The Person behind the chastening*
(a) The chastening is an expression of love.
(b) The chastening is an evidence of life.

B. *The purpose beyond the chastening*
(a) The intention of God which can be seen.
(b) The submission of God which will be sought.

C. *The perils within the chastening*
(a) A worthlessness can be ascribed to such discipline.
(b) A weariness can be allowed with such discipline.

Disciplined by God (2)

Hebrews 12.5–18

A. *The evidence revealed by it*
(a) Evidence of a living relationship between Father and child.
(b) Evidence of a loving relationship between Father and child.

B. *The endurance required for it*
(a) How unpleasant chastening can be.
(b) How unprofitable chastening can prove.

C. *The experience resulting from it*
(a) The gain to ourselves.
(b) The grip on ourselves.

Esau – the man who lost so much for so little

Hebrews 12.16: 'Esau, who for a single meal, parted with his birth-right' (Moffatt)

A. *What he loved*
(a) His importance in the community.
(b) His indulgence of his appetites.

B. *What he lacked*
(a) He lacked discernment.
(b) He lacked discipline.

C. *What he lost*
(a) The destiny he was meant to fulfil.
(b) The delight he was meant to give.

'Be not forgetful to entertain strangers'

Hebrews 13.2

A. *The strangers we are bound to meet*
(a) They may be people we have never met before.
(b) They may be experiences we have never had before.
(c) They may be truths we have never heard before.

B. *The suspicions we are apt to feel*
(a) There is wisdom which justifies such an attitude.
(b) There are warnings which encourage such an attitude.
(c) There is a welcome which transcends such an attitude.

C. *The surprises we are going to get*
(a) A new environment which God wants us to enter.
(b) A new enrichment which God wants us to accept.
(c) A new enjoyment which God wants us to have.

The unchanging Christ

Hebrews 13.8: 'Jesus Christ the same yesterday, today and forever'

A. *His pardon for my sins never changes*
(a) The dying which secured my pardon.
(b) The doubting which can spoil my pardon.

B. *His presence in my heart never changes*
(a) How certain the fact has been.
(b) How clouded the fellowship may be now.

C. *His provision for my need never changes*
(a) The faithfulness on which I can rely.
(b) The fearfulness in which I stand rebuked.

D. *His purpose for my life never changes*
(a) The perfection of his purpose.
(b) The completion of his purpose.

James to Jude

James

A prayer for wisdom

James 1.5–8

   A.   *Faith's bewilderments*
   (a) The existence of problems.
   (b) The importance of prayer.

   B.   *Faith's encouragements*
   (a) The manner of God's giving.
   (b) The measure of God's giving.

   C.   *Faith's requirements*
   (a) A singleness of heart.
   (b) A steadfastness of will.

'Receive the Word'

James 1.21–25

A. *The receiving of the word*
(a) The soil in which the seed will grow.
(b) The seed from which the plant will grow.

B. *The revealing of the truth*
(a) The truths I must grasp.
(b) The temptations I shall meet.

C. *The rejoicing of the heart*
(a) The obedience we must give.
(b) The experience we will have.

'Be ye doers of the word, and not hearers only' (1)

James 1.21–25

A. *An ability which is claimed for the word*
(a) The weeds which must be removed.
(b) The seeds which must be received.

B. *An absurdity which is seen in the Church*
(a) The respect for the word.
(b) The rebuke from the Lord.

C. *An authority which must reign in our lives*
(a) A thoroughness which is required.
(b) A happiness which will result.

'Be ye doers of the word, and not hearers only' (2)

James 1.22

A. *The enjoyment of the word which we can know*
(a) The traditions we cherish.
(b) The travesty we condone.

B. *The endorsement of the word which we can say*
(a) How easy to utter words on our lips.
(b) How empty of meaning words can be in our lives.

C. *The application of the word to our lives*
(a) There must be a continuance of our obedience.
(b) There will be a contentment in our hearts.

Mastering the tongue (1)

James 3.1–13

A. *The maturity which the tongue will reveal*
(a) A surprising test.
(b) A searching truth.

B. *The ministry which the tongue fulfils*
(a) The direction which the tongue can give to lives.
(b) The damage which the tongue can do to lives.

C. *The mastery which the tongue demands*
(a) The inconsistency which dishonours the name of Christ.
(b) The impossibility which demands the grace of Christ.

Mastering the tongue (2)

James 3.1–13

A. *The direction which words can give to life: 'the bit . . . the rudder'*
(a) How insignificant words can seem.
(b) How influential words can prove.

B. *The damage which words can do in life: 'fire . . . poison'*
(a) Accidental damage through fire.
(b) Intentional damage through poison.

C. *The disappointment which words can cause in life: 'the fountain . . . the fruit-tree'*
(a) The expectations which people can have.
(b) The experiences which people can have.

D. *The deliverance from words which we must find in life*
(a) The mastery which seems impossible.
(b) The remedy which proves infallible. *Matt. 12.34*

Mastering the tongue (3)

James 3.1–13

A. *It is so small*
(a) How deceptive.
(b) How dangerous.

B. *It is so strong*
(a) Man's confidence in his power.
(b) Man's impotence in this matter.

C. *It is so serious*
(a) The dishonour it can cause.
(b) The disappointment it can create.

Mastering the tongue (4)

James 3.1–13, Psalm 139.4: 'There is not a word in my tongue but thou, oh Lord, knowest it altogether'

A. *James is dealing with something intensely practical*
(a) Something in which we are all daily involved.
(b) Something with which God is deeply concerned.

B. *James is dealing with something immensely powerful*
(a) The direction which words can give to lives.
(b) The damage which words can do to lives.

C. *James is dealing with something incredibly possible*
(a) This is something which we cannot do.
(b) This is something which Christ can do.

Mastering the tongue (5)

James 3.1–13

A. *The blunders which we should fear*
(a) The importance of words in the lives of men.
(b) The influence of words on the lives of men.

B. *The dangers which we should face*
(a) The destruction of which James writes.
(b) The distinctions of which James writes.

C. *The answers which should be found*
(a) Our inconsistencies which lead to disappointment for others.
(b) Our inability which calls for the enablement of Christ.

The problem of unanswered prayer

James 4.2

A. *The practice has been discontinued*
(a) In the life of the Christian.
(b) In the life of the Church.

B. *The person has been disqualified*
(a) A right relationship with God has never been established.
(b) A wrong relationship with God has never been adjusted.

C. *The petition has been denied*
(a) There can be a delay in the giving of the answer.
(b) There can be a refusal in the wisdom of God.

Pride, the first and worst of sins

James 4.6: 'God resisteth the proud'

A. *The verdict is passed on it in Scripture*
(a) The severity of the sentence: Prov. 6.16.
(b) The subtlety of the presence.

B. *The venom which is spread by it in the world*
(a) The homage which pride must have.
(b) The damage which pride can do.

C. *The vision which is fuelled by pride in our minds*
(a) Where the vision is to be found.
(b) Why the vision is to be feared.

'What is your life?'

James 4.14

   A. *It is powerful*
   (a) It will affect others naturally and inevitably.
   (b) It can affect others spiritually and eternally.

   B. *It is passing*
   (a) How swiftly time will pass.
   (b) How surely time will end.

   C. *It is precious*
   (a) I have only one life.
   (b) God has only one me.

   D. *It is purchased*
   (a) The claim which man makes.
   (b) The claim which God makes.
   (*With acknowledgements to R. H. Pope*)

Sins of omission

James 4.17: 'To him that knoweth to do good, and doeth it not, to him it is sin'

   A. *Something is assumed here*
   (a) There has been enlightenment.
   (b) There has been enablement.

   B. *Something has been allowed here*
   (a) How wide the failure can be.
   (b) How wrong the picture will be.

   C. *Something is affirmed here*
   (a) How personal sin is.
   (b) How practical salvation is.

'Be patient'

James 5.7–11

   A.   *A patience which toils: the patience of the labourer in the field*
   (a) The diligence which his work demands.
   (b) The dependence which his work reveals.

   B.   *A patience which trusts: the patience of the prisoner at the bar*
   (a) The voices which disturb.
   (b) The verdict which decides.

   C.   *A patience which triumphs: the patience of the sufferer in the world*
   (a) The bewilderment which baffles the mind.
   (b) The enrichment which blesses the soul.

The prayer of faith

James 5.16: 'The effectual fervent prayer of a righteous man availeth much'

   A.   *The faith on which prayer is based*
   (a) Fellowship with God has been restored.
   (b) Fellowship with God has been preserved.

   B.   *The flame with which prayer will burn*
   (a) The intensity of the manner of our praying.
   (b) The intensity of the motive of our praying.

   C.   *The force through which prayer will bless*
   (a) Its origin is divine.
   (b) Its outcome is dynamic.

1 Peter

Suffering – a prelude to glory

1 Peter Chapter 1

A. *An indifference to the world to which they had once belonged*
(a) The truth which they had come to see about the world.
(b) The treatment which they had had to suffer in the world.

B. *An importance to the Lord to whom they now belonged*
(a) The place given to them in the mind of God.
(b) The price paid for them in the cross of Christ.

C. *An insistence on the way in which they now behaved*
(a) Their response to the will of God.
(b) Their resources in the Spirit of God.

Christian obedience

1 Peter 1.2: 'Elect unto obedience'
John 2.5: 'Whatsoever he saith unto you, do it'

A. *In obedience lies the purpose of our redemption by God*
(a) This involves an acceptance of the cross.
(b) This involves an allegiance to the Crown.

B. *In obedience lies the proof of our devotion to God*
(a) The substitutes which we find for our obedience.
(b) The standard which we must accept for our obedience.

C. *In obedience lies the pathway to our experience of God*
(a) There will be the experiment which faith will make in obedience.
(b) There will be the experience which faith will reach in obedience.

'Blessed be the God and Father of our Lord Jesus Christ'

1 Peter 1.3–6

    A.   *The work which God has done*
    (a) The failure which God has met with love.
    (b) The future which God has filled with light.

    B.   *The watch which God will keep*
    (a) The ceaselessness with which the watch is kept.
    (b) The faithfulness with which the watch is kept.

    C.   *The way which God will take*
    (a) The trials through which God will lead.
    (b) The triumphs to which God will lead.

The Christian's inheritance

1 Peter 1.3–5

    A.   *The glory of the Christian's inheritance*
    (a) The quality of our inheritance.
    (b) The security of our inheritance.

    B.   *The gateway into the Christian's inheritance*
    (a) The entrance I must gain.
    (b) The evidence I can see.

    C.   *The guarantee of the Christian's inheritance*
    (a) There will be no moment when I need fear that God will forget.
    (b) There will be no matter in which I need fear that God will fail.

Facing the Fire

1 Peter 1.3–9

A. *The prospect ahead*
(a) What assures them.
(b) What awaits them.

B. *The protection around*
(a) There will be no moment in which God will forget.
(b) There will be no matter in which they need fail.

C. *The presence above*
(a) The reasons for their trials.
(b) The results of their trials.

'Kept by the power of God . . . unto salvation'

1 Peter 1.5

A. *The power by which we are being kept*
(a) The hesitation which can be caused by our fearfulness.
(b) The liberation which will be based on his faithfulness.

B. *The perils from which we are being kept*
(a) The heredity within which will not be removed.
(b) The hostility without which will not be relaxed.

C. *The person for whom we are being kept*
(a) Our desire for the pleasure of the One loved.
(b) Our delight in the pleasure of the One loved.

The Christian lives a different life

1 Peter 1.3, 33

    A.   *The different source from which it has come*
    (a) The spiritual birth he experiences.
    (b) The spiritual growth he can expect.

    B.   *The different society in which it will grow*
    (a) The life of the family entered.
    (b) The life of the family enjoyed.

    C.   *The different standards to which it will look*
    (a) The Father to whom the Christian looks.
    (b) The fashions from which the Christian turns.

'The precious blood of Jesus'

1 Peter 1.19

    A.   *A way opened*
    (a) The basis of entry.
    (b) The blessing of entry.

    B.   *A walk cleansed*
    (a) It involves a coming to the light.
    (b) It involves a cleansing by the Blood.

    C.   *A war won*
    (a) The accuser we face.
    (b) The answer we have.

The word of God in the life of the Christian (1)

1 Peter 1.22–23

    A.   *The Christian will be purified by the truth of it*
    (a) Purified from sin.
    (b) Purified for service.

    B.   *The Christian will be vivified by the touch of it*
    (a) The word of God is a word which lives.
    (b) The word of God is a word which lasts.

    C.   *The Christian will be satisfied by the taste of it*
    (a) There is nourishment in it.
    (b) There is enjoyment in it.

The word of God in the life of the Christian (2)

1 Peter 1.22–23

    A.   *The claim which the word of God makes*
    (a) That it lives.
    (b) That it lasts.

    B.   *The change which the word of God brings*
    (a) The change of birth.
    (b) The change of growth.

    C.   *The chance which the word of God must have*
    (a) There must be a hearing of the word.
    (b) There must be a heeding of the word.

Growing on the milk of the word (1)

1 Peter 2.2–3: 'Desire the sincere milk of the word, that ye may grow thereby'

A. *An approach which I must make to the word*
(a) There is a condition to fulfil.
(b) There is a challenge to be faced.

B. *An appetite which I should have for the word*
(a) The purity of the food.
(b) The intensity of the fight.

C. *An appeal from the past which I will heed*
(a) The experiences of the past.
(b) The expectations for the future.

Growing on the milk of the word (2)

1 Peter 2.2–3

A. *The power of the word to strengthen*
(a) It will strengthen faith.
(b) It will strengthen love.

B. *The power of the word to cleanse: Ephesians 5.26*
(a) The world defiles.
(b) Sin defiles.

C. *The power of the word to enlighten: Psalm 119.105*
(a) It will show the dangers to avoid.
(b) It will show the direction to take.

Growing on the milk of the word (3)

1 Peter 2.2–3

   A. *Read it through*
   (a) This will take time.
   (b) This will need a way.

   B. *Think it over*
   (a) Think it over prayerfully.
   (b) Think it over expectantly.

   C. *Write it down*
   (a) Why? Because we can forget.
   (b) Where? In a wide-margin Bible or a notebook.

   D. *Live it out*
   (a) We are not to be hearers only.
   (b) We are to be doers also.

   E. *Pass it on*
   (a) It will enrich your fellowship.
   (b) It may encourage your brethren.

Growing on the milk of the word (4)

1 Peter 2.2–3

   A. *We are to be hungry for Scripture*
   (a) The nourishment which God has provided.
   (b) The development which God has planned.

   B. *We are to be hungry for sanctity: Matthew 5.6*
   (a) The vision we must have.
   (b) The victory we may share.

   C. *We must be hungry for souls: John 4.32–34*
   (a) How sensitive Christ was to human need.
   (b) How satisfied Christ was in meeting that need.

The Church – a spiritual house

1 Peter 2.4–10

A. *The Person to be found there*
(a) The attraction of Christ.
(b) The rejection of Christ.

B. *The purpose to be fulfilled there*
(a) How varied are the purposes for which a house is built.
(b) How vital that the purposes should be fulfilled.

C. *The pictures which will be seen there*
(a) The excellence to be found in Christ.
(b) The difference to be seen in Christians.

The principle and practice of abstinence

1 Peter 2.11–12

A. *The reasons for it*
(a) The concept of the Christian life involves this.
(b) The conflict in the Christian life demands this.

B. *The resentment through it*
(a) The goodness revealed.
(b) The goodness reviled.

C. *The results from it*
(a) The day when trouble comes.
(b) The day when trust wins.

Obeying the authorities

1 Peter 2.13–17: 'Submit yourselves to every ordinance of man for the Lord's sake'

A. *Recognition of the need for an authority*
(a) Its source in the will of God.
(b) Its service for the good of man.

B. *Confusion through the want of an authority*
(a) What such confusion will create.
(b) What such confusion will demand.

C. *Submission to the rule of an authority*
(a) How that submission can be secured.
(b) What that submission will silence.

Grace in the life of the Christian

1 Peter 2.18–25

A. *The picture of grace*
(a) What grace accepts.
(b) How grace arrests.

B. *The pattern of grace*
(a) The silence of perfect restraint.
(b) The presence of perfect righteousness.

C. *The purpose of grace*
(a) The purpose for us.
(b) The purpose through us.

Life in the Christian home

1 Peter 3.1–7

- A. *Christians should live attractively*
- (a) He warns against superficial ideas of loveliness.
- (b) He wants a deeper concept of true loveliness.

- B. *Christians should live effectively*
- (a) The difficulties to be faced in the home.
- (b) The opportunities to be found in the home.

- C. *Christians should live co-operatively*
- (a) The sources of their lives are the same.
- (b) The standards in their lives are the same.

Christian marriage

1 Peter 3.7: 'Heirs together'

- A. *The hopes which can fill our minds*
- (a) The child of God's right to romance.
- (b) The child of God's road to romance.

- B. *The hurts which can break our hearts*
- (a) What may the reasons be?
- (b) What can the results be?

- C. *The help which can meet our need*
- (a) The pressures which can break us.
- (b) The presence which can bind us.

What to look for in a Christian
1 Peter 3.8–12

    A.   *His concern for the Church*
    (a) For the people of God to be found in the Church.
    (b) For the purpose of God to be fulfilled in the Church.

    B.   *His conflict with the world*
    (a) What the Christian should expect.
    (b) What the Christian should express.

    C.   *His contact with the Throne*
    (a) He will live carefully.
    (b) He will live confidently.

The lordship of Christ
1 Peter 3.15

    A.   *The rights on which his claim is based*
    (a) His rights as Creator.
    (b) His rights as Redeemer.

    B.   *The reign in which his will is done*
    (a) The difference I will see in my life.
    (b) The assurance I will have in my heart.

    C.   *The room in which his throne is set*
    (a) The unseen action which acclaims his lordship.
    (b) The unchanged attitude which accepts his lordship.

The help which we find in fellowship

1 Peter 4.7–11, 5.1–11

> A. *True fellowship is marked by diligence*
> (a) How gladly fellowship shares.
> (b) How humbly fellowship serves.
>
> B. *True fellowship is marked by vigilance*
> (a) Here we see the power which will assail.
> (b) Here we see the prayer which will avail.
>
> C. *True fellowship is marked by confidence*
> (a) The adequate resources which are available.
> (b) The ultimate results which are achieved.

Hospitality

1 Peter 4.9: 'Use hospitality one to another without grudging'

> A. *A work which we can all do*
> (a) The encouragement we can see here.
> (b) The requirements we can sense here.
>
> B. *A warmth which we can all show*
> (a) The contacts we have.
> (b) The constraint we know.
>
> C. *A wealth which we can all share*
> (a) The opportunity which this ministry will hold.
> (b) The intimacy which this fellowship can bring.

Humility – the finest of graces

1 Peter 5.5–6

A. *How attractive humility is: 'be clothed with humility'*
(a) The appreciation of others which humility displays.
(b) The availability to do anything which humility reveals.

B. *How receptive humility is: 'God . . . giveth grace to the humble'*
(a) The correction which humility accepts.
(b) The commissions which humility receives.

C. *How decisive humility is*
(a) The trust which God will place in the humble.
(b) The time which God will choose for the humble.

Know your enemy

1 Peter 5.8: 'Your adversary the devil'

A. *He seeks to discredit the Christian: 'the accuser of the brethren' (Rev. 12.10)*
(a) The attacks we should expect.
(b) The answers we can give.

B. *He seeks to deceive the Christian: 'the deceiver of the whole world' (Rev. 12.9)*
(a) How clever the attacks may be.
(b) How complete the answer will be.

C. *He seeks to destroy the Christian: 'as a roaring lion' (1 Peter 5.8)*
(a) The tragedies which can be seen.
(b) The triumph which can be shared.

2 Peter

Remembrance, one of life's gentler ministries

2 Peter 1.12–15

A. *A ministry which is practical*
(a) His appreciation of these Christians.
(b) His apprehension for these Christians.

B. *A ministry which is powerful*
(a) The instrument which is called on.
(b) The stimulant which is called for.

C. *A ministry which is possible*
(a) There is a negligence which he wants to avoid.
(b) There is a permanence which he wants to achieve.

Has man a future?

2 Peter 1.19

A. *The shadows in which faith lives*
(a) The insecurity which man must face.
(b) The inhumanity which man has shown.

B. *The Scriptures to which faith looks*
(a) The light thrown upon the matter by the Scriptures.
(b) The light trusted by the saint in the Scriptures.

C. *The sunrise for which faith longs*
(a) The expectancy which awaits a returning Lord.
(b) The eternity which awaits the redeemed soul.

The Second Coming of Christ

2 Peter 3.4: 'The promise of his coming'

A. *When will he come?*
(a) The information which has been denied to us.
(b) The indications which should be discerned by us.

B. *How will he come?*
(a) Suddenly, in a moment.
(b) Visibly, as a Person.

C. *Why will he come?*
(a) To complete a picture.
(b) To conclude a story.

1 John

The communication of the gospel

1 John 1.1: 'heard . . . seen . . . handled'
John 1.14

A. *Communicating the gospel audibly*
(a) The audience must be secured.
(b) The accuracy must be stressed.
(c) The authority must be sensed.

B. *Communicating the gospel visibly*
(a) The activity of the love of Christ.
(b) The adequacy of the power of Christ.
(c) The agony of the passion of Christ.

C. *Communicating the gospel tangibly*
(a) How close the examination.
(b) How clear the conclusion.
(c) How complete the analogy.

Walking in the light

1 John 1.7

A. *The conditions with which we are faced*
(a) There must be a coming to the light.
(b) There must be a continuing in the light.

B. *The communion to which we are called*
(a) Fellowship with God.
(b) Fellowship with Christians.

C. *The corruption from which we are cleansed*
(a) A mystery which the cross enshrines.
(b) A ministry which the cross effects.

Stages of spiritual development

1 John 2.12–13

  A.   *Spiritual infancy: 'Little children' – the pardon I have*
  (a) The gladness which the birth of a child will create.
  (b) The sadness which failure in growth will bring.

  B.   *Spiritual adolescence: 'Young men' – the power I need*
  (a) The conflicts of adolescence.
  (b) The claims of adolescence.

  C.   *Spiritual maturity: 'Fathers' – the person I know*
  (a) The privilege of intimacy which maturity enjoys.
  (b) The pressures of responsibility which maturity accepts.

What the Second Coming of Christ means to a Christian (1)

1 John 3.1–3

  A.   *The expectation of his coming*
  (a) How important this hope is as a truth.
  (b) How ignorant our hearts are as to the time.

  B.   *The preparation for his coming*
  (a) I would want to be found holy.
  (b) I would want to be found busy: Matt. 24.46.

  C.   *The transformation at his coming*
  (a) The transformation in the Lord we love.
  (b) The transformation in the lives we live.

What the Second Coming of Christ means to a Christian (2)

1 John 3.1–3

    A.   *The purity we are to seek*
    (a) The motive for it.
    (b) The measure of it.

    B.   *The urgency we are to show*
    (a) A limit which has been set.
    (b) A regret which would be sad.

    C.   *The relevancy we are to sense*
    (a) Related to the seeming inactivity of our God.
    (b) Related to the seeming inadequacy of our gospel.

The church – the community in which people count

1 John 3.13–18

    A.   *The witness which Christian love is*
    (a) The life of God which has been received.
    (b) The love of God which must be released.

    B.   *The sacrificial demands which Christian love meets*
    (a) The illustration of this love we find in Christ's life.
    (b) The implications of this love we face in our lives.

    C.   *The practical concern which Christian love shows*
    (a) How observant love will be.
    (b) How diligent love will be.

A plea for sacrificial living

1 John 3.16: 'Hereby perceive we the love of God, because he laid down his life for us: and we ought to lay down our lives for the brethren'

A. *The Christian is seen here as a debtor*
(a) The trust received by him.
(b) The toil required of him.

B. *The Christian is seen here as a brother*
(a) Family life calls for co-operation.
(b) Family life calls for consideration.

C. *The Christian is seen here as a lover*
(a) How costly was the love shown to us.
(b) How costly is the love seen in us.

Expressing Christian love

1 John 4.7–21

A. *Love and our identity as Christians*
(a) The divine love as received by the Christian.
(b) The divine love as revealed in the Christian.

B. *Love and our activity as Christians*
(a) The revelation of divine love we can see.
(b) The obligation of divine love we must face.

C. *Love and our maturity as Christians*
(a) The restraint of fear.
(b) The release of love.

'God is love'

1 John 4.8

    A. *Love thinks of those it loves*
    (a) Love will want to please.
    (b) Love will want to plan.

    B. *Love talks to those it loves*
    (a) What love will want to say.
    (b) What love will want to share.

    C. *Love toils for those it loves*
    (a) The needs of life.
    (b) The hands of love.

'God sent his Son into the world'

1 John 4.9–10, 14

    A. *The initiative which love takes*
    (a) We see the movement which love takes.
    (b) We see the excitement which love creates.

    B. *The intention which love has*
    (a) The enrichment for us.
    (b) The involvement for him.

    C. *The invitation which love awaits*
    (a) The restraint which love accepts.
    (b) The response which love awaits.

Overcoming fear with love (1)

1 John 4.18: 'There is no fear in love; but perfect love casteth out fear: because fear hath torment'

A. *John writes of a tyranny*
(a) An insufficiency of which my heart is afraid.
(b) An imagination in which my thoughts are active.
(c) An intention of which my heart is afraid.

B. *John writes of a remedy*
(a) The lavishness of love's giving.
(b) The limit of love's thinking.
(c) The loveliness of love's planning.

C. *John writes of a certainty*
(a) The reality upon which love rests.
(b) The intimacy in which love grows.
(c) The authority by which love rules.

Overcoming fear with love (2)

1 John 4.18

A. *The progress which has stopped*
(a) The intention which has been feared.
(b) The inaction which has proved fatal.

B. *The principle which is sound: 'There is no fear in love'*
(a) There will be no doubts to hinder our obedience.
(b) There will be no delay to halt our obedience.

C. *The problem which is solved*
(a) The evidence which will convince us of love's reality.
(b) The experience which will come with love's response.

'We love him, because he first loved us'

1 John 4.19

 A. *The actions of the love of God which are arresting*
 (a) The initiative which love takes.
 (b) The intentions which love has.

 B. *The aspects of the love of God which are appealing*
 (a) How unchanging is the constancy it will show.
 (b) How unending are the discoveries it will bring.

 C. *The answer to the love of God which is awaited*
 (a) A reluctance which is hurtful.
 (b) An acceptance which is joyful.

Can I be sure that I am a Christian?

1 John 5.13: 'These things have I written unto you . . . that ye may *know* that ye have eternal life'

 A. *How I may feel about it as a sinner*
 (a) The charges I may sometimes meet.
 (b) The changes I may sometimes feel.

 B. *What I can learn about it from the Scriptures*
 (a) It is desired for me in Scripture: 1 John 5.13.
 (b) It is declared by men in Scripture: 2 Timothy 1.12.

 C. *Where I must look for it in the Saviour*
 (a) I must think of his work for me as my Saviour.
 (b) I must rest on his word to me as my Saviour.

527

2 John

Glimpses into the heart of an old minister

2 John

A. *The delight he finds in his flock*
(a) The truth had been learned by them.
(b) The truth was being lived by them.

B. *The desire he has for his flock*
(a) He stresses the love which truth includes.
(b) He stresses the life which love involves.

C. *The demand he makes of his flock*
(a) The anxiety he feels for them.
(b) The activity he fears for them.

3 John

Glimpses into the life of a New Testament Church

3 John

A.   *We find fidelity to the truth here*
(a) We see John's delight in Gaius' progress.
(b) We see John's desire for his prosperity.

B.   *We find charity for the church here*
(a) Note the welcome shown to others.
(b) Note the witness shared with others.

C.   *We find hostility to the work here*
(a) The motive in the heart of the man.
(b) The manner of the life of the man.

D.   *We find integrity in the life here*
(a) Note the obligation laid upon his readers.
(b) Note the illustration sent to his readers.

The message of John's Third Epistle

A. *The supremacy of truth in the mind of John*
(a) As the basis of Christian experience.
(b) As the bond of Christian unity.

B. *The generosity of love in the heart of Gaius*
(a) Without reproach as to its quality.
(b) Without restraint as to its object.

C. *A travesty of grace in the attitude of Diotrephes*
(a) The conceit John discerned.
(b) The conduct he deplored.

D. *The inadequacy of letters in the fellowship of believers*
(a) The details which characterise true fellowship.
(b) The difficulties which confront such fellowship.

Jude
Autumn trees without fruit
Jude 12

A. *The promise recalled*
(a) The privilege of a spiritual environment.
(b) The profession of a spiritual experience.

B. *The poverty revealed*
(a) The poverty of a purpose not fulfilled.
(b) The tragedy of opportunities not grasped.

C. *The penalty recorded*
(a) The condition they were in.
(b) The contempt they deserved.

D. *The process required*
(a) The delay which would be permitted.
(b) The desire which would be pursued.

Revelation

What does it mean to be a Christian?

Revelation 1.5: 'Unto him who loved us, and washed us from our sins in his own blood, and hath made us kings and priests unto God'

A. *It is like the liberation of a slave*
(a) The chains by which we are bound.
(b) The Christ through whom we are freed.

B. *It is like the coronation of a king*
(a) The destiny of a king.
(b) The dignity of a king.

C. *It is like the ordination of a priest*
(a) The Presence to which he has access.
(b) The service in which he is active.

The Lord's Day

Revelation 1.10: 'I was in the Spirit on the Lord's Day'

A. *The authority which rules over this day*
(a) The ordering hands of the Saviour.
(b) The obedient heart of the servant.

B. *The opportunity which comes with this day*
(a) The opportunity for worship.
(b) The opportunity for witness.

C. *The results which flow from this day*
(a) The fulfilment of the purposes of God it should hold.
(b) The fellowship with the people of God it should bring.

The church at Ephesus (1)

Revelation 2.1–7: 'Thou hast left thy first love'

A. *The position in which the church was found*
(a) It was in a privileged position.
(b) It was in a perilous position.

B. *The condition to which the church had fallen*
(a) Words of commendation.
(b) Words of condemnation.

C. *The decision with which the church was faced*
(a) The imperative of the will of God.
(b) The alternative of the wrath of God.

The church at Ephesus (2)

Revelation 2.1–7

    A. *Here we have love's tragedy*
    (a) The efficiency which was undenied.
    (b) The intimacy which was undesired.

    B. *Here we have love's memory*
    (a) The heights recalled.
    (b) The hurt received.

    C. *Here we have love's recovery*
    (a) The words to heed.
    (b) The way to take.

Christ 'in the midst of the seven golden candlesticks'

Revelation 2.1

    A. *Christ is observant of the Church*
    (a) What does he see in the Church?
    (b) What does he say to the Church?

    B. *Christ is available to the Church*
    (a) The guidance the Church will need.
    (b) The grace the Church must have.

    C. *Christ is revealed in the Church*
    (a) The functioning of the light seen.
    (b) A forgetting of the light sensed.

Faithfulness despite suffering

Revelation 2.8–11

A. *A Christ who is undeniably alive*
(a) The person he is.
(b) The pressures he sees.

B. *A church which was understandably afraid*
(a) The courage the church must have in its trials.
(b) The control which Christ will keep in his hands.

C. *The crown which is indisputably assured*
(a) The purpose we can trace in our sufferings.
(b) The promise we can trust in our sufferings.

Being a nominal Christian

Revelation 3.1–6

A. *A church in which spiritual life was assumed*
(a) The possibility which exists of making such an assumption.
(b) The tragedy which results from making such an assumption.

B. *A church from which spiritual life was absent*
(a) The stillness which reigns in death.
(b) The sickness which results from death.

C. *A church to which spiritual life was available*
(a) There must be contact with the Author of life.
(b) There must be consent to the advent of life.

Life's open doors

Revelation 3.8: 'Behold, I have set before thee an open door'

A. *The opening experienced*
(a) The hand by which the door is opened.
(b) The hour at which the door is opened.

B. *The opposition encountered*
(a) The intention of men.
(b) The prevention by God.

C. *The opportunity envisaged*
(a) The prospects of service.
(b) The promise of power.

The church at Laodicea (1)

Revelation 3.14–22

A. *The contrast of which Christ speaks*
(a) The thoughts they had.
(b) The truth he knew.

B. *The consent for which Christ waits*
(a) What he desires.
(b) When they decide.

C. *The control through which Christ reigns*
(a) The room I make in my life.
(b) The place he takes in my life.

The church at Laodicea (2)

Revelation 3.16

A. *The tragedy of which Christ speaks*
(a) How complacent they were.
(b) How ignorant they were.

B. *The remedy with which Christ comes*
(a) The love he would show to them.
(b) The life he would share with them.

C. *The urgency with which Christ asks*
(a) He asks them to repent.
(b) He asks them to receive.

Christ at the door (1)

Revelation 3.20: 'Behold I stand at the door, and knock: if any man hear my voice, and open the door, I will come in'

A. *Where Christ stands*
(a) The initiative of love which brings him there.
(b) The intention of love which keeps him there.

B. *What Christ seeks*
(a) He wants us to have an encounter with himself.
(b) He wants an entrance for himself.

C. *What Christ says*
(a) Here is a promise we can trust.
(b) Here is the position he must take.

Christ at the door (2)

A. *A picture which is arresting*
(a) I am arrested by the presence of Christ at the door.
(b) I am arrested by the patience of Christ at the door.

B. *A promise which is assuring*
(a) The word for which Christ waits.
(b) The word on which faith rests.

C. *A presence which is abiding*
(a) The difference his presence will make to my life.
(b) The permanence his presence will have in my life.

Christ at the door (3)

A. *The assessment which Christ makes of us*
(a) How different this is.
(b) How demanding this is.

B. *The acceptance which Christ seeks from us*
(a) Consider the reason.
(b) Consider the request.

C. *The assurance which Christ gives to us*
(a) How simply we must act.
(b) How surely Christ will come.

The recapture of the castle of King Self by Prince Jesus

A story for children, illustrated by a model if possible

Revelation 3.20

A. *The first wall of indifference, commanded by Captain I-Don't-Know*
(a) They have never read God's word.
(b) They have never heard God's truth.

B. *The second wall of indifference, commanded by Captain I-Don't-Care*
(a) They are too busy.
(b) They are quite happy.

C. *The wall of cowardice, commanded by Captain I'm-Afraid*
(a) They are afraid of what people will say.
(b) They are afraid of what Jesus will do.

D. *The wall of procrastination, commanded by Captain I'll Wait*
(a) The delay they want to make.
(b) The danger they do well to heed.
(*Acknowledgements to R. Hudson Pope.*)

The sovereignty of Christ

Revelation 19.16: 'King of Kings'

A. *The threat which men have felt from him (cf. Herod)*
(a) The reaction of worship from some.
(b) The reaction of worry from others.

B. *The thrust which men have faced in him (cf. Palm Sunday)*
(a) An offer which was unmistakeable.
(b) An outcome which was unbelievable.

C. *The throne which men have found for him (cf. Good Friday)*
(a) A picture of savage mockery.
(b) A picture of serene majesty.

The judgment of unbelievers

Revelation 20.11: 'I saw a great white throne'

A. *A certainty to face*
(a) The presence of God.
(b) The purpose of God.

B. *An accuracy to find*
(a) The records of God's dealings with us.
(b) The records of our dealings with God.

C. *A destiny to fear*
(a) The tragedy of being lost.
(b) The security of having Christ.

The Church as the Bride of Christ (1)

Revelation 21.2: 'As a bride adorned for her husband'

A. *A loveliness which the Bridegroom will see in his Bride*
(a) Love's desire for such beauty.
(b) Love's delight in such beauty.

B. *A lavishness which the Bridegroom will shower upon his Bride*
(a) The happiness which such lavishness is meant to achieve.
(b) The costliness which such lavishness is bound to involve.

C. *A loneliness which the Bridegroom will share with his Bride*
(a) There will be a sharing with each other.
(b) There will be a caring for each other.

The Church as the Bride of Christ (2)

Revelation 21.2

A. *A loveliness which the Bridegroom will see in his Bride*
(a) What the word has to say.
(b) What the world needs to see.

B. *A lavishness which the Bridegroom will shower upon his Bride*
(a) The dimensions of divine love's giving.
(b) The intention in divine love's giving.

C. *A loneliness which the Bridegroom will share with his Bride*
(a) The new Presence which will be in her life.
(b) The new people who will be brought into her life.

What does heaven hold for the believer?

Revelation 22.3–5

A. *A life of perfect sinlessness: 'There shall be no more curse'*
(a) Earth speaks of the presence of sin.
(b) Heaven speaks of the absence of sin.

B. *A life of perfect government: 'the throne of God and of the Lamb'*
(a) On earth we see the tragic rule of man.
(b) In heaven we will see the perfect rule of God.

C. *A life of perfect service: 'His servants shall serve him'*
(a) The longing for service which love knows in heaven.
(b) The limiting of service which love knows on earth.

D. *A life of perfect communion: 'they shall see his face'*
(a) The reality of communion with God on earth.
(b) The quality of communion with God in heaven.

E. *A life of perfect possession: 'His name shall be in their foreheads'*
(a) The threats we face on earth.
(b) The truth we will face in heaven.

F. *A life of perfect blessedness: 'There shall be no night there'*
(a) The hurts we have known on earth.
(b) The light we shall have in heaven.

G. *A life of perfect glory: 'and they shall shine for ever and ever'*
(a) The path of suffering here.
(b) The place of splendour there.

Obedience in the life of the Christian

Revelation 22.14: 'Blessed are they that do his commandments'

A. *The place given to it*
(a) It has a prominent place in God's word: Genesis 2.16.
(b) It has a permanent place in God's word: Revelation 22.14.

B. *The price asked in it*
(a) Obedience to God means the renunciation of self.
(b) Disobedience to God means a rejection from service.

C. *The prize gained through it*
(a) The rewarding intimacy with God.
(b) The resulting influence for God.

God's last and best word to man

Revelation 22.21: 'Grace'

A. *What we can see in Christ*
(a) Grace speaks of the magnitude of our need.
(b) Grace speaks of the attitude of his love.

B. *How we are saved by Christ*
(a) What the grace and love of God did for us in Christ.
(b) What the grace and love of God do for us through Christ.

C. *Where we must stand in Christ*
(a) Grace is the ground upon which we must remain: Romans 5.2.
(b) Grace is the ground on which we can rejoice.